THE RECONSTRUCTION
OF HUMANITY

THE Reconstruction of Humanity

PITIRIM A. SOROKIN

Boston • THE BEACON PRESS • 1948

KRAUS REPRINT CO.
New York
1971

THIS BOOK IS
REVERENTLY DEDICATED
TO THE DEATHLESS

MOHANDAS K. GANDHI

PREFACE

If this plan for personal, social, and cultural transformation is carried through, international and civil wars are likely to be eliminated, interpersonal and intergroup conflicts largely abolished, vast creative forces released, and an unprecedented renaissance of human values ushered in.

If the plan is replaced by a mere patching up of the tattered fragments of our existing social order, new wars and other catastrophes will inevitably ensue, and inglorious self-destruction will terminate the creative career of humanity.

The book is a nontechnical introduction to a series of technical researches carried on at the present time by the author in co-operation with a few eminent and young scholars. Though each of its main statements can be backed by a vast body of evidence, most of this together with the large array of relevant literature is omitted, so as to make the book available to intelligent lay readers. The full body of evidence and literature will be presented in special publications of the technical researches mentioned.

I wish to express my sincere gratitude to Eli Lilly and the Lilly Foundation for their generous financial help in connection with these researches.

PITIRIM A. SOROKIN

Harvard University
Cambridge, Mass.

CONTENTS

PART FIVE

PERSONAL FACTORS OF CREATIVE ALTRUISM

THE RECONSTRUCTION

OF HUMANITY

THE ETERNAL QUEST CONTINUES

Bleeding from war wounds and frightened by the atomic Frankensteins of destruction, humanity is desperately looking for a way out of the deathtrap. It craves life instead of inglorious death. It wants peace in place of war. It is hungry for love in lieu of hate. It aspires for order to replace disorder. It dreams of a better humanity, of greater wisdom, of a finer cultural mantle for its body than the bloody rags of its robot civilization. Having foolishly maneuvered itself into a deathtrap, and facing the inexorable problem, "To be or not to be," it is forced to pursue, more desperately than ever before, its eternal quest for survival and immortality.

During the catastrophes of this century, humanity has child-ishly followed in this quest one leader after another and has credulously tried various plans of salvation. In vain! None of the leaders and none of the plans have delivered the goods they promised. Instead of peace they have produced two world wars. Instead of happiness and plenty they have brought mankind into an inferno of misery. These facts irretrievably condemn these leaders and their plans as dismal failures, guilty of irresponsible promises, of inability to prevent catastrophe, of ignorantly lead-ing humanity toward destruction.

As a result of this bankruptcy, humanity must bestir itself to discover new cures for its deadly ills. Once more it is chal-lenged to feverish activity in finding and trying new plans of salvation. More imperatively than heretofore must it choose new leaders.

And yet, observing the kinds of leaders it is choosing, one cannot refrain from gloomy forebodings! Tested by the full experience of humanity itself they appear to be inadequate and their plans fallacious. These blunders must be corrected before

3

it is too late. Otherwise humanity is doomed to drift toward an inglorious and painful Calvary devoid of either redemption or transfiguration.

The subsequent pages aim to reveal these shortcomings. Criticism of the current plans is followed by a constructive blueprint. Both — the criticism and the constructive suggestions — are offered in the humblest spirit of malice toward none and charity for all.

PART ONE

QUACK CURES FOR WAR
AND IMPOTENT PLANS FOR PEACE

CHAPTER ONE

POLITICAL CURES

I. DEMOCRACY

Among the most popular plans for eliminating war and for establishing lasting peace are political prescriptions. They are offered by a legion of social doctors. The main ingredient of all such prescriptions is the claim that through a change of certain political conditions the disease of war can be cured and peace can be ensured. In their supplementary ingredients these prescriptions vary. Some doctors add to the common ingredient a monarchic, others a republican element. Some add a dash of autocratic, fascistic, or totalitarian régimes; others, one of democracy. Some believe in many small state powers; others, in a few big ones. The monarchic, autocratic, fascistic, and totalitarian varieties are unpopular at the present time. As such they can be passed over without criticism. Instead we shall consider those political cures that at present are subscribed to by thousands of leaders and millions of ordinary persons.

Among these the most popular is democracy. A host of statesmen and scholars, business leaders, ministers, and plain men and women are convinced that *a republican and democratic system of government guarantees peace and eliminates war.* This belief is offered in hundreds of variations. It underlay the First World War, supposedly fought to make the world safe for democracy and peace. It has been the main motto of the Second World War, in which the formula of "democratic and peace-loving nations" has identified peace with democracy. It lies at the foundation of the policy of "democratic re-education" of the Germans and Japanese as the best guarantee of their future peacefulness. It is used as the justification of the sacrifice of the millions of victims of these wars. It is the reason for the

7

establishment of the United Nations and for the current foreign policies of democratic countries.

There is no doubt that a genuine and virile democracy does offer a potent cure for many social troubles. It arrests many a social infection, invigorates many a vital process; and builds up the mental, moral, and physical health of the nations. However, it does not cure all diseases and does not stimulate all the vital processes. In addition, if democracy is contaminated by poisonous elements its therapeutic power largely evaporates.

Most of the democracies, in fact, have been of this low-grade, contaminated variety. Beginning with the Athenian democracy and ending with the Dutch, the English, the French, the Belgian, and even the United States democracy before the abolition of slavery, each of these systems was actually a small oligarchy built upon a vast stratum of slaves, serfs, and exploited, disfranchised, and autocratically ruled colonial Helots. Some twenty thousand Athenians constituted an oligarchic minority superimposed on several hundreds of thousands of unfree or semi-free persons deprived of practically all political and most civil rights. Some thirty to forty millions of English citizens formed a small oligarchy superimposed upon approximately three hundred million disfranchised colonials. The same is true of some six millions of Dutch citizens compared with approximately sixty million colonial semi-serfs; and so on. Similarly, virtually all the democracies of history have been vitiated by many other elements incompatible with the essence of genuine democracy.

This contamination, together with the fact that even the best medicine is never an antidote for all diseases, explains why so-called democratic political régimes have hardly ever exerted a restraining effect upon war and a positive influence upon peace. A long series of well-ascertained facts demonstrates that *republican and democratic nations have been no less belligerent or more peaceful than monarchic and autocratic ones.*

If we measure the belligerency of the respective nations by their historic war record, we find that such comparatively democratic nations as ancient Greece, England, France, the Netherlands, and the United States waged war, on an average, during

57, 56, 50, 44, and 49 years, respectively, (including main Indian wars) in every hundred years of their history. On the other hand, the figures for such relatively autocratic nations as ancient Rome, Germany, Russia, Italy, Spain, and Austria are 41, 28, 46, 36, 67, and 40 years respectively.[1] If anything, the frequency of wars is slightly higher in the totality of the democratic countries than in that of the autocratic nations.

The same result is obtained if we measure the burden of war by the relative casualties for a given unit of population of the specified nations, as follows:

For Democratic Countries
Centuries

	XX*	XIX	XVIII	XVII
England	66.5	5.0	30.1	20.0
France	92.0	51.0	45.8	36.6
Holland	0.0	5.7	84.4	161.0

For Autocratic Countries
Centuries

	XX*	XIX	XVIII	XVII
Spain	2.2	11.0	11.8	?
Italy	52.4	—	—	—
Russia	41.1	11.1	21.5	7.9
Germany	94.7	13.1	—	—
Austria	48.0	5.8	94.0	130.0

* Only up to 1925.

A similar conclusion is reached on the basis of the following data. From 1480 to 1940 there were about twenty-six hundred important battles. Of these battles Great Britain participated in 22 per cent; France in 47 per cent; the Netherlands in 8 per cent; Russia in 22 per cent; Germany (Prussia) in 25 per cent; Austria-Hungary in 34 per cent; Turkey in 15 per cent; Spain in 12 per cent.[2] These data do not display the alleged peaceful-

---

[1] For detailed investigations of all the wars in the history of Greece, Rome, and later European countries from 600 B.C. to 1925 A.D., see P. A. Sorokin, *Social and Cultural Dynamics* (New York, 1937), III, 348-352. (This book will hereafter be referred to as *Dynamics*.)

[2] Q. Wright, *A Study of War* (Chicago, 1942), p. 220.

ness of democratic nations as compared with the autocratic ones.

Furthermore, before 1914 the twentieth century was more democratic than the previous centuries of Europe and other Western continents. Yet, as we shall see, this most democratic century has proved to be the most belligerent and bloody of all the twenty-five centuries of Western history.

Moreover, moving from the autocratic Middle Ages to the increasingly democratic modern centuries, we move at the same time from the small professional armies of the Middle Ages toward the ever vaster, universally drafted national armies of modern times, and from small wars as the "sport of kings" toward "total" wars involving millions — indeed, practically the entire civilian population. With the increasing democratization of humanity, wars have not decreased but have enormously increased in their magnitude, destructiveness, and scientific bestiality.

A long series of similarly ugly facts may be adduced to prove beyond any reasonable doubt that the superior peacefulness of democratic régimes as compared with the autocratic ones is a mere myth, sharply contradicted by the evidence.[3] After the victory of the democratic nations in the First World War, Great Britain, France, the United States, and Belgium dismally failed to eliminate war or even to reduce its frequency. The Treaty of Versailles and the Allied postwar domination did not lead to a century of comparative peace, as in the case of the Vienna Congress of autocratic Russia, France, Austria, and England in 1815. Instead, the postwar domination of the democratic nations resulted only in a short period of nonbelligerency from 1918 to 1939 and ended in the most terrific explosion in the whole of human history. The same reasons explain why at the present time, after the victory of the democratic bloc of nations, we enjoy no real peace. Only some two years have elapsed since the armistice; and the air is already thick with war sentiments. A feverish race in the most destructive armaments is already under

---

[3] See *Dynamics*, III, chaps. 9-11; Q. Wright, *op. cit.*, chap. 22; A. J. Toynbee, *A Study of History* (Oxford, 1935-1939), IV, 143 ff.

way, accompanied by diplomatic war, mutual intimidation, and economic unrest.

This means that a contaminated democracy is not a potent cure for war! The "democratic cure for war" is a quack remedy, and the doctors that confidently prescribe it are ignorant "medicine men," no matter how great may be their achievements in other fields.

These conclusions are reinforced by a consideration of *civil wars and internal disturbances.* A systematic study of all the important civil wars, revolutions, and riots in the history of ancient Greece and Rome and of eight of the principal later European countries, from 600 B.C. up to 1925 A.D., shows that *democratic nations and periods have been no less turbulent, violent, and bloody in their internal disturbances than the autocratic nations and periods.* The popular belief that democracy is a cure for internal anarchy, that it ensures an orderly and lawful process of social change, that democratic revolutions are less sanguinary, cruel, and destructive than revolutions under an autocratic régime—this notion is again nothing but a myth sharply contradicted by the ugly facts.

From 600 B.C. up to 1925 A.D. in the history of the foregoing nations there were approximately 1623 important disturbances (small and large civil wars). Their frequency, magnitude, and destructiveness have been no less in democratic nations and periods than in autocratic nations and periods. In such comparatively democratic countries as ancient Greece, France, England, and the Netherlands one important disturbance occurred on an average in every 5.4, 8.1, 7.9, and 12.1 years respectively. Similar data for the more autocratic countries, such as Rome, Byzantium, Germany and Austria, Russia, and Spain, are respectively 5.8, 17.5, 7.5, 5.9, and 6.1 years. No appreciable difference is shown by the two classes of nations in this respect.

Finally, the fourth century B.C. was the most turbulent in the history of Greece. The same century was, all in all, possibly the most democratic period in her entire history. In Rome the most turbulent period was the first century B.C. The same century was at least as democratic as any other period of Roman history.

In Europe the most turbulent centuries (in decreasing order of turbulence) were the twentieth, the second part of the eighteenth and the first half of the nineteenth, the thirteenth, and the fourteenth. Of these the thirteenth and fourteenth centuries were, on the whole, more democratic than the preceding centuries; the eighteenth and the nineteenth were more democratic than the period from the fifteenth to the seventeenth century; and prior to 1914 the twentieth century was more democratic than any of the proceding centuries of European history.[4]

The total body of evidence clearly demonstrates that *there is no close causal relationship between international and civil wars on the one hand and autocratic or democratic, monarchical or republican, political régimes on the other.*

II. THE UNITED NATIONS

Another fashionable type of political alleged cure for war is *the United Nations.* In the last few years the belief in this remedy has grown rapidly, and at the present time, in the opinion of millions, the United Nations is the only cure for war and the only hope for a lasting peace. Hundreds of societies devoted to "One World" and "World Federation" are feverishly active in speech-making and printed propaganda. Millions of dollars are spent for these "cures." Hundreds of quack doctors are flourishing in this epidemic of credulity. Humanity seems to have found again "the surest cure for war."

However commendable this enthusiasm may be, it is bound to fade and to lead to new disillusionment. The League of Nations was likewise launched in an atmosphere of the highest hopes and greatest expectations. Nevertheless, after some twenty years of inglorious existence it died in impotence and was soon relegated to oblivion. There is little reason to believe that the United Nations will fare better. If anything, its inner organization is more defective than that of the League of Nations; and its social environment is less favorable to its growth than that of the Geneva institution.

---

[4] For detailed study see *Dynamics,* III, chaps. 12-14.

The United Nations Organization is shot through and through with cancerous self-contradictions. On the one hand, it is based upon the principle of equality of all nations; on the other, the great powers are legally and actually unequal to the small powers. It is democratic in the sense of giving an equal vote to all the nations; and it is most undemocratic in making the vote of one Cuban or Icelander equal to the votes of some twenty to forty Americans, Russians, or Chinese. Its majority vote in terms of the number of the nations voting for a given proposition often turns into a small minority vote when counted according to the number of individual citizens represented by such a majority vote. The small nations claim equal status with the great powers in regard to *rights and privileges;* but they insist on a sharp inequality so far as economic, military and other burdensome *duties* are concerned. It is based on the principle of unanimity of the great powers; yet it rests on a principle of majority and minority votes that precludes such unanimity. Even its policy of deciding problems by majority vote is flagrantly contradicted by the veto principle, by virtue of which a single great power can annul the decisions of the majority.

The organization of its voting units is also self-contradictory. It is devoid of any consistent principle. Thus, a bloc of Latin American and Arab states has one-half of all the votes of the United Nations, although representing only a small fraction of the total human population. The highly unequal small powers and several big nations, such as the United States and China, have each only one vote; on the other hand, the British Commonwealth and Soviet Russia have, respectively, six and three votes. Owing to this peculiar characteristic of the voting units the majority votes of the United Nations are rendered highly precarious in their moral, legal, and social authority. Such a haphazard organization affords an excellent opportunity for a degeneration of the United Nations into a mere screen for cynical power politics of this or that bloc of nations representing but a small portion of humanity, strong or weak in its military power, and undistinguished in its creative achievements.

Again, the United Nations is supposed to represent humanity

as a whole. Each individual member is meant to vote and act for the welfare of all mankind rather than for that of his particular clique. Actually its members are first and foremost the delegates of the states, appointed and given mandatory instructions by the states for the defense of parochial state interests, regardless of whether these coincide with or contradict that of humanity as a whole or of its major part.

Self-contradictory are also its powers and functions. On the one hand, it is merely a sort of "advisory council" to the sovereign states. Its decisions are not mandatory for any sovereign state nor can they be enforced as long as it lacks a powerful military and police force of its own. It does not possess even an "exterritorial piece of land" for the control of its own buildings and personnel. It is entirely dependent upon the generosity of the member states, which are supposedly subordinate to it and controlled by it. On the other hand, the United Nations is not supposed to constitute a mere debating forum whose decisions are not binding upon its member states. Thus it is neither strictly a debating society nor an organ of world government enacting and enforcing its laws.

Even as "the highest tribunal of human conscience" the United Nations is an abortive child. Made up only of the representatives of *states* it is bound to fail even in this function; for of all the important groups — religious, ethical, scientific, economic, and so forth — the state group is the most Machiavellian and cynical in its policy of the *raison d'état*, in its power politics, in its application of the rule that might is right. Its representatives, when they act as diplomats, ministers, executives, generals, admirals, and other state agents rather than as private persons, are the most perfidious and nihilistic embodiments of naked power politics. No matter how noble and ethical they may be in their private capacities, when they assemble as state representatives their standards inevitably fall to this level. Although even as a mechanism of power politics the United Nations is largely impotent.

To repeat. In these and many other respects the United Nations is shot through and through with self-contradictions. It is a house divided against itself. No organization incessantly tortured with such self-contradictions can function successfully. From this standpoint even the League of Nations was better organized than the United Nations.

Likewise *the social and cultural environment of the United Nations is hardly more favorable to its growth than that of the Geneva institution.* As will be indicated later, the process of disintegration of almost all the main values of humanity, ethical and religious, economic, and political, has increased rather than decreased since 1918.[5] All the legal and moral norms of human conduct and relationships, beginning with the Sermon on the Mount and ending with legal and purely utilitarian norms of Victorian decency, are now more precarious and "relativized" than they were even in 1914-1918. Their controlling and binding power is less effective today than it was then. Interpersonal, intergroup, and international contracts (such as the marriage vow, management-labor contracts, and solemnly concluded international treaties) have been violated much more frequently by persons, groups, and state powers during the last score of years than during the nineteenth century and at the beginning of the twentieth century. Bethmann-Hollweg's reference to the treaty guaranteeing the neutrality of Belgium as a mere "scrap of paper" shocked the whole world in 1914. Owing to violations of such treaties during the period 1918-1947 by practically all governments, we have become so accustomed to them that we regard them as something normal. The frequency of violation of contracts between labor and management has increased so sharply that they fail to shock us any longer. The violation of solemn marriage vows through desertion and divorce has grown so rapidly that it has ceased to be a scandal. And so it is in the field of all other norms, values, and contracts.

If these have lost their binding and controlling power, if they are flouted increasingly, on the slightest pretext, and if we all have become double-crossers, then no agreements reached by the United Nations, no contracts entered into by it, can really be

---

[5] Cf. *Dynamics* and P. A. Sorokin, *The Crisis of Our Age* (New York, 1941). (This book will hereafter be referred to as *Crisis*).

binding upon the parties. They are certain to be broken whenever such a violation appears profitable. If, as is suggested by the mutual recriminations of the Allies, the recent Teheran, Yalta, Potsdam, and Moscow agreements have been violated by yesterday's comrades in arms, and if the Atlantic Charter has been repudiated and forgotten by its signatories, what reason have we to believe that the semi-Platonic declarations of the United Nations (or, rather, the "Disunited Nations") will be more respected?

The United Nations can hardly prosper in such an unhealthy atmosphere. As the highest tribunal of the ethical conscience of humanity it cannot function because of the defects of its own organization; nor can it function as a moral force in the unmoral and cynical world of today. As a power machine it cannot work successfully because it lacks the necessary power; being vitiated by innumerable contradictions, it cannot employ the concerted power of mutually harmonious states; nor can it apply even the calculated egoistic common sense of the policy, "Grab and let the others grab," so well exemplified by the unholy diplomats of the "Holy Alliance" and the Congress of Vienna.

As a result of these internal and environmental defects, the United Nations has already displayed all the weaknesses of the League of Nations and many additional ones. It has already revealed its impotence to settle any serious conflict among the great powers. The great and small powers ignore it in connection with most important problems. Even when they do submit to it such matters as the trusteeship of the Pacific islands or the annexation of South-West Africa by the Union of South Africa, they explicitly declare that, regardless of the decision of the United Nations, these territories will be annexed anyhow. When such a procedure is practiced, it speaks for itself: no further evidence of a quasi-contemptuous attitude toward the United Nations and no better proof of its impotence are needed.

Hence it has already lost the moral prestige it enjoyed at the moment of its inception. The "incidental" majority of its Security Council has not been able to resist the temptation of misusing its majority position for the pursuit of selfish interests.

By placing on the agenda the Russian-Persian conflict and refusing to consider the Anglo-Persian conflict and the bloody British-Dutch-French-Indonesian strife; by airing and denouncing the policies of the Slavic bloc and passing by in silence the much more autocratic and imperialistic colonial policies of the big and small colonial empires (the Anglo-American policies in the Middle and Far East; the policies relating to Greece, Palestine, Egypt, and French Indo-China; and a host of other undemocratic and rapacious policies of colonial countries); through these and many similar partialities, the United Nations has degenerated into a mere screen for the power politics of the artificial and incidental majority of world states. In spite of its brief existence it has already succumbed to the fatal sickness of the League of Nations as a similar screen for the selfish interests of Britain and France.

To sum up: Through such one-sided actions the moral prestige of the United Nations has already been seriously impaired; and if these actions continue (and there is no assurance that they will not), its moral prestige is bound to sink still lower. Having neither moral authority nor adequate physical power, it cannot perform the miracle of eliminating war and erecting a temple of eternal peace. The roots of its failure are deep in the very soil of contemporary society and culture. Single-handed, it cannot radically change the world. In a modified form, and as part of a much vaster system of social, cultural, and personality changes, the United Nations may play an important role in the realization of its great mission. Otherwise it is bound to repeat the life course of the ill-starred League of Nations!

III. WORLD GOVERNMENT

This conclusion is beginning to be shared by an ever-growing number of leaders and common people. Their increase accounts for the movement in favor of a *world government* as a more effective cure for war and a more adequate way to a lasting peace. The central points of this plan consist of two principles; the establishment of a genuine world government and the abolition of the national sovereignty of the existing states. This scheme is free from many of the contradictions of the United Nations. If realized, it can achieve a great deal more than the United Nations can achieve. As part of a vast ensemble of social and cultural changes necessary for the elimination of war some sort of world government is indispensable. Taken alone, however, without other changes, it would offer no better an antidote for war than democracy or the United Nations.

For the present and the near future such a system can hardly be realized. Almost all the proponents of a world government insist on their own special conditions. These conditions are invariably constructed so as either to make the nation of each partisan dominant, or to promote its economic, political, and other interests at the expense of those of other countries. Almost all the American advocates of a world government assume, explicitly or implicitly, that the United States shall play the dominant role in such an organization and that the pattern of the United States government shall be the form of the world government. They reject the principle of proportional representation based on the relative number of the citizens of the various countries; for under such an arrangement India, China, Russia, and other Asiatic countries would have a greater number of representatives than the United States. For similar reasons they reject other bases of representation in the government of the "One World" which would not secure for the United States the preponderant role. Instead, they propose, in a high-falutin' form, such conditions of representation as would ensure this role to the United States, in spite of this fact that some of these conditions violate the principles of democratic government.

The same attitude applies to the partisans of "One World" in other countries. They are "ardent and open-minded internationalists" provided that their particular brand of world government is accepted. If the brand is rejected, they become ardent nationalists. In other words, a large part of the movement for "One World" is a camouflaged imperialism of nations and groups bent on promoting their special economic, political, and cultural interests and unwilling to make any genuine sacrifices on behalf of the cause of world government. Their position is similar to that of the United States Senate in its resolution expressing willingness to submit to the World Court any matter except the important problems considered as purely domestic, which should be decided exclusively by the United States.

Such factors preclude the possibility of a *free* realization of the movement. All the nations and groups that have anything to lose by the plan would resist it. It is thinkable, of course, that they could be *coerced* by the dominant powers. Such coercion, however, would amount to a conquest of the weaker nations by the stronger ones. As such it would defeat the main objective and central value of world government as an instrument of peace and freedom. Under such conditions the world government would become a sort of world *tyranny,* which might turn into the worst tyranny the world has ever known.

Under the existing social and cultural conditions, including the egoism of contemporary individuals and groups, it is hardly possible to organize freely a real world government. The nations and groups that have anything to lose through such an organization would resist and reject it. If they were coerced, the world government would become a tyranny of the strong groups over the weak ones. Such coercion would lead to endless wars. Hence the entire plan would result in dismal failure.

Besides this difficulty the plan for a world government reveals serious shortcomings. Its most fatal weakness is the assumption that the cause of wars is the existence of a multitude of sovereign states and that as soon as these are abolished, and one sovereign world government is established, lasting peace will ensue. This belief is very old and has been set forth many times.[6] Recently, among its other proponents, E. Reves repeated it, and a galaxy of eminent authorities sponsored it. We are told that "wars between groups of men forming social units always take place when these units — tribes, dynasties, churches, cities, nations — exercise unrestricted sovereign power. Wars between these social

---

[6] S. J. Hemleben, *Plans for World Peace through Six Centuries* (Chicago, 1943).

units cease the moment the sovereign powers are transferred from them to a larger or higher unit." [7]

In spite of the clear enunciation of these "laws" and of the host of authorities supporting them, the propositions in question are fallacious. From 500 B.C. up to 1925 A.D. in the history of Greece, Rome, and later European countries there were 967 international wars. Within the same period in the history of the same countries there were about 1623 civil wars, that is, wars occurring within the limits of a given sovereign state. The major civil wars were as devastating as the large-scale international wars.[8] This means that, contrary to Reves' "laws," wars occur not only between sovereign states or other sovereign groups but even more frequently between the nonsovereign parts of the same state or group. It means also that the abolition of sovereign states and the establishment of a world government cannot eliminate civil wars. Moreover, if many civil wars have occurred in comparatively small and homogeneous nations, such as Greece, Rome, and eight later European countries, they would occur much more frequently within the framework of the entire body of humanity, made up of countless heterogeneous groups with diverse and even opposing interests. A *purely external unification of all mankind under the sovereign rule of a world government would merely substitute "civil" wars for "international" wars, without decreasing their total number and frequency, their destructiveness, or their bloodiness and inhumanity.* If anything, such a change would be likely to increase their frequency and especially to intensify their bestiality, since civil wars, on the whole, have been more inhuman than international wars. Hence, the replacement of a multitude of sovereign states by a single world government would in itself prove inefficient and inadequate as a cure for war.

The alleged "laws" of Reves are contradicted by many other facts. If his "laws" were valid, we should expect that with the subjection of a multitude of sovereign states and other groups to the vast empires of Genghis Khan or Timur, the Gupta or Maurya

---

[7] E. Reves, *The Anatomy of Peace* (New York, 1945), p. 121 *et passim*.
[8] See *Dynamics*, III, 283 ff., 306 ff.

dynasties, Alexander the Great, Mohammed, Napoleon or Hitler, wars would decline through the decrease of sovereign groups. As a matter of fact, they sharply increased. Conversely, the periods marked by an increase in the number of sovereign states should show, according to Reves' "laws," an intensification of war. As a matter of fact, such periods as the Middle Ages, when there was a greater number of European states than after the fifteenth century, or the period from 1815 to 1914, when a large number of new sovereign states appeared (Greece, Bulgaria, Serbia, Rumania, Belgium, Luxemburg, Norway, Italy, Chile, Bolivia, Peru, Ecuador, Brazil, and most of the other Latin-American states) — such periods were marked by either a very low level of war, as in the Middle Ages or by a notable decrease in belligerency, as during the period 1815-1914.

Furthermore, if the incorporation of many sovereign groups into a single empire, such as the Roman Empire, sometimes leads to a temporary *pax Romana*, with its decrease of international wars, such a unification is followed by an increase of civil war between the various coercively unified groups. In addition, a decrease of international war does not inevitably occur in such periods of unification; and when, as in Rome, it does occur, it proves to be short-lived and is attended by a disintegration of the empire, with a consequent increase of international and inter-group wars.

Several fallacious assumptions underlie Reves' propositions. The first is that "freedom in human society is exclusively the product of the state. It is, indeed, unthinkable without the state. . . . Experience demonstrates that during all our history there has been one method alone to approach this ideal. This method is: law. Human freedom is *created* by law."[9]

If these propositions were sound, we should have to conclude that for millennia mankind lived without any freedom, since the state as a specific group appeared comparatively late in human history; that for millennia all the tribes and clans were in incessant *bellum omnium contra omnes* and that within each tribe the members were ceaselessly engaged in slaughtering or despoiling

---

[9] Reves. *op. cit.*, p. 66.

one another; that man possessed no legal or moral norms, since these are *created only by the state;* and so on. Reves explicitly declares that no freedom (or law) exists in the jungle, in the pre-state stage of humanity.[10]

It would be superfluous to point out that all these propositions, both factually and logically, are sheer nonsense. The body of ethnological and anthropological evidence shows that practically all primitive tribes have their norms of law and that these norms function fairly efficiently in controlling their behavior. The evidence demonstrates, further, that law is not created by the state but existed long before the state emerged, indeed, that it is the necessary prerequisite for the emergence of the state itself. Intertribal and intratribal (or civil) wars have been neither more frequent nor more devastating than the interstate and civil wars waged since the emergence of the state. It is significant that out of some 403 preliterate peoples studied by Hobhouse, Wheeler, and Ginsberg, only two tribes were found whose history was free from war, and these tribes happened to be marked by the "lowest" level of "civilization," consisting of primitive hunters and collectors of the gifts of nature in distinction from the "more advanced" pastoral and agricultural tribes.[11]

Moreover, not all the laws enacted by the state have created or even amplified freedom. A large proportion of state laws, especially those of the tyrannical, monarchical, autocratic, or totalitarian states, have led to a curtailment of freedom, and even to slavery or serfdom. We must not forget that slavery and serfdom were often established and always sanctioned, protected, and enforced by state laws. If such laws promoted the freedom of the masters, to the vast disfranchised masses of slaves, serfs, and unfree and semi-free groups they meant the loss of their freedom.

There is no need to argue these elementary platitudes, well known to any competent anthropologist, sociologist, or historian,

---

10 *Ibid.*, p. 66 *et passim.*

11 L. Hobhouse, G. Wheeler, and M. Ginsberg, *The Material Culture and Social Institutions of the Simpler Peoples* (London, 1915).

in order to perceive the fallacy of the Reves' assumptions. Equally erroneous is his conception of the differentiation of humanity into groups. Explicitly or implicitly he contends that among the various groups into which mankind is differentiated — racial, sex, age, kinship, nationality (or language), territorial, religious, political, and economic or occupational groups, such as the family, the clan, the tribe, the nation (in contradistinction to the state), the caste, the social order, and the social class — the state group is always paramount and sovereign. He holds that it is the most powerful group, controls all the others, creates all the laws, protects all the freedom that is enjoyed, and invariably serves only beneficial purposes. Hence he believes that as soon as the sovereignties of the separate states are abolished in favor of a single world state, war will be eliminated and lasting peace will be established.

This traditional conception of the social differentiation of humanity and of the supremacy of the state among the nonstate groups is fallacious. The facts show that the state is only one among these various groups; that it emerged relatively late in human history; that law is created by each of these groups, often without permission or sanction on the part of the state; that the state has not been, *de facto* or even *de jure,* the only sovereign group (for instance, the medieval Christian Church was more sovereign than the medieval state and exercised supremacy over it); and so on.[12]

For all these reasons, even if we succeeded in uniting all the states in a single world state, this would not lead to an elimination of war among the nonstate groups, between these groups and the world state, or between the heterogeneous parts of the world state itself. Besides, the laws enacted by such a world state would be effective only if they were approved and supported by all the nonstate groups. Otherwise, according to Tacitus' *Quid leges sine moribus,* they would remain impotent, devoid of any efficacy or controlling power, like the notorious Volstead Act of the prohibition era in this country.

---

[12] Cf. P. A. Sorokin, *Society, Culture, and Personality: Their Structure and Dynamics* (New York, 1947), chaps. 10-16. (This book will hereafter be referred to as *Society.*)

The totality of the foregoing evidence is sufficient to prove why, taken alone, the establishment of a world government or the abolition of state sovereignties could in no way either eliminate or decrease war or lead to a just and lasting peace.

If neither democracy nor the United Nations nor a world government offers an adequate cure, still less adequate are other, less thoroughgoing and more narrow, political remedies, such as this or that specific type of democratic régime, the abolition of the veto power in the United Nations or the equalization of its great and small powers, and a federated variety of world government.

One can only regret the enormous amount of time, energy, and money spent on behalf of such insignificant details. Such concentration on petty minutiae, to the exclusion of weightier considerations, betrays the utter confusion and derangement of the public mind and that of its leaders.

Let us now turn to the politico-economic cures for war and factors of peace.

CHAPTER TWO

ECONOMIC CURES AND PLANS

I. CAPITALISM

In our economically minded age various economic cures for war are as popular as the political ones. Among these a restoration of the capitalist economy of "free enterprise" is regarded by many as a sure antidote for war and a builder of peace. The social doctors point out that capitalist economy led to an enormous development of productive forces and prosperity throughout the nineteenth century, especially in the United States; raised the standard of living throughout the Western world from two to five times; swept away the remnants of feudalism and serfdom; gave economic and political freedom to the masses; was responsible for an unprecedented multiplication of scientific and technological inventions; and secured a century of comparative peace, from 1815 to 1914. Unshackle free competive enterprise from the chains of governmental control, and prosperity and peace will automatically be restored.

This prescription has several fatal weaknesses. First, the allegedly peaceful capitalist system of economy did not prevent the First World War, which was conceived in the womb of the capitalist society of the nineteenth and the early twentieth centuries. In that period there were no communist, socialist, or totalitarian economies. The war was a child of the imperialist economy of competitive free enterprise. Since capitalism could not prevent this catastrophe and was largely responsible for it, there is no reason to believe that it can prevent wars in the future.

Its second weakness is attested by the very fact of the decline of capitalism during the twentieth century. If it had possessed only the virtues attributed to it by its partisans, it could not have declined; for humanity would not have been foolish enough to reject the most beneficial system in favor of vicious noncapitalist systems. Since the system of free competitive economy withered, it must have contained in itself not only virtues but serious defects. Foremost among these were its own germs of self-destruction and its vitiation of cultural and social values. No external force or agency destroyed it. The governments and ruling classes of the nineteenth and the early twentieth centuries were favorable to it; so also were the well-to-do and middle classes; favorable to it must likewise have been the farmer-peasant and labor classes, since they were supposed to be greatly benefited by it.

The first mortal blow was dealt to it by its own agents, capitalists and large-scale entrepreneurs; for it was the captains of industry who launched the economy of big corporations, trusts, and cartels. This economy split the very cornerstone of capitalism, that of private property. In its full-fledged form private property means the right of possession, use, management, and disposal of the property in question, and also the duty to bear the risk of its mismanagement. The economy of corporations shattered this: in every corporation those who own it, its thousands of share-holders and bondholders, neither use its property nor manage nor dispose of it; on the other hand, those who manage and dispose of it, the board of directors and the officials, do not own even a significant portion of its property. In the two hundred largest corporations in the United States, the directors, presidents, vice-presidents, and treasurers together do not own even 20 per cent of the shares and bonds. In an overwhelming majority of cases they do not own even 2 per cent of the property they manage and dispose of. Actually, then, they are not the pro-prietors but the officials and trustees of the *public* property of the corporations. Nevertheless, they treat it as their own property, and the business as their own "free enterprise." They allocate to themselves fabulous salaries and stock issues, often giving no compensation to the real owners, the thousands of small share-holders and bondholders. In addition, they do not bear the risk of a real owner: not infrequently, when the corporation goes into the red they still draw their fabulous salaries and lucrative bonds at the cost of the actual owners. When a corporation becomes bankrupt, they do not suffer either the financial or the legal consequences of the bankruptcy. Thus they are, in effect, irresponsible economic barons who arbitrarily exploit the public ownership without the responsibility of either a real owner or a governmental official. Therefore, their plea for a restoration of "capitalist free enterprise" is really an appeal for the inviolability of their privileged position as irresponsible economic barons, not a plea for bona fide private property and a system of genuine capitalism based upon it.

It was precisely the "pioneers of corporation economy," the Rothschilds and Rhodeses, Rockefellers and Carnegies, and not the communists or socialists who dealt the mortal blow to the full blooded capitalism of the nineteenth century. With the establishment and rapid growth of big corporations at the end of the nineteenth century they invalidated private property, shattered authentic capitalism, crushed thousands of small, truly capitalistic enterprises, and inaugurated the fatal decline of capitalist economy.

Since corporation economy is not a real capitalist economy, its maintenance is not the maintenance of genuine free enterprise. Since corporation economy is already a system of publicly owned property, its further development can only be away from private property and bona fide capitalism in the direction of its further socialization, with its managers stripped of their irresponsible and autocratic position and reduced to the status of responsible government officials. If sound political evolution for the last few centuries has consisted in replacing irresponsible political autocrats by responsible democratic governments, a similar economic evolution must supplant irresponsible managerial autocracy by means of responsible democratic agents of publicly owned corporations. Such an evolution means not a restoration of capitalism and free competitive enterprise but a complete replacement of these by a system of public — co-operative, socialized, nationalized, or communized — economy.

If the prescription in question means a restoration of real private property and capitalism, it is clearly not feasible; for no one could resurrect these defunct institutions, which have committed suicide through the development of the system of corporation economy. Neither technologically nor economically is it possible to return to the system of comparatively small enterprises in most branches of economic production. None of the small businesses can meet the requirements of national and international trade, which demand production on an enormous scale, with correspondingly huge outlays for efficient equipment, labor, managerial personnel, and the like. Large-scale production and reconstructed corporations are here to stay, and no one can abolish them.

If the prescription envisages the maintenance of the present corporation economy, with its basic defects, this would not mean a restoration of capitalism. Nor would a maintenance of the present system be either possible or desirable. Lacking the merits of real capitalism and those of authentic public property, such a system is bound to suffer increasingly from the fatal defects of a public economy ruled by an irresponsible managerial autocracy. Since this system conceived and produced the First and, in part, even the Second World War, there is not the slightest chance that it can prevent future wars and ensure humanity the blessings of peace.

The capitalist and corporation economies possess many other traits which operate in favor of war rather than against it. Being incarnations of the principle of competition, from its mildest to its most cut throat forms, they engender in individuals and groups the spirit of mutual struggle rather than of mutual aid, the ethos of aggressiveness instead of love. They pit individual against individual, group against group, as inexorable rivals. Thus they generate international and civil wars, interpersonal and intergroup conflicts.

They produce the same result in many other ways. By its very nature the culture of capitalist and corporation economy is economically minded, materialistic and hedonistic. In spite of its lip service to the values of the Kingdom of God, its real God is Mammon. Its paramount values are embodied in wealth and material comfort, sex indulgence, epicurean food, strong drink, luxurious clothing and houses, conspicuous consumption, and worldly fame. Its heroes are power-drunk victors of the commercial, industrial, and financial world, the prize ring, or the field of battle.

Stressing these values as paramount, such a culture inevitably generates incessant conflicts. The demand for these values in capitalist society is far greater than the supply, and this scarcity leads to continuous and bitter struggle for a maximum share for every individual and group.

Moreover, this capitalist culture is responsible to a great extent for the degradation of man himself. It turns persons into mere commodities in a competitive labor market. Out of medieval artisans it created proletarians, mere marketable robots, condemned to sell their labor and at the same time doomed to perpetual insecurity. In the periods of depression inherent in the capitalist economy, millions of proletarians are unemployed, thus being deprived of even the minimum means of subsistence. Throughout the period of the Industrial Revolution capitalism shamelessly exploited the labor of women and children. During its whole existence it has degraded and demoralized millions among colonial populations: the very improvement in the standard of living of the European population during the capitalist era has been achieved through a pitiless exploitation of the much larger populations of colonies and unindustrialized backward countries (as the sources of raw material, including human material). Creating glaring inequalities, it has split society into antagonistic rich and poor classes "living in the same spot and always hating and conspiring against one another." [1]

Even through the creation of prosperity the capitalist economy and culture have not proved an efficient antidote for international and civil wars. A study of the causes of war and revolutions shows that these have not uniformly decreased during periods of prosperity or increased in periods of depression and impoverishment, nor have the more prosperous nations and other

[1] Plato, *Republic*, viii.

groups been less belligerent, revolutionary, or aggressive than the poorer nations and groups. Contrary to the prevalent opinion, the factors of prosperity and comparative poverty are not the important causes of wars and revolutions. Indeed, the majority of wars and revolutions, as well as of strikes, tend to occur when the respective societies are moving in the direction of greater prosperity, not during periods of depression.[2]

Even granting that the capitalist economy and culture have exerted certain peaceful influences, their war-making tendencies have been more pronounced. Direct confirmation of this conclusion is found in the undeniable fact that with the emergence and growth of capitalist economy, wars and revolutions have not decreased but (with some fluctuations) have rather increased. Capitalism as a system of economy began to emerge in Europe in the thirteenth century, exhibiting a steady growth up to the beginning of the twentieth century. The indexes of the movement of war and revolution in Europe from the eighth to the twentieth century show that in the thirteenth and fourteenth centuries civil wars increased enormously in comparison with those of the precapitalist period of the eighth to the thirteenth century; then they subsided during the centuries of the vigorous growth of capitalism; in the eighteenth and at the beginning of the nineteenth century they again flared up; and after the comparatively orderly second half of the nineteenth century they "shot into the stratosphere," rendering the twentieth century thus far the most turbulent period in the entire history of Europe.

International wars began to grow during the thirteenth century and steadily multiplied up to the end of the seventeenth century. Then they slightly subsided, showing an upward trend again in the second half of the eighteenth and at the beginning of the nineteenth century. The period from 1815 to 1914 was a comparatively peaceful one, followed by unprecedented explosions of war in the twentieth century. This inductive verification corroborates the foregoing analysis. It clearly demonstrates that if the capitalist and corporation economies are not wholly belligerent, they are utterly unable either to reduce or to eliminate war.

---

[2] See *Dynamics*, III, chaps. 10-14; *Society*, chaps. 31-33.

II. COMMUNIST, FASCIST, AND SOCIALIST ECONOMIES

With the decline of capitalism and the rise of various totalitarian systems of economy, various brands of the latter are offered as radical cures for war. However different these brands may be in their secondary traits, they are similar in essence in that they all present a "planned economy" controlled by the state government. The totalitarian economies replace the "anarchy of free enterprise," controlled by a multitude of private owners (individuals and groups), by so-called "planned economy" controlled by a communist, socialist, fascist, nazi, or other type of totalitarian government. Communist and socialist régimes abolish the private ownership of land and other important means of production, which are nationalized or communized. Under fascist, nazi, and other régimes the legal abolition of private ownership is not so thoroughgoing, applying to only a part of the instruments of production. Factually, however, the governmental control of production, distribution, and consumption of economic commodities is very comprehensive in even these varieties of totalitarian economy. In all such economies not the private individuals and groups but the state government decides what and how much is to be produced; how the product is to be distributed; by whom it is to be consumed and in what quantities; the scale of prices; the level of wages and other remunerations; the place of work and the amount to be performed; the kind of labor each citizen has to engage in; and so on. In completely totalitarian economies practically all the citizen's economic activities and most of his other behavior and relationships are rigidly controlled by the government. In partly totalitarian economies only the larger portion of his activities is regimented, the rest being left to the control of individuals and groups.

Such a governmentally managed economy has been the dominant trait of all totalitarian régimes: the economy of the Pharaohs in certain periods of Egyptian history; the economy of China in some periods of her history; that of ancient Sparta and Lipara; of ancient Peru and Mexico; of the Roman Empire after 300 A.D.; of Byzantium throughout its history; of early communist and socialist experiments, such as the Taborite state in Bohemia; and of absolute monarchies and the "police states" (or Polizei- staaten) of the seventeenth and eighteenth centuries. Contem- porary or recent examples are furnished by Soviet Russia, Fascist Italy, and Nazi Germany; by the British, Czech, and French nationalized war economies; and by the wartime economy of the New Deal. The degree and the extent of governmental control of business in all these régimes have varied, but in all of them such control has been rigorous and far-reaching.

In other respects, especially in ideology, such economico- political régimes have differed sharply. The ideology of the totalitarianism of the Pharaohs was different from that of com- munist, socialist, or nazi totalitarianism, just as that of the Inca system differed from that of other totalitarian governments. The contemporary communist ideology diverges notably from that of the fascist, nazi, and other wartime totalitarian economies.

In addition to their respective ideologies, these régimes differ from one another in several other important traits. Only the communist, socialist, fascist, and other contemporary or recent varieties need to be considered in respect to their claim of offering remedies for war. Do these politico-economic systems actually ensure peace? The answer is in the negative. Their claims are wholly unwarranted by the existing body of evidence.

The recently emerged communist, nazi, fascist, socialist, and wartime varieties of totalitarianism have shown themselves to be inherently militant. First of all, *they are notoriously militant in their domestic relations.* Communism, Fascism, and Nazism arose and achieved their dominance through violence, including revolution and large-scale or small-scale civil wars. They have all maintained themselves through incessant coercion, the extermi- nation, imprisonment, banishment, intimidation, or mutilation of their opponents. Their ideology explicitly reveals their militant nature, whether it is the ideology of the class struggle (that of the proletariat versus all other classes), of the "master race" against the slave races, or of the self-chosen élite in opposition to the sheeplike masses. The laws and especially the criminal codes enacted by these régimes display the same militancy: the Soviet,

Fascist, and Nazi criminal codes prescribe capital punishment and other severe penalties for a host of violations of laws and decrees. The firing squads and gallows of such régimes are always busy; their prisons and concentration camps are invariably overcrowded; they maintain a vast army of slave labor, and they show scant respect for human life or liberty.

Other recent varieties of totalitarian economy, such as the wartime English, Czech, French, and American economies, arose without any serious domestic conflict; but they were the offspring of international war. Only under such emergency conditions could they emerge and flourish. They too are characterized by coercive regimentation and by explosive tendencies manifested in strikes, in intense antagonism between radicals and conservatives, in wholesale arrests and the like. In this sense they, too, are militant in their domestic relations.

Totalitarian systems are militant likewise in their international relations. The régimes of the Pharaohs, of ancient Sparta or Lipara, of China at the beginning of our era and in the eleventh century A.D., of the Roman Empire of Diocletian and his successors, of Byzantium, of ancient Mexico and Peru, of the Taborite state in Bohemia, of the "police states" of the seventeenth and eighteenth centuries, and the recent Fascist, Nazi, Communist and Labor Socialist régimes are all marked by aggressive belligerency and by militant imperialism. If anything, their history exhibits more wars than that of the nontotalitarian governments.

The pronounced international aggressiveness of Fascism and Nazism is not something exceptional but is typical of totalitarian régimes, inherent in their very nature. This becomes readily comprehensible when one understands the conditions under which they arise and develop. *Whenever a given society is confronted by a grave emergency (war, famine, an acute depression, a devastating plague, a disastrous flood or earthquake, and so on) govermental control and regimentation invariably tend to increase, extending over many areas of economic and other relationships hitherto controlled by private individuals and groups. And the greater the emergency, the greater the expansion of governmental control and regimentation, the more pronounced the swing toward totalitarianism. Conversely, when the emergency passes, the amount of governmental regimentation tends to decline and the politico-economic régime swings away from totalitarianism in the direction of free enterprise and voluntary co-operation.* Since war has constituted possibly the most frequent and most critical emergency, it is not surprising that major wars have invariably been followed by an upward trend of totalitarianism.

The processes of "totalitarian conversion" in grave emergencies and "antitotalitarian reconversion" under nonemergency conditions depend very little upon the existing form and personnel of the government. If a government carries out the necessary measures, it remains in power; otherwise it is replaced (either through the ballot or through revolution) by a more totalitarian régime in war, and a less totalitarian régime in peace. Only the secondary traits of the operations depend upon the specific nature and personnel of the existing government, such as the skill with which the measures are executed, the degree and magnitude of the swings in either direction, whether the transition takes the form of a democratic "New Deal" or that of the decrees of the Pharaohs, whether the ideology is that of communism, socialism, or democracy, of the divine right of kings, of a sacred war for the Fatherland, or of God and religion.

The swings toward and away from totalitarianism take place under these conditions regardless of the inclinations of the government. Hence it was not Franklin D. Roosevelt who was responsible for the New Deal or the wartime increase of government regimentation, but, rather, the great depression which set in during President Hoover's administration, followed by the emergency of the Second World War. If, instead of a Democratic administration, we had had at that time the most conservative Republican administration, the swing toward an increase of governmental regimentation would have taken place anyhow. As a matter of fact, immediately after the crash of 1929, the Hoover administration at once introduced numerous Federal controls of banking, money, and other economic relations which had hitherto not been regimented. Conversely, after the armistice the Democratic administration of President Truman dropped most of the wartime regulations. Similarly, the emergency of the First World War led the Czarist government of Russia to institute far-reaching governmental regimentation. When this emergency was reinforced by that of civil war, famine, and pestilence, a trend toward full-fledged totalitarianism was inevitable, assuming in this case the form of extreme Communism. When, in 1921, the First World War and the acutest phase of the civil war were over, and only the emergency of famine and destruction remained, a swing away from extreme totalitarianism occurred in the form of the so-called "New Economic Policy," introduced by Lenin and the same communist government. With a diminution of emergencies of every sort during the period 1930-1939, the mitigation of communist totalitarianism continued until the trend was abruptly reversed by the terrific explosion of the Second World War. If in future, in Russia or any other country, every emergency should disappear, we should expect a drastic "reconversion" of the contemporary compulsory totalitarian régimes in the direction of nontotalitarian economic and political systems, regardless of the personnel of the government in power. If, on the other hand, the present emergencies continue, we must expect most of the existing governmental controls to be retained and, if the emergencies become more acute, even increased. Otherwise the régime in power will be ousted (either peacefully or through the use of force) in favor of one more responsive to the exigencies of the situation.

This law of fluctuation of the extent and intensity of governmental control, of fluctuation of politico-economic régimes between the poles of extreme totalitarianism and *laissez faire, laissez passer,* is one of the few valid social laws,[3] though even the majority of specialists, to say nothing of the rank and file, are still unaware of it. Without a knowledge of this law it is im-

---

[3] For the detailed evidence, see *Dynamics,* III, chaps. 6 and 7; P. A. Sorokin, *Man and Society in Calamity* (New York, 1942), chap. 7. (This book will hereafter be referred to as *Calamity.*)

possible thoroughly to understand basic social changes and to avoid needless blunders and baseless accusations.[4]

Knowing the conditions under which totalitarian politico-economic régimes emerge and develop, we are now in a position to grasp their inherently militant nature. They are the offspring of war and other emergencies. They appear and flourish only under conditions of social distress, especially those of war. Hence they cannot be peaceful systems. Still less can they eliminate war and inaugurate an era of permanent peace, domestic or international. But in the absence of notable emergencies totalitarianism invariably declines.[5]

The above reasons suffice to dismiss all cures of war compounded of totalitarian varieties of politico-economic régimes. They cannot cure the diseases of war and other social conflicts. Indeed, they tend to aggravate them.

Since neither the capitalist or corporation economy nor totalitarian economic régimes can assure peace, still less can it be achieved through minor variations of these systems, such as special tariff measures, money and banking reforms, new schemes of taxation, novel export and import arrangements, modifications of transportation and trade, transformations in trusts and cartels

---

[4] For instance, such popular books as F. A. Hayek's *The Road to Serfdom* (Chicago, 1944) completely ignore this law. Hence the author's ponderous denunciation of totalitarian economies is but a journalistic effusion akin to berating a thermometer for showing that a patient has a high temperature. Similar ignorance is evinced by the chambers of commerce and other groups who have enthusiastically acclaimed the book. Their acclamation is but the blind emotional outburst of persons suffering from the discomfort of regimentation without understanding its origin, the conditions under which it can be reduced, or the most effective cures. Mere denunciation of a planned totalitarian economy, or wishful thinking to the effect that it can be eliminated merely through the restoration of a Republican majority in Congress or a similarly ineffectual method, will be of no avail. The only remedy lies in overcoming the underlying social emergency.

[5] Its disappearance does not necessarily mean a return to the capitalist or corporation economy. A genuinely free co-operative economy, a freely established system of national public economy contrast as sharply with the totalitarian economy (which is always coercive) as the capitalist economy does. If war and similar grave emergencies can be overcome, it is probable that the future economy will be mainly one of free public ownership — co-operative, national, even international. Only in part is it likely to remain one of small enterprises owned by private individuals and minor groups.

or in the personnel of business firms, or the establishment of prices and wages on a different basis. Certain minor ailments such measures might cure, if soundly conceived and applied; but they could never secure the blessings of peace and a creative social order.

CHAPTER THREE

SCIENTIFIC, EDUCATIONAL, RELIGIOUS, AND OTHER CURES AND PLANS

I. SCHOOLING, SCIENTIFIC DISCOVERIES, AND TECHNOLOGICAL INVENTIONS

In our credulous age the most potent panacea for war is held by many to be education, in the sense of literacy, schooling, science, and technological inventions. The more rapidly they increase, the sooner will peace be assured. Such is the almost universal belief of contemporary humanity, from university presidents and professors, engineers and inventors, to the illiterate bushman dazzled by the miracles of science and technology.

If education had been purely constructive, if science and technology had served only the God of Creation and not the Mammon of Destruction, if their fruits had not been misused, they might have constituted a potent remedy. Unfortunately school education has contained within itself many a destructive element. It has all too frequently been a mere superficial veneer, making neither for true intelligence nor for ennoblement of character. Science and technology have created not only beneficial inventions but also the most destructive devices for mass murder and for the extermination of cultural values. The fruits of science and technology have invariably been misused.

The contemporary misuse of these disciplines constitutes the gravest threat to the life, peace, and happiness of humanity. Hence in their present form neither literacy and schooling nor science and technology can eliminate or even reduce wars.

These are strong statements. They sound sacrilegious in our age of deified science. Yet they are accurate and verifiable. Here is a sufficient minimum of evidence. Since the twelfth century A.D. the percentage of literacy, the number of schools, colleges, and universities, and the volume of scientific discoveries and technological inventions have exhibited a fairly steady growth. Especially rapid has been their progress during the last two centuries. If these factors were genuine cures for war and revolution, we should expect that such conflicts would decline as we move from the illiterate, almost unscientific, and technologically primitive twelfth century on toward the increasingly literate, scientific, and technological nineteenth and twentieth centuries. As a matter of fact, however, war and revolution have, with some fluctuations, shown an upward trend. The highly literate, scientific, and technological twentieth century has been thus far the bloodiest, the most turbulent, and the most belligerent of all the twenty-five centuries of Western history since the rise of ancient Greece.

The following figures summarize the relationship between wars, revolutions, scientific discoveries, and technological inventions during the centuries in question.[1]

Centuries	Index of Magnitude of War (Measured by War Casualties per Million of Europe's Population)	Index of Magnitude of Internal Disturbances in Europe	Number of Universities and Colleges, Technical Schools, and Theological Institutions in the Western World	Number of Such Institutions Founded	Number of Scientific Discoveries and Technological Inventions per Century
XII	2 to 2.9	763	5	5	12
XIII	3 to 5.0	882	18	13	53
XIV	6 to 9.0	827	30	12	65
XV	8 to 11.0	748	57	27	127
XVI	14 to 16.0	509	98	41	429
XVII	45	605	129	31	691
XVIII	40	415	180	51	1574
XIX	17	766	603	423	8527
XX (1900-1925)	52	295	753	150	862 (only for 1900-1908)

The foregoing data show a constant multiplication of scientific discoveries and inventions from century to century, a fairly steady growth of the institutions of higher learning founded in each century, and a rapid and uninterrupted increase in the

---

[1] The data on the number of universities, etc., are taken from the official *Minerva Jahrbuch der Gelehrten Welt* (Berlin, 1930) and W. Lunden, *The Dynamics of Higher Education* (Pittsburgh, 1939), chap. 15. Other data are from *Dynamics*, II, chap. 3, and III, chaps. 9-14, which should be consulted for the details and for the method of computation of the indexes of war and internal disturbances.

number of such institutions. The nineteenth and twentieth centuries break all the records for the number of inventions and discoveries and of institutions of higher learning.

The data demonstrate also that war has not declined but, with some fluctuations, has sharply increased as we move from the twelfth to the twentieth century. The index for this century covers only the first quarter. If the wars between 1925 and 1947 were included, the index for the first half of this century would soar into the stratosphere, exceeding all the indexes of war for all the preceding centuries taken together.

Revolutions and other major internal disturbances have moved more erratically. After the high level of the twelfth to the fifteenth century inclusive, they underwent a notable decline between the sixteenth and the eighteenth century. In the nineteenth they again flare up, and in the first quarter of the twentieth century reach an unprecedentedly high level. If all the important domestic disturbances that occurred in the subsequent period of 1926-1947 were included, the first half of this century would give an index exceeding that for any whole century preceding.

Similar results are reached by a comparison of the culture of the most primitive tribes, the lower hunters and collectors of gifts of nature, with that of the more "advanced" higher hunters and the pastoral and agricultural tribes. With such an "advance of civilization" neither the frequency of war nor the cruelty of treatment of the vanquished decreases.[2]

These inductions demonstrate clearly that neither the growth of school education nor the multiplication of technological inventions and scientific discoveries has led to a decline of wars and revolutions. As a matter of fact, they have been attended by an enormous increase in war and revolution during the most literate and scientific century of all history. The explanation is that these alleged cures are either inherently impotent as remedies for social conflicts or that they have been misused in such a way as actually to promote these calamities.

This conclusion is supported by a vast body of other evidence.

---

[2] Cf. L. Hobhouse, G. Wheeler, M. Ginsberg, *The Material Culture and Social Institutions of the Simpler Peoples* (London, 1915), p. 232.

The evidence proves (1) that with an increase in education, scientific discoveries, and inventions, crime has not decreased; that comparatively illiterate persons, nations, and groups are not more criminal than literate ones; and that criminals are no less intelligent (in terms of schooling and mental tests) than non-criminals; (2) that there is a very remote relationship, if any, between education, I.Q., school grades, and other forms of measured intelligence, on the one hand, and egoism or altruism and antisocial or co-operative traits, on the other; (3) that even the intellectual élite of the past four centuries, distinguished for their genius, have hardly been ethically superior to the rank and file.

The widely accepted opinion that science, technology, and education invariably exert only moral, pacific, and socially ennobling effects is a sheer myth. The highly dangerous, antisocial effect of misapplied science and technology is now evident to everyone. Witness the atomic bomb (which has already snuffed out some two hundred thousand innocent lives), bacteriological warfare, and other satanic instruments of destruction. If in the future there are atomic and bacteriological wars, misused science and technology will be primarily responsible for the annihilation of the human species. A Biblical myth declares that at the dawn of human history the misused "tree of knowledge" cost humanity its Garden of Eden: a similar misuse now threatens to destroy the very tree of human life.

A morally and socially responsible science and technology, serving only a creative God and not the demons of destruction, a system of education inspiring human conduct with love and man's intellect with a true wisdom — such science, technology, and education would indeed promote creative peace. But in their present form they cannot perform this function.

II. RELIGION

If Christianity and its norms of conduct as they are enunciated in the Sermon on the Mount, were really practiced by Christians, and if Confucianism and Taoism, Hinduism and Buddhism, Judaism and Jainism, Mohammedanism, and other religions, with their moral commandments, were actually realized in the overt behavior of their followers, then they would exert a decisive influence upon the inhibition of war. Through the universal practice of love, hatred, antagonism, and injustice would be eliminated, and abiding harmony would prevail throughout the entire human universe.

Unfortunately there has been a vast discrepancy between what the followers of all these religions have preached and what they have actually practiced. In the West, among the Christians of the past few centuries, this chasm has steadily deepened and widened. Hundreds of millions of adherents of these religions learn the credo and the commandments; attend divine service, with its ritual and ceremonies; observe the prescribed rites and prayers; make donations for church buildings; rejoice over the expansion of their religion — over the increase in its membership and the multiplication of its churches, schools, and other institutions; and now and then are willing to promote its dominance through machinations, political pressure, or even the sword. In all these respects the leading religions have been successful in influencing the behavior of their members. They have, however, failed in the cardinal point, in making the overt conduct of their followers conform to the Golden Rule, to the principle of love toward their fellows, to the ethical norms of the Sermon on the Mount. This is especially true of Christianity during the last few centuries. Its external growth has been phenomenal. It has been diffused to all the four corners of the globe, achieving millions of converts on every continent, has vastly multiplied its funds, its real property, its agents, and its press facilities; and has notably improved the training of its priests and missionaries.

This growth has, however, not been accompanied by a decrease in wars or revolutions. On the contrary, during the past few centuries the most belligerent, the most aggressive, the most rapacious, the most power-drunk section of humanity has been precisely the Christian Western world. During these centuries Western Christendom has invaded all the other continents; its armies, followed by its priests and merchants, have subjugated, robbed, or pillaged, most of the non-Christian peoples, beginning with the preliterate tribes and ending with the non-Christian nations. Native American, African, Australian, and Asiatic populations have been subjected to this peculiar brand of Christian "love," which has generally manifested itself in pitiless extermination, enslavement, coercion, destruction of the cultural values, institutions, and way of life of the victims, and the spread of alcoholism, venereal disease, commercial cynicism, and the like. Incidentally the West did bring them a modicum of *real* Christianity, help and protection (in the form of hospital and medical services), loving sympathy, education, freedom and democracy. But these blessings were but "a drop in the bucket," a mere by-product, so to speak.

Somewhat similar has been the conduct of Christians toward one another during these centuries. With the Reformation they split into various factions, sects, and denominations, engaging, in the name of Christ, in endless religious wars, Protestants being pitted against Catholics, Catholics against Protestants and Eastern Orthodox Christians, and so forth. Likewise, in spite of the external growth of Christianity, secular civil and international wars involving Christians have not decreased during recent centuries, nor have crimes and other antisocial actions against individuals shown any abatement or proved any less numerous or atrocious than among non-Christian peoples.

To sum up: Christianity has failed to realize the vision of "Glory to God in the highest, and on earth, peace, good will toward men." It has not been able either to eliminate war or to make Christians less belligerent than non-Christians.

The immediate reason for such a failure is the chasm between the ideological preaching or speech reactions of Christians and their behavioral practice. Giving only lip service to the supreme injunction of Christianity, all-giving and all-forgiving love for God and man, and little practicing it, they are the victims of their own belligerency and aggressiveness, hatred, greed and lust of power, and other antisocial and antimoral traits. The criminality of Christians is no less pronounced than that of persons belonging to no religious denomination or even of avowed atheists and materialists.

What has been said of Christianity may be said, with the

proper modifications, of other religions. However lofty their ideals and norms of conduct, they have failed to mitigate war and other forms of conflict because they have not practiced what they have preached. In proselytizing they have tended to use the gospel of love to mask the sword of destruction and degradation. Likewise, their followers have failed to eradicate among themselves war, enmity, exploitation, and enslavement.

The leading world religions have had ample time to demonstrate their potentialities in shaping the overt behavior of human beings in the direction of love and harmony. As long as the chasm between preaching and practice remains, there is no reason to believe that the religions of the present time or of the future can eliminate war and ensure a lasting peace.

III. LEGAL AND ETHICAL CURES

What has been said of religion applies to law and ethics as inhibitors of war and other conflicts. Even if legal and moral norms prescribe altruistic conduct and prohibit war, they can be effective factors of peace only if they indeed influence the overt actions of persons and groups; that is, if they are practiced and enforced. Otherwise they remain simply impotent speech reactions.

Mere enforcement of legal norms prescribed by the state is, however, insufficient if these official norms do not correspond to the legal and ethical *convictions* of persons and groups. In such conditions the enforcement of the official law either becomes impossible or defeats the goal of peace and harmony. The ineffectiveness of the Volstead Act is one of innumerable cases of that sort. If tomorrow some state should enact a law establishing slavery, and if the state should mobilize all its police and judicial powers for its enforcement, such a law would be doomed to remain a dead letter, or if it were enforced by all the means at the disposal of the state, the result would be a civil war. Conquerors have been prone to impose such laws upon conquered populations, laws contradictory to the legal and moral convictions of the conquered. If the conquerors did not impose the most pitiless sanctions upon the conquered, their laws remained void of effectiveness. If they backed their laws by stern punishments and enforced them by the most drastic means, the result was hatred on the part of the vanquished toward the victor and endless attempts to overthrow his régime; that is, war instead of peace. If the conqueror was able to maintain his bloody domination for a long period, all attempts of the vanquished to free themselves from his yoke proving fruitless, the result was often the gradual extinction of the vanquished population or its physical, mental, and moral deterioration.

The history of the expansion of the white man's dominion is replete with such facts. For instance, the native population of New Zealand in 1841 was 104,000; in 1858, 55,467; in 1864, only about 47,000. The white man's civilization proved truly deadly to the conquered New Zealanders! At the time of Cook's visit the native population of Tahiti was between 150,000 and 200,000; in the sixties of the nineteenth century it was only about 15,000.[3] In our own day Hitler's cohorts exterminated millions of the rebellious vanquished. The excellently equipped armies of the white man are doing much the same thing in Indonesia, Indochina, South-East Africa, and elsewhere to populations that rebel against the domination and laws imposed by "democratic, civilized" governments of the Netherlands, France, and Great Britain. In such cases the enforcement works; but instead of bringing peace and happiness it produces hatred, bestiality, endless war, and finally extermination. In other cases the enforcement itself is found to be impossible. Thus the legal and ethical norms in question become a mere dead letter.

In general, if a law or ethical norm is not deeply rooted in a person's convictions and in his emotional and volitional nature, becoming a potent inner mentor and guide to his actions, such a law is doomed to be ineffective, no matter how rigorous may be the external enforcement. Most of us refrain from committing murder, rape, or theft not because we fear imprisonment or the electric chair, but because our "built-in" legal and moral con-

---

[3] For an enormous collection of similar data, see A. N. Engelgardt, *Progress kak evolutzia jestokosti* [Progress as the Evolution of Cruelty] (St. Petersburg, 1904); W. H. R. Rivers, *Essays on the Depopulation of Melanesia* (Cambridge, England, 1922); G. LeFevre, *Liberty and Restraint* (New York, 1931).

victions powerfully inhibit such actions, rejecting them as disgusting, criminal, or sinful. If our social order depended solely upon the police and external coercive enforcement, there would be perpetual disorder. To repeat: the enforcement of law by coercive means, when it contradicts the inherent legal convictions of the people, has never been able to prevent bloody conflict and establish lasting peace.

Moreover, law and ethics directly defeat this purpose and actually promote conflict when the legal and ethical norms prescribe antisocial conduct and relationships. A large proportion of law norms in various societies throughout history have been precisely of this type. They have introduced and enforced slavery and serfdom; they have prescribed the punishment or even extermination of those who disapproved of the legal norms of the ruling class, however selfish and however harmful to the subordinate majority these norms might be. Many legal and moral norms have demanded and enforced mass murder of all enemies in international or civil wars. They have decreed the imprisonment, execution, or banishment of all dissenters from the established state or church government, or of those opposed to the dominant political faction, race, nationality, social order, caste, or ruling social class.

A considerable part of the ethical norms of various hedonistic, materialistic, and utilitarian ethical systems, based on the principle of the struggle for existence, have also been of this character. They have recommended and inspired the most selfish, antisocial, and destructive forms of conduct and relationships. As such they have been not inhibitors of war but direct instigators of interpersonal and intergroup conflicts.

In the light of the foregoing considerations the utter vacuity of such formulas as "Peace and freedom are created by law" or "Law is the all-powerful factor of order and peace" must be clear. Only when we know what *kind* of law is meant, — whether ennobling or antisocial, just or unjust, conducive to the welfare of all or merely to the selfish interests of a few at the cost of the many, — only then do such formulas become meaningful. Only altruistic, ennobling, and just law norms, firmly rooted in the inner nature of human beings and groups and actually practiced by them, can constitute effective factors of peace and inhibitors of war. Such norms do not, however, arise automatically. They are possible only under certain cultural and social conditions. What these conditions are will be discussed later. Without a knowledge of these specifications and conditions the magic word, "Law," means nothing. If the law is antisocial, it works for war. In that case *summum jus* becomes *summa injuria.*

At the present time many norms of national and international official law are antisocial, serving the selfish interests of a few at the expense of humanity at large or of a majority of the populations. A portion of these norms are enforced, but lead to war instead of peace; the rest cannot be enforced and remain a dead letter. A very large percentage of the just law norms in the present codes are ineffective in the sense of not being practiced by the persons or the nations and other groups that profess them. They are not embodied in the inner nature of men, or only superficially so, residing chiefly in the ideologies of individuals and groups and not being given proper effect in their overt actions. As such they are violated at the first pretext.

Much the same effect has been produced by the wholesale "relativization" and degradation of legal and ethical norms that has occurred in the Western culture of the past four centuries. This culture has rebelled against all absolute and universal values and norms.[4] It has pronounced these to be merely relative, man-made conventions, incessantly changing, assuming the most diverse and even opposite forms in different groups and periods. It has degraded all ethical and legal norms by branding them as "rationalizations," "derivations," or "smoke screens," or as "repressions of the superego" veiling the egoistic interests and lusts of persons and groups: their economic interests, according to Marx; the libido and sadistic instincts, according to Freud; and similar drives and complexes according to a host of psychologists, biologists, sociologists, and anthropologists. Official law is declared specifically to be nothing but a clever invention of the ruling minority to exploit the stupid majority. Thus all ethical

---

[4] See *Dynamics,* II, chaps. 7, 13-15; also *Crisis,* chaps. 3-5.

and legal norms have been robbed of their intrinsic value and prestige, being debased to the level of means for the exploitation of the superstitious majority by a hypocritical minority.

At the present time there is no value or norm, whether relating to God or to the institutions of marriage or private property, that is equally accepted by all and regarded as universally binding on all, on communists and anticommunists, rich and poor, Catholics and atheists, Southern white Senators and Negroes, labor-unions and employers, fascists and democrats, Germans and non-Germans, Semites and Gentiles, "civilized" and "primitive" man. What one party declares legal, another calls "outrageous"; what one faction values as "sacred," another brands as "super-stitious"; what is "right" to one group is "wrong" to another. The norms of various groups are at war with and undermine one another. In this war they have made themselves mere "con-ventions" that can be transgressed at any time without com- punction. All-round cynicism and nihilism reign supreme. Na-turally, such legal and moral norms cannot effectively control human behavior.

No wonder, then, that with the increasing relativization and degradation of law and ethical norms during the modern period, especially the twentieth century, wars and revolutions have shown an upward trend, as well as the delinquency of the generations born and reared in this atmosphere of devitalized, debased, and contradictory norms! No wonder that contracts and vows, obligations and loyalties, have been more and more frequently repudiated; by the parties to a marriage, as attested by the rapidly mounting rate of divorces and desertions; by labor and management, as indicated by the increasing waves of strikes and lockouts; by governments, as evinced by the multi-plication of breaches of international law, treaties, and agree-ments; and so forth! Even the Supreme Court of the United States exhibits this relativization of law: during the past few years its unanimous decisions have notably decreased in number and the frequency of split decisions (by a slight majority) has sharply increased. No wonder, also, that under these conditions force has become the supreme arbiter of what is right and what is wrong in almost all major national and international disputes!

As long as such a state of law and ethics prevails, there is no hope of building lasting peace through these agencies.

IV. Prosperity

In our economically minded age prosperity is believed to be a sure panacea for all evils. To it are ascribed almost magical properties. It is well-nigh deified. Naturally it is endowed also with radical curative powers in relation to war.

In our discussion of capitalist and other economic alleged cures, it was pointed out that such beliefs are essentially superstitious. If poverty below the subsistence level engenders inter-individual and intergroup conflicts, prosperity above this level either is a relatively negligible factor of war and peace or else, when it leads to a sharp contrast between excessive riches and marginal poverty, promotes strife. This conclusion is sustained by a series of crucial facts.

The standard of living of the Western countries improved from two to five hundred per cent during the period 1800-1914, rising more rapidly as we approach 1914. Yet such a unique prosperity did not prevent the European explosion of 1914-1918. A systematic study of all the wars and revolutions from 500 B.C. up to 1925 A.D. in the history of ancient Greece and Rome and that of later European states shows that wars and revolutions occurred both in periods of rising prosperity and of impoverishment, and among both prosperous and poor nations, without any preponderance in periods of poverty or among poor nations. If anything, revolutions and wars occurred somewhat more frequently when the respective countries showed an upward trend of prosperity.[5] A study of strikes [6] in the United States and Canada for the periods 1881-1919 and 1920-1941 demonstrates that they too are more prevalent in periods of rising prices or prosperity than in those of depression.

---

[5] Cf. *Dynamics*, III, chaps. 9-13.

[6] A. Hansen, "Cycles of Strikes," *American Economic Review* (1921), pp. 616-621; J. V. Spielmans, "Strike Profiles," *Journal of Political Economy* (1944), pp. 319-339.

Similarly, with the increase of prosperity that marked the period 1800-1914, crimes failed to decline in number, nor were they fewer in the more prosperous countries as compared with the less prosperous countries that remained above the level of physiological necessity.

When rising, general prosperity is attended by an intensification of the contrasts between the richer and the poorer nations or between the richer and poorer strata of a given population, such prosperity tends to heighten the antagonism between the less favored and more favored nations, social classes, and groups. Furthermore, we shall see in chapter five that morally the more prosperous classes are hardly better than the poorer ones that are above the subsistence level.

The totality of such evidence dispels the faith in the magic curative properties of prosperity and its ability to abolish wars. With cultural and social conditions remaining what they are, we might conceivably have a society made up exclusively of multimillionaires; yet such a prosperity would not appreciably reduce wars, revolutions, and other conflicts.

V. The Fine Arts

Some are suggesting the fine arts, literature, the drama, music, painting, sculpture, or architecture, as the looked-for cure. There is no doubt that the fine arts exert tangible effects upon one's mentality and conduct. Whether this effect operates in favor of war or of peace depends upon the character of the fine arts. A truly noble type of the fine arts works for peace rather than for war. A low-grade, vulgar, sensual, erotic, and pathological type demoralizes and enervates. It stimulates man's lowest impulses and thus breeds egoism, sensuality, cynicism, and interpersonal and intergroup antagonism. A large proportion of the contemporary fine arts are precisely of this low-grade, demoralizing, and desocializing type. The bulk of the movies and shows, crooning and jazz, and many best sellers are mainly negativistic and debasing, moving in the subsocial sewers of sex pathology, crime, insanity, and muck raking vulgarity. Their characters are chiefly criminals, mistresses, prostitutes, sexual perverts, alcoholics, the insane, hypocrites, and the like.[7] Such an art obviously cannot create a noble and peaceful humanity. It tends, on the contrary, to intensify human demoralization and conflicts.

VI. OTHER CURES

The negative conclusions reached in regard to the discussed cures apply likewise to a long series of other alleged cures ranging from the innocuous to the downright absurd. *The invention of still more destructive weapons than the atomic bomb, and a monopolistic accumulation of these instruments of warfare in the hands of one nation or of one committee (national or international), are suggested as the road to peace.* The advocates of this plan believe that the realization of the very destructiveness of warfare waged with such a device would operate as a sobering deterrent.

It is hardly necessary to emphasize the naïve and highly dangerous character of this superstition. The increasing destructiveness of implements of warfare has never eliminated or even decreased war but, on the contrary, has merely intensified its magnitude and frightfulness. With the invention of gunpowder the percentage of war casualties per unit of manpower rose from 2.9 in the thirteenth century to 4.6 per cent in the fourteenth, and to 5.7 per cent in the fifteenth. With the subsequent invention of more efficient means of warfare the percentage rose to 16.3 in the nineteenth century, to 38.9 during the First World War, and to still higher figures during the Second World War.[8] Between the twelfth century and the First World War the strength of the military forces increased by about 36 times, while the casualty rate increased 539 times.

To hold that the destructive power of atomic bombs will stop war is equivalent to a belief that the more devilish the devil is, the more saintly he becomes! To expect that the monopolization of such means by one nation would abolish war is to forget the entire experience of human history. The attempt to conquer the world and through such domination to

---

[7] See chapter 8. Cf. *Dynamics.*
[8] For the details, see *Dynamics*, III, 336 ff.

establish universal peace is an old story. It has been repeated many times in human history; but it has never worked. Other nations have somehow always managed to procure armies and other destructive agencies equal to those of the world conqueror. The very sponsors of the latest plan to eliminate warfare through fear of an inferno themselves assure us that monopolistic control of the atomic bomb can at best be maintained for only a few years. There is, in fact, no assurance that such a monopoly still exists. Moreover, the power holding the monopoly could never withstand the temptation to misuse it for selfish purposes. The United States has already employed the atomic bomb unnecessarily: there is no guarantee that if we were pressed we would not employ it on a large scale. The same applies to any other nation. If no nation is going to use such lethal devices, why are all of them intent on manufacturing them and holding them in reserve? Why this mad race for armaments, the insane struggle for strategic bases, and all the other rivalries that within one year after the armistice had already poisoned the relationships of previous comrades-in-arms and turned them into quasi-enemies?

Likewise the other much-discussed plans for controlling the implements of war are utterly impractical. For instance, if a national monopoly of such weapons is futile, no less impotent is the plan to entrust their control to an international committee. If a committee of a monopolistic nation cannot be trusted, why should we trust an international committee, made up of persons in no respect better than the members of a national committee? Does the international character of such a body miraculously prevent its misusing the means entrusted to it? Don't we daily witness, in the deliberations of the United Nations, international majorities outrageously abusing their majority position at the expense of the vital interests of the minority? To believe that a mere transfer of control of such means of warfare from the hands of a national committee into those of an international committee would preclude their misuse is a sheer superstition!

The very existence of such satanic implements of warfare places every nation in a deadly dilemma: *either to strike first,* destroying perhaps hundreds of millions of innocent men, women, and children, or to run the imminent risk of *being annihilated by some other nation.*

Another potent preventive of war is alleged to consist in the *unlimited freedom of newspaper correspondents, columnists, radio commentators, and the like to write and speak as they please.*

Genuine freedom of thought and of the press is a great boon when it is not abused. If it *is* abused, this very freedom becomes a vicious war-breeding force. Considering that besides competent, wise and responsible reporters, columnists, and commentators there are many who are incompetent in respect to most of the things they discuss (for instance, they write and talk about a country or problem which they have studied for only a very brief period); that the rank and file of them are not blessed with great native ability; that many are biased, having some axe to grind or certain vested interest to promote, some of them cynically selling their services to the highest bidder; considering all this, such agents of "free public opinion" tend to misinform rather than to inform; to hand out misleading "scoops" rather than disseminate truth; and to engender distrust, envy, hatred, and enmity rather than sympathy, love, and good will. Hence this supposed remedy either does not work at all or else operates in such a way that with one hand it sows the seeds of peace while with the other it spreads the germs of war.

Other proposed cures are either of trifling importance or so utterly fatuous and stupid that it would be a waste of time even to survey them. One example (and there are hundreds) will suffice, namely, the establishment of a symbol of internationalism in the form of a seal or button. The Christian Cross is just such a symbol; yet throughout the two thousand years of its use it has been unable to banish war!

VIII. Conclusion

It should now be quite clear that none of the foregoing plans can assure peace. Taken alone, they are either fallacious or inadequate. Their principle defect is that they either neglect *the decisive factor of altruism and love, without which war cannot be eliminated, or are unable to make the overt behavior of persons and groups, with their social and cultural institutions, more altruistic than they are now.* Whatever the other prerequisites of a creative and lasting peace may be, it cannot be achieved without a substantial increase of love, sympathy, and free cooperation in the overt relationships of persons and groups.

This conclusion leads us to a further step in our study, namely, the investigation of the forces and conditions which render human beings, groups, and social and cultural institutions altruistic. Only by understanding these forces and conditions can we draft an adequate plan for the elimination of social conflicts and for the establishment of a harmonious and creative social and cultural order.

PART TWO

Insufficient Factors of Altruism

CHAPTER FOUR

ALTRUISM:
ITS FORMS, GRADATIONS, AND CREATIVITY

I. No Peace or Survival without Altruism

No human group can survive without a minimum of altruistic conduct among its members. If newborn infants were not cared for, they would die, and their death would end the existence of the group. This care is not always pleasant; and in many cases it brings no profit to those who perform it. A thoroughly egoistic person, devoid of love or sympathy, would prefer to be free from such burdensome duties. But such freedom, universally practiced, would lead to the extinction of the group. The increase of childless marriages in our time has already resulted, in most of the Western societies, in a stationary population, and in many cases, a declining population. Egoistically inspired, the practice of freedom from burdensome childbearing and the care of children is already bringing the Western world to the brink of suicide.

Similarly, without a minimum of altruism, all the sick, incapacitated, and aged members of a group would soon die. For a thoroughgoing egoist there is no reason to engage in such an unpleasant activity as the care of the aged and infirm. Only love, sympathy, and compassion can motivate it. Hence *a society consisting of only thoroughly egoistic members could not survive.*

Likewise *no peaceful or creative society could be made up of wholly egoistic members.* Devoid of mutual sympathy and a sense of duty, they would be engaged in an incessant struggle, now mild, now sharp and bloody. Suspicion, distrust, and mutual plots would flourish: *Bellum omnium contra omnes* would be the rule. A peaceful, harmonious, and creative society can exist only when its members possess at least a minimum of love, sympathy, and compassion ensuring mutual aid, co-operation, and fair treatment. Under these conditions its members are united in one collective "we" in which the joys and sorrows of one member are shared by others. In such a group a member is not an isolated "atom," but a vital part of a creative community. In such an atmosphere duties are performed gladly; burdens are borne easily; life is lived meaningfully; and serenity and peace of mind tend to prevail.

These self-evident truths are mentioned because in our days they are all too frequently forgotten. Most of the plans discussed in the preceding chapters barely mention an increase of altruism as a condition of lasting peace. Implicitly or explicitly they put their trust in some specific remedy which is supposed magically to create a harmonious society out of a gang of murderers and double-crossers.

II. Definition, Forms, and Gradations of Altruism

Without any pedantic definition, through our own direct experience we know what constitutes love or altruism. In most cases we can unerringly point out what kind of conduct is altruistic or egoistic, and we instantly recognize the sublimity of a given act of altruism or the callousness of an observed act of selfishness.

The Roman law gives the following formula of the minimum of altruistic conduct: "Neminem laedere et suum cuique tribuere" ("Do good to others, harm no one, and render to each his own"). Exercise your legal rights and perform your legal duties when they do not harm anyone else and when they do not violate the rights and duties of others — such is the essence of marginal altruism, slightly above the purely legal conduct prescribed. It is marginal because, with the exception of not harming anyone, it is confined within the limits of the obligatory legal conduct, by various punishments prescribed for its violation. Such a legal conduct is neither egoistic nor clearly altruistic. It does not contain any elements of love or generosity. Real altruism begins only when this minimum is transcended: when an individual freely sacrifices his rightful interests in favor of the well-being of another, refraining from harming him, even though his legal right entitles him to do so, and helping him in various ways, though no law demands of him such action. In this sense altruistic conduct is always above the purely legal conduct exacted by statutes. In contrast to obligatory legal conduct, altruistic conduct is always free from any external compulsion. It is freely chosen and it is also the purest form of free conduct known.

Genuine altruism is pure also in its motivation: altruistic actions are performed for their own sake, quite apart from any considerations of pleasure or utility. Aristotle and Cicero already clearly distinguished true friendship (altruism) from pseudo friendships motivated by the anticipation of pleasure or profit. Real friendship is an absolute end in itself. In pseudo friendships one loves a friend "not in so far as the friend beloved *is* but in so far as he is useful or pleasurable. Such friendships are of course very liable to dissolution when they are no longer pleasurable." [1]

The sublimest form of altruism is formulated in the Sermon on the Mount: "Love your enemies, do good to them that hate you, bless them that curse you. Greater love hath no man than this, that a man lay down his life for his friends." [2] This formula clearly indicates also the free, superlegal nature of altruistic conduct: "Whosoever shall smite thee on thy right cheek, turn to him the other also"; and "If any man will sue thee at the law, and take away thy coat, let him have thy cloak also." [3]

The above formulae of the marginal and sublimest forms of altruistic conduct define its nature and basic properties. They enable us to distinguish altruistic conduct from nonaltruistic and antialtruistic behavior. They indicate also the main forms and gradations of altruistic conduct.

A. Conduct opposed to altruistic conduct is *antialtruistic* or *egoistic*. Such are actions of hatred, enmity, and the like.

B. Conduct that does not actually contradict altruism but is

---

[1] Aristotle, *Nicomachean Ethics* (Everyman's Library), viii, 1156 a; cf. Cicero, "On Friendship." *The Offices* (Everyman's Library), p. 179.

[2] Luke 6:27-31; John 15:13.

[3] Matthew 5:39-41. For a detailed definition, analysis and classification of altruism, see *Society*, chaps. 4-7.

devoid of its characteristics is *nonaltruistic*. Strictly legal conduct, especially when the legal norms entitle one to exercise a right harmful to somebody else, is nonaltruistic, purely legal conduct. Social workers or officials rendering certain help to others are merely performing a duty for which they are paid. Their actions are only legal, marginal altruism.

c. Altruism preached but not practiced is a sham, or *hypocritical, pseudo altruism*. Real altruism must manifest itself not merely in speech reactions and ideology but in overt actions.

d. When altruistic actions are performed freely, for their own sake, they constitute *genuine altruism*. When they are performed for the sake of pleasure or utility, — not because of the inherent value of altruism itself, — they are forms of *impure altruism*. In genuinely altruistic actions, of course, a certain amount of pleasure or utility may and usually does follow as a *by-product*. However, they are not the reason for the performance of the altruistic acts, as in impure altruism. Genuinely altruistic acts are performed even when some suffering or disadvantage is incurred by the doer.

e. Again, we must distinguish *wise and creative altruism from blind altruistic passion*. In the former the action is devoid of harmful effects for the other party. It is altruistic both *subjectively and objectively*. In a blind love passion subjectively altruistic actions prove harmful to the other party: while their subjective end is altruistic, their objective nature is nonaltruistic. A mother spoiling her child by catering to all its fancies and failing to inhibit its dangerous whims affords an example of such a blind passion. Krylloff's fable furnishes another example, that of a bear throwing a stone at a fly that annoys the sleeping hermit (the bear's friend) and hitting instead the forehead of the hermit. The bear's intentions were wholly altruistic; but the objective consequences of its altruism are disastrous for the hermit.

f. Altruistic conduct varies widely in respect to the *extensity of the field to which it is applied and the intensity of the altruism itself*. One may apply his altruism to only a few persons, remaining either antialtruistic or nonaltruistic toward the rest of humanity. Or one may be altruistic toward many persons — indeed, toward the whole of mankind and all living creatures. In the first case the scope of one's altruism is very narrow; in the second it is wide, perhaps unbounded.

The intensity of altruism ranges from a minor act of sympathy, perhaps motivated by the expectation of pleasure or profit, to the boundless, all-giving, and all-forgiving love formulated in the Sermon on the Mount. Between these poles the intensity assumes many specific forms, as is suggested by the following terms: friendliness, kindness, benevolence, compassion, loyalty, devotion, respect, admiration, reverence, adoration, and infatuation. The duration of altruism varies from a short-time to an indefinitely long period of altruistic conduct.

c. The foregoing aspects of altruism permit a rough but valid gradation of persons and groups according to the magnitude, purity, duration and intensity of their altruism.

At the top of the scale of altruists are *the persons the scope of whose love is widest, being coterminous with the whole universe and God; the intensity of whose love is highest; whose love is wisest and most creative, and whose acts are motivated only by love itself, continuous and durable.* The greatest altruists of humanity, such as Buddha, Jesus (as a man), and Saint Francis of Assisi, represent the highest type of altruists. They were free from antialtruism and largely from nonaltruism; they loved even their enemies; their sphere of love was unlimited; their love was most intense; their altruism was of the most creative, wisest, and purest type. At the bottom of the scale stands a person imbued with intense hatred embracing the widest possible scope — devoid of altruism toward anyone or anything. Satan is often depicted as such an antialtruist, endowed with unlimited hatred.

In between these poles of love and enmity there are numerous intermediate types. We all know persons who intensely love their family or their own little group, hating at the same time many persons and groups, and remaining callously indifferent toward the rest of humanity. All who thus limit their love to their own group (their family or their friends, their religious group or their trade-union, their nation or their political party).

regarding the rest of the world as mere instruments for the advantage of themselves and their group belong to the type of *intragroup altruists and extragroup egoists.*

There are many who seemingly love all humanity without intensely loving any individual. Their love of humanity is so slight, costs them so little, and is so little practiced that it is closely akin to nonaltruistic indifference. Being neither hot nor cold, they occupy the borderline between the egoists and the low grade altruists.

Then there are many whose conduct is limited to the confines of the *legal norms,* rarely transcending these in the direction of a real altruism. They are law-abiding persons. As such they feel self-righteous, regarding themselves as honest and solid citizens. Their conscience is at rest even when they demand the "pound of flesh" they are entitled to by law, foreclose a property mortgage, beat their slaves or serfs, and so on. Such Scrooges are on the borderline between altruistic, nonaltruistic, and antialtruistic persons.

III. VARIETIES AND METHODS OF CREATIVE ALTRUISTS

The Hindu system of yoga distinguishes three main varieties of yogi and three ways of achieving union with the Absolute, or realizing man's own divinity and capacity for supreme love. (*a*) *Karma yoga,* leading to this goal through unselfish work performed incessantly for the benefit of all the human beings and other living creatures amidst whom a yogi lives. Such a yogi does not become a hermit or ascetic, priest or monk; he achieves his purpose through his altruistic actions amidst the busy, throbbing life of the everyday world. (*b*) *Bhakti yoga,* or the path of devotion to and love for the Absolute and hence in relation to all living creatures. Ordinarily the Bhakti yogi becomes a hermit or ascetic. As one of the first steps toward achieving love for the Absolute, he practices love for all living creatures and scrupulously refrains from harming them. (c) *Jnana yoga,* or the path of union with the Absolute through the highest creative activity in the fields of science and philosophy, religion and ethics, the fine arts, and so on, motivated by the purest desire of achieving union with the Absolute and of realizing the latent divinity within the yogi himself.[4]

The foregoing account of the great altruists and of the way of life which they have employed delineates fairly well the principal types and methods. Not only in the East but also in the West some persons have become great altruists through incessant deeds of love performed in the course of their daily work as laborers, peasants, teachers, doctors, and the like. Even such altruists as Saint Francis of Assisi did not retire to a hermitage but lived and functioned in the very heart of the busy workaday world. All normal human beings getting their living through honest work have a chance to practice the highest type of altruism, and many of them, in the most diverse callings, do so.

Other examples of altruists are furnished by scientists engaged in work that benefits others, giving to it all their energies regardless of remuneration, and sacrificing for it their health and other utilitarian values; by poets, dramatists, artists, and composers performing the same functions in their respective fields of creativeness; and by eminent philosophers, moralists, educators, and inventors similarly motivated. They all function as great altruists in respect to that portion of their work which they freely perform for the greater glory of God or for the greater welfare of humanity and which actually benefits a large number of human beings, although the rest of their activities may be devoid of these traits.

Finally, the great ascetics and hermits, true religious leaders, and mystics perform the functions of highest altruism through striving to achieve a union with God, or the Absolute. Saint Anthony, Pachomius, Saint Jerome, Sri Ramakrishna, Saint Benedict, and other noted Eastern and Western ascetics, hermits, mystics, and founders of monastic orders, as well as genuine religious and moral leaders, have manifested their lofty altruism through this particular method — that of striving for a union with God and thus embracing in love the whole of humanity and the whole cosmos.

---

[4] Cf. Swami Pavitrananda, *Common Sense about Yoga* (Advaitu Ashrama Mayavati, 1944); Swami Vivekananda, *Raja-Yoga* (Mayavati, 1930); J. H. Woods, *The Yoga-System of Patanjali* (Cambridge, Mass., 1914); Swami Akhilananda, *Hindu Psychology* (New York, 1946).

To sophisticated philistines their conduct may appear to be egoistically centered on their own salvation. The philistines are quite mistaken in such an interpretation. The goal of union with the Absolute already contains within itself as the first step, unlimited love for man and the entire world. In addition, as Bergson pointedly observes, these ascetics, hermits, and mystics serve the cause of altruism in a specific way by furnishing examples of human beings inseparably identified with the *creative élan* itself, or, in other words, with the Absolute.[5] These altruists who have fallen in love with the Absolute have exerted incalculably altruistic effects upon humanity.

Thus there are many types of altruistic persons and many ways to become altruists. The highest types of altruists are great creators. Saint Francis of Assisi and Saint Anthony were as eminent creators of altruistic values as were Beethoven and Sir Isaac Newton in their fields. The values of Karma, Bhakti, and Jnana and the manner of their creation are different, but they all represent the highest peaks of creativity, all ennobling man morally, enlightening him mentally, and elevating him aesthetically. In this sense the highest altruism and the highest creativity are inseparable.

IV. Altruistic Forms of Social Organization and Relationships

Since genuine altruism manifests itself not only in ideology and speech reactions but also in overt actions and relationships, its social manifestation always assumes *some form of co-operative organization involving mutual aid and collective altruistic relationships.* In accordance with the purity, extensity, intensity, and wisdom of the altruism of the members, co-operative organizations range from a marginally altruistic type of organization to the most extensive, purest, and highest form of co-operation. In marginal co-operative organizations whether a pair of friends, the family, a business concern, a political party, a state, a trade-union, or a religious group, a low grade altruism prevails among its members

---

[5] Henri Bergson, *Les Deux Sources de la Morale et de la Religion* (Paris, 1932), 225 ff.

who band together for the pursuit of their common interests through *competition* with other organizations, a struggle against a common enemy, or the exploitation of the rest of humanity. Though such marginal, low-grade altruistic co-operative groups widely vary in the extensity, intensity, purity, and wisdom of their altruism, they are all *co-operative organizations existing for the purpose of competition with the outside world.* In this sense they all blend some in-group altruistic elements with extragroup nonaltruistic and antialtruistic elements. If co-operation within the group embodies certain altruistic values, competition in all its forms contains nonaltruistic and antialtruistic values. The members of a murderous gang (who, by co-operating, render to one another certain altruistic services), co-operative business firms, competitive sporting teams, and competitive educational, scientific, philosophical, ethical, and religious institutions, all such organizations exhibit this impure or mixed form of altruism in varying degrees. *Only a co-operative organization free from every competitive element, with the widest scope for its altruism, and exhibiting the most intense, the purest, and the wisest forms of love, represents the highest altruistic type.* Its end is altruism itself. Its ethos is free from any cult of success and rivalry, from any pride or sense of superiority. It is imbued with the spirit of humility. Its members freely do their best because of their devotion to love itself. To do their best they require no compulsory legal sanctions, neither reward nor punishment, neither victory nor defeat, neither fame nor the fear of unpopularity. There have been few, if any, such institutions or groups. But certain approximations to them have now and then occurred, chiefly in the form of family, religious, and some other small groups.

The majority of co-operative organizations have belonged to an intermediate type between the marginal and the highest form of altruism. The overwhelming majority have been nearer to the marginal type; only a minority of social groups and organizations have approached the ideal type.

V. CONCLUSION

The foregoing gives us a sufficient working notion of altruism — of its forms and gradations; of its paths and methods; of the types of great creative altruists; and, finally, of altruistic organizations. Let us now turn to a consideration of what forces make for altruism and what are the roots of altruism itself.

CHAPTER FIVE

INSUFFICIENT FACTORS OF ALTRUISM

I. THE BIOLOGICAL NATURE OF MAN

Is altruism rooted in the biological nature of man or is it an acquired form of conduct? Is man's biological nature essentially altruistic or egoistic? All in all, the human organism seems to contain both altruistic and egoistic forces. The biological struggle for existence impels it to perform egoistic actions. On the other hand, the struggle for the preservation of the species, and often even for the self-preservation of the individual organism, induces acts of mutual aid and co-operation and other forms of altruistic behavior. In various degrees this is true of almost all species, especially of those whose offspring are born helpless and in need of nurture and for whom life in large groups offers better chances of survival than the roving life of those associated only sporadically and briefly with a few others. Charles Darwin himself stressed this law of co-operation and mutual aid, side by side with that of the struggle for existence, although for some time this aspect of his theory was neglected by many Darwinians. In 1880, the Russian zoologist Kessler made it clear that the law of mutual aid or co-operation is as fundamental a biological law as that of the struggle for existence. Later on Peter Kropotkin, in his *Mutual Aid* and then in his *Ethics,* demonstrated this principle convincingly. Since that time an enormous body of evidence has been produced showing that the principle of co-operation has possibly been even more important in the evolutionary process than that of the egoistic struggle for existence. From the simplest protozoa up to man, mutual aid in various forms is found to function among all species, especially among those that have to nurture their offspring. For man mutual aid has been the condition of survival of the species. Owing to its helplessness, a newborn child has to be taken care of for a number of years. The very biological interdependence of the two sexes of *homo sapiens* dictates their living together, their co-operation, their mutual love. Before human culture and weapons were developed, men could defend themselves against stronger species and many destructive forces only by living in large groups with co-ordinated collective activities. The lack of self-sufficiency of the human individual in many other respects led to the same result.

Since the altruistic conduct of man, side by side with egoistic actions, has deep roots in his biological nature, all the theories that proclaim the purely egoistic nature of the human organism are untenable. Among such fallacies is the Freudian theory that perceives in the human organism (in the "id") only sex drives and sadistic or masochistic instincts. On the other hand, all theories that insist on the purely altruistic nature of the human organism are equally one-sided.

A large body of observations shows that the elementary forms of aggressiveness as well as of sympathy appear in a child at as early an age as from four to eight months. For example, children smile at the smiles of others. From one to four years many aggressive as well as sympathetic actions emerge in their relationships. For instance, during 216 hours of observation 169 episodes of altruistic conduct occurred in the behavior of 52 out of 70 children at the age of from two to four years,[1] and in the behavior of 54 nursery-school children one conflict occurred on an average every 5 minutes.[2]

II. SOMATIC FACTORS OF ALTRUISM AND EGOISM

Experimental and observational studies of children show further that some of them are definitely more altruistic or egoistic than others.[3] Daily observations of adult persons reveal similar

---

[1] L. B. Murphy, *Social Behavior and Child Personality* (New York, 1937), p. 121 ff.

[2] A. T. Jersild and T. V. Markey, *Conflicts between Preschool Children* (New York, 1935), p. 53 ff.

[3] Cf. L. B. Murphy, *op. cit.*; A. T. Jersild and T. V. Markey, *op. cit.*; J. G. Mengert, "A Preliminary Study of the Reactions of Two-Year-Old Children," *Journal of Genetic Psychology* (1931); E. H. Green, "Friendship and Quarrels

contrasts. The question thus arises why human beings and groups differ so widely in their altruism and egoism. Why do some persons overflow with love toward all mankind, whereas others seem to be imbued for the most part with unquenchable hatred and selfishness? Are such differences inherent in the biological constitutions of individuals and groups, or are they caused by dissimilar environmental conditions?

The answers to these questions vary widely. Many have claimed that such differences are due mainly to dissimilarity in the somatic or biological factors. In contrast to this many others have found the explanation almost exclusively in environmental factors. A third theory relies on both somatic and environmental factors. Excluding certain biologically abnormal human organisms whose insane and often homicidal conduct is undoubtedly caused by their defective constitution, the answer to these questions seems to be somewhat as follows.

It is possible that some of the egoistic or altruistic differences in individuals and groups are due to the dissimilarity of their somatic (or bodily) constitutions. However, the attempts to demonstrate this, especially to determine exactly what kind of somatic differences are responsible, have proved quite inconclusive. Many theorists long claimed that the responsible somatic factors were as follows: the color of the skin, hair, and eyes; height and weight; the shape of the cranium; the texture of the hair and the configuration of the nose and other facial features; the specific structure of certain glands or of the nervous system; or a combination of these and other bodily traits. All such theories have turned out to be fallacious.[4]

Their failure led to much more complex and subtle varieties of these claims. The recent theories of somatic factors of human egoism and altruism do not take a single specific bodily trait as the key factor. Instead, they take the whole body, measure it in many directions, consider several other bodily characteristics,

among Preschool Children," *Child Development* (1933); H. C. Dawe, "An Analysis of Two Hundred Quarrels of Preschool Children," *Child Development Monographs*, No. 5 (1934).

[4] P. A. Sorokin, *Contemporary Sociological Theories* (New York, 1928), chap. 5.

put all these measurement data and characteristics together, and create a type of somatic constitution. Proceeding thus, they produce several somatic types. They claim that each somatic type is connected with certain mental, moral, and social characteristics, including such traits as criminality or sociality, egoism or altruism. The recent works of E. Kretchmer, E. A. Hooton, W. H. Sheldon and S. S. Stevens, C. C. Seltzer, C. W. Heath and others afford the best examples of theories of that kind.[5] Sheldon, for instance, gives us three main somatic types: (1) broad in the hips and relatively narrow in the shoulders, fattish and "round" (endomorphic); (2) broad in the shoulders, with narrow hips, strongly muscled, and well built (mesomorphic); (3) slender, somewhat flat-chested, and small-boned (ectomorphic). Among the many temperamental and other psychosocial characteristics ascribed to these somatic types are the following: sociality, tolerance, complacency, a pleasing character, amiability (the endomorphic type); aggressiveness, callousness, ruthlessness, assertiveness, love of domination and lust for power (the mesomorphic type); love of privacy, secretiveness, sociophobia, solitude, unpredictability, and so on (the ectomorphic type). C. Seltzer finds that persons whose bodies are somewhat disproportionate in the relationships of their chest depth, hip breadth, face breadth, and so on, display a lack of purpose and sense of values, lack of integration of their personality, asociality, and so on, more frequently than persons with normal bodies.

So far as the measurements of bodies and somatic types are concerned, these works are excellent. However, when we consider the alleged causal connection between certain somatic types and certain mental, moral, and social characteristics (including

[5] E. Kretchmer, *Physique and Character* (New York, 1925); E. A. Hooton, *Crime and the Man* (Cambridge, Mass., 1939); *Young Man, You Are Normal* (New York, 1945); W. H. Sheldon, *The Varieties of Human Physique* (New York, 1940); W. H. Sheldon and S. S. Stevens, *The Varieties of Temperament* (New York, 1942); C. C. Seltzer, "Body Disproportions and Dominant Personality Traits," *Psychosomatic Medicine* (1946), "The Relationship between the Masculine Component and Personality," *American Journal of Physical Anthropology* (1945); C. W. Heath, *What People Are* (Cambridge, Mass., 1945).

criminality and noncriminality, sociality and asociality, egoism and altruism), the theories in question are weak and unconvincing. Most of such traits are ascribed to a given somatic type with practically no supporting evidence. In other cases there is very little indication as to precisely how the temperamental and other characteristics were measured. In the somatic studies of various forms of criminality (murder, rape, theft, etc.) the explanation is much more clumsy and defective than an interpretation based on various environmental factors. In addition, the somatic theories themselves are somewhat contradictory: one ascribes a certain temperamental trait to a given somatic type, whereas another theory ascribes it a quite different type. Finally, a large number of studies of altruistic persons (devoted friends exhibiting acts of mutual service and sympathy) reveal no connection between the altruistic actions in question and this or that somatic type or bodily trait.

Thus the biological, or somatic, causation of altruism and egoism is still unproved. It is possible that there is some connection; but what it is and how close it is is virtually indeterminate.

Moreover, on the basis of a large number of experimental, semiexperimental, statistical, clinical, observational, and historical studies[6] we must conclude that *no close and definite relationship has been established between altruism or egoism, on the one*

---

[6] An abridged list of such studies: M. A. May and H. Hartshorne, *Studies in the Nature of Character* (New York, 1928-1930); L. B. Murphy, *op. cit.*; W. Boeck, *Das Mitleid bei Kindern* (Giessen, 1909); M. E. Bonney, "A Sociometric Study of the Relationship of Some Factors of Mutual Friendship," *Sociometry* (1946); R. Potashin, "A Sociometric Study of Children's Friendship," *Sociometry* (1946); A. T. Jersild and T. V. Markey, *op. cit.*; Jan D. Suttie, *The Origin of Love and Hatred* (London, 1935); E. Webb, "Character and Intelligence," *British Journal of Psychology Monographs*, Supplement No. 3 (1915); J. B. Maller, *Co-operation and Competition* (New York, 1929); P. A. Sorokin, "An Experimental Study of Efficiency of Work," *American Journal of Sociology* (1930); E. V. C. Berne, *An Experimental Investigation of Social Behavior in Young Children* (Iowa City, 1930); E. A. Graves, *The Effect of Competition* (unpublished study, University of Minnesota, 1934); P. J. Greenberg, "Competition in Children," *American Journal of Psychology* (1932); F. Hoppe, "Erforg und Misserfolg," *Psychologische Forschung* (1930); B. V. Belyaeff, "The Problem of the 'Collective' and Its Experimental-Psychological Study," in Russian *Psychologiya* (1929, 1930, 1932); I. Evergettoff, "Observations of Manifestations of Sociality in Early Childhood," in

hand, and such somatic characteristics as age, sex, race, health (apart from certain specific forms of mental and physical disease), *physical strength, cephalic index, weight, height, and color.* There is no even remotely adequate evidence that males are more altruistic or egoistic than females, or vice versa; that some races are more altruistic or egoistic than others; that healthy or physically strong persons are more unselfish than persons with poor health, or vice versa; that handsome people are more selfish than homely ones, or vice versa; that certain age groups are more altruistic or egoistic than other age groups; and so on.[7]

This means that the importance of somatic factors in this connection is not supported by the available body of evidence. Even if they do play a tangible role, it seems to be quite secondary in comparison with the influence of all the actions and reactions experienced by a person throughout his life under the impact of the totality of environmental forces amidst which he is born and reared and spends his adult life.

Let us now glance at various psychological factors which are

Russian *Mètody obiektivnago izucheniya rebenka* (1924); P. R. Farnworth and A. Behner, "A Note on the Attitude of Social Conformity," *Journal of Social Psychology* (1931); J. L. Moreno, *Who Shall Survive* (Washington, 1934); R. Updegraff and E. K. Herbst, "An Experimental Study of Social Behavior," *Journal of Genetic Psychology* (1933); M. A. May and L. W. Dobb, *Competition and Co-operation* (New York, 1937); J. C. Hsia, *A Study of Sociability of School Children* (New York, 1928); M. Meade, ed., *Co-operation and Competition among Primitive Peoples* (New York, 1927); E. Bogardus and P. Otto, "Social Psychology of Chums," *Sociology and Social Research*, XX; E. Bogardus, "Social Distance," *ibid.*, XXII; R. C. Challman, "Factors Influencing Friendship," *Child Development* (1932); E. G. Flemming, "Best Friends," *Journal of Social Psychology* (1932); C. H. Winslow, "A Study of the Extent of Agreement," *Journal of Social Psychology* (1937); H. M. Richardson, "Community of Values as a Factor in Friendship," *ibid.* (1940); E. V. Van Dyne, "Personality Traits and Friendship Formation," *ibid.* (1940); R. G. Pintner, Forlano, and H. Friedman, "Personality and Attitudinal Similarities," *Journal of Applied Psychology* (1937). If we add to these and similar studies the studies of causes of crime, revolutions, and wars, as the most acute forms of interindividual and intergroup antisociality, there is abundant evidence of the lack of any close connection between somatic factors, on the one hand, and altruism or egoism, on the other.

[7] In technical terms the coefficients of correlation between each of these somatic factors and sociality, altruism, or sympathy are found to be very insignificant — below .2. Most of them are close to zero, between .01 and .07.

claimed to be in part inherent and for which an important role is claimed in many theories of the causation of altruism and egoism.

III. INTELLIGENCE

Since somatic factors seem to be unimportant in making human beings altruistic or egoistic, the attention of investigators has naturally shifted to intelligence as a possible major factor. A large number of statistical, experimental, observational, clinical, and historical studies have been made to find out the relationship between intelligence and varieties of altruistic and selfish conduct. In some of these studies the samples of human material were very numerous, embracing thousands of individuals. The persons studied have included babies, nursery school children, elementary school and high school pupils, adolescents, college students, and adults. Intelligence itself has been measured by I.Q. and other forms of mental tests, by mental age, by school grades, by the amount of schooling, by personal achievement and the like.

What is the conclusion to be drawn from these studies? Contrary to a widely accepted opinion, *intelligence as measured by the foregoing techniques does not appear to be a significant factor in making human beings either altruistic or egoistic. Some slight relationship between these two phenomena possibly exists, higher intelligence slightly favoring altruism; but this relationship appears to be neither uniform nor consistent.*

The first confirmation of this conclusion is furnished by studies of the *relationship between intelligence and criminality,* as the most acute form of egoistic conduct. More than 163,000 cases were investigated from this standpoint. In earlier days, before such studies were undertaken, it was thought that most criminals were feeble-minded, or at least moronic, stupid, and of low intelligence. At the present time, in the light of a vast body of evidence, this conception is no longer regarded as tenable. Although the feeble-minded and persons of very low intelligence contribute in proportion to their number a slightly higher share of criminals than persons with normal intelligence, nevertheless the percentage of low intelligence, feeble-mindedness, and illiteracy is approximately the same in each population among the criminal and noncriminal elements. C. F. Chassell has carefully summed up the results of the bulk of such studies.[8] In the first place, the results of various studies of the relationship between delinquency and intelligence are contradictory, some exhibiting a positive and others a negative relationship, some a close and others a very remote relationship. In technical terms,[9] the coefficients of correlation between these variables range from minus .52 to plus .76, most of the best studies being near to zero (for instance .04 in the Army mental test of 18,711 delinquent cases). The contradictoriness of the results and the low coefficients in the most reliable studies indicate the absence of a close causal connection between criminality and intelligence or mental ability. The coefficients of colligation between *delinquency and illiteracy* fluctuate from minus .09 to plus .24; between *delinquency and amount of schooling*, from minus .12 to plus .19; between *criminality and school progress*, from .46 to .52; between *delinquency and educational achievement* about minus .46. Considering that the coefficient of colligation is a still less reliable symptom of causal relationship than the coefficient of correlation, the foregoing coefficients of colligation indicate a lack of close relationship between intelligence and delinquency.

Similar are the results of the studies of the relationship *between intelligence and morality* (including altruism and egoism). The coefficients of correlation between these phenomena are contradictory in various studies and range from minus .35 to plus .84, remaining very low (about .1 to .3) in the most careful studies.[10]

These results are well confirmed by the data on the trend of

---

[8] C. F. Chassell, *The Relationship between Morality and Intellect* (New York, 1935).

[9] If the causal relationship between the variables studied is close, the coefficient of correlation must be near to 1, though even such a coefficient does not guarantee that the variables are causally connected. To have symptomatic significance, it has to be above .5, exceeding many times the so-called standard deviation and probable error.

[10] Cf. C. F. Chassel, *op. cit.*, pp. 25-133, 377-470. Cf. also many of the works listed in footnote 6 of this chapter.

wars, revolutions, and crimes, and the growth of scientific discoveries and inventions and of institutions of higher learning from the twelfth to the twentieth century, as indicated in Chapter Three. The figures demonstrate that an increase of schooling, literacy, scientific discoveries, and inventions is not followed by a decrease of wars, revolutions, and crimes, as the most antisocial forms of conduct.

The conclusion is corroborated further by a series of experimental and observational studies that reveal a *very slight relationship between familiarity with the norms of altruistic and honest conduct and overt altruistic behavior.* For instance, in a series of experimental studies by H. Hartshorne, M. May, and F. Shuttleworth, though the children were aware of the moral norms prohibiting deceit and advocating social service, mutual aid, and sympathy in their overt conduct they made scant application of these rules of good conduct. The coefficient of correlation between their moral awareness and their overt conduct was very low, between minus .020 and plus .346. "No definite relations between conduct and ideas about conduct were discovered." [11]

We daily observe persons and groups who profess high moral standards but whose moral conduct remains on a low plane. The overwhelming majority of Christians, when slapped on one cheek, fail to offer their other cheek. In general, they practice the norms of the Sermon on the Mount as little as non-Christians, sometimes even less. A scholar may be thoroughly conversant with all the ethical systems, writing excellent treatises on ethics, and yet be as egoistic as the rank and file. In brief, the mere inculcation of ideas of altruism and saintliness is insufficient to elicit corresponding conduct. One may embrace these ideals intellectually, brilliantly analyze them and develop their implications, and effectively demonstrate their validity; yet, more often than not, one fails to apply them in one's overt conduct.

Finally, a tentative study of historical men and women of intellectual genius discloses that many of these, aside from the essentially altruistic character of their creative works, were of

[11] H. Hartshorne, M. May, and F. K. Shuttleworth, *Studies in the Nature of Character* (New York, 1930), pp. 157-165.

quite average stature in their morality and altruism, while others were actually below the average standard of the rank and file of their contemporaries. Whether the proportion of moral delinquency among persons of intellectual genius is greater or smaller than among the bulk of the population has not been determined. But the very fact that, with the above exceptions, many intellectual geniuses have been notable egoists, sometimes conspicuously antisocial, points to the lack of any close connection between intellectuality on the one hand and altruism or egoism on the other. Like health or physical strength, intelligence as such seems to be a neutral factor in respect to altruism or egoism. Whether it operates to serve altruism or the reverse depends upon the environmental forces, family, schooling and the educational character of the various agencies amidst which the individual is born and reared. If all such agencies mold it in an altruistic direction, it will serve the cause of altruism; otherwise it will promote the cause of personal or group egoism. As we shall see, many educational influences in our modern society operate in both directions.

IV. Religious, Ethical, and Political Ideologies

As long as the discrepancy between the ideologies of persons and groups and their overt conduct persists, it is relatively unimportant what kind of religious, ethical, political, or other doctrines they profess; for an unapplied ideology is not a major factor of altruism or egoism. That is why an avowedly religious person often behaves no more altruistically than an avowed atheist; why there is little difference between the overt conduct of partisans of an extremely materialistic and those of an extremely idealistic philosophy; of ardent advocates of capitalism, socialism, communism, fascism, democracy, and autocracy; of proponents and opponents of anti-Semitism; of those proclaiming the doctrines of racial superiority and equality; or of purely ideological pacifists and militarists. This general principle explains why, for instance, we do not find much difference in the belligerency of autocratic and democratic countries and of Christian and non-Christian countries (cf. Chapters One to Three).

Only when religious, ethical, political, economic, artistic, and other ideologies are so deeply rooted in persons and groups that they are consistently *practiced,* only then do they become effective factors of altruism and egoism.

Unfortunately, intellectually sophisticated modern persons apply their altruistic ideologies much less consistently than primitive tribes, unsophisticated children, and simple persons in general. The ideologies and overt actions of the latter are far more intimately connected. In their thinking and speech their whole organism participates; their thoughts and speech reactions are an integral part of their overt actions. Their ideas and utterances are not employed to mask their actual conduct, nor are their overt activities readily performed in contradiction to their ideologies and speech reactions. They ordinarily say what they think and do what they say they do. "Whosoever shall not receive the kingdom of God as a little child, he shall in no wise enter therein," Jesus pointedly observed, stressing children's practice of what they profess, in contradistinction to the behavior of sophisticated hypocrites.[12]

But modern adults can, with no moral compunction, manipulate their thoughts and speech reactions independently of their overt behavior. They can profess almost anything without appreciably practicing what they preach.[13] Owing to this chasm, different persons may entertain quite opposite ideologies, and yet their overt conduct may be equally altruistic or egoistic. A person may substitute an atheistic ideology for a religious one, or adopt a materialistic philosophy in place of an idealistic one, without any significant change in the altruism or egoism of his overt behavior. Such "autonomous" ideologies and speech reactions are not important factors as determinants of altruism or egoism; hence the relative impotence of most of the purely ideological indoctrination employed in the interest of a multitude of causes. In spite of thousands of daily sermons on Christian love and millions of invocations of the name of "Our Lord,

---

12 Luke 18:17.

13 See the series of excellent observations on this in W. Galt, "Our Mother Tongue," *Psychoanalytic Review* (1943); T. Burrow, *The Biology of Human Conflict* (New York, 1937); *Society,* chaps. 17-19.

Jesus," in spite of the most powerful propaganda against anti-Semitism and other racial and religious discrimination, overt Christian altruism has shown no tangible increase nor have anti-Semitism and racial and religious tension perceptibly decreased.

V. "Emotional Stability"

"Emotional stability" has been much in vogue during the last few decades. It is regarded as a factor making for integrity, honesty, altruism, and other desirable social traits. It is recommended as a potent cure for mental illness, hatred, crime, war, strikes, and other personal and social maladjustments. During the war some of its advocates went so far as to urge that soldiers should fight unemotionally, without a sense of hatred toward the enemy, employing only rationally calculated actions. High emotionality, "emotional heat and outbursts," and emotional instability are regarded unfavorably, as the source of many personal and social evils. This fashion has gone so far that if a scientific book betrays emotion, such emotionality is deemed sufficient evidence that the book is unscientific.

Is this vogue sound? Is so-called "emotional stability," as it is measured by various tests designed for that purpose, indeed a force operating in favor of altruism? Have the great altruists of history actually been unemotional calculating machines? Does "emotional stability," in this sense, really eliminate or decrease egoism? The answer to all these questions is in the negative.

The existing studies of the connection between altruism and emotional stability do not show any close relationship. The coefficients of correlation between these variables run low,— around .15,—which means a lack of any genuine causal ties between emotional stability or instability and sympathy, social service, honesty, and other forms of altruistic conduct.

Many great altruists, notably Jesus and Saint Francis of Assisi, have been distinctly emotional, showing intense compassion for the sorrows of others and heatedly denouncing the vices of egoism. The tone of the sermons of Jesus is highly emotional throughout. Again, witness the incessant singing and emotional ebullitions of Saint Francis, the fluctuations between moods of black despair and those of beatific joy which have been a common trait of the experience of most of the major altruists and mystics before they have reached the final stage, that of union with the Absolute. According to the existing psychological tests of "emotional stability" they would be ranked as highly emotional persons with a low index of stability.

On the other hand, the Nazi policy of extermination of millions of the conquered was carried on quite cold-bloodedly, with a calm, scientific efficiency aimed at eliminating the maximum number of enemies of "inferior" races, groups, and individuals. The same applies to the inhuman experiments on prisoners performed by Nazi scientists. Equally unemotional was the invention, in scientific laboratories, of the most inhuman and deadly instrument of destruction on record, the atomic bomb, and its use in the annihilation of the inhabitants of Hiroshima and Nagasaki. Likewise, efficient modern gangs of murderers generally slay their victims relatively unemotionally, not necessarily with a sense of hatred but for cold-blooded pecuniary advantage.

In brief, the vogue discussed is but a superstition, idealizing so-called "emotional stability," or unemotionality, without any valid reason. Contradicted by a vast body of specific factual evidence, it is repudiated also by still more general considerations.

Without intense love, sympathy, empathy, compassion, and other emotional participation in the joys and sorrows of others we cannot be deeply moved to actions of altruism, generosity, or sacrifice. For any vigorous activity we need always a strong emotional support. The mere idea of an action, not backed by emotional force, is insufficient to impel us to perform an act, much less, to carry it through with vigor and perseverance. If our legal or moral convictions remained merely the intellectual apprehension of rules of conduct, we should hardly be able to put them into practice, vigorously defending our rights when they are violated or discharge our duties when these are burdensome.[14] Without emotions we cannot be truly indignant at

[14] For evidence, see *Society*, chap. 4

violations of the rules of decency; cannot indefatigably fight against injustice; cannot wholeheartedly pursue any purpose.

To sum up: Emotionality is a most powerful force in human behavior. As long as a person pursues vigorously any objective, his ideas of action must be backed by strong emotions; and the more difficult the task to be performed, the greater must be the driving force of the respective emotions. Taken *per se,* emotions are neither good nor bad, neither altruistic nor egoistic. Like any motive power, they can propel a bomber showering devastation upon cities or an airplane flying on a charity mission. The emotion of hatred induces chiefly egoistic actions, whereas the emotion of love ordinarily engenders altruistic actions. What is important is not emotional stability or instability as such but the *kind* of emotion and the character of the cause which it serves. If emotions are of an altruistic nature, and if they serve the cause of love, sympathy, and mutual aid, the stronger they are the better.

VI. Economic Conditions

Here we have to repeat much of what has been said respecting economic conditions as factors of war and peace. If they fall below the level of physiological necessity, as in the case of famine or extreme poverty, they tend to accentuate the altruism of a small minority and to brutalize the majority (the law of polarization, to be discussed later).[15] Above that level, taken alone, they do not exert uniformly either altruistic or egoistic effects. The widespread notion that an improvement of economic conditions necessarily leads to a corresponding ennoblement of human conduct is largely a myth. The existing studies of the relationship between the economic status of children and their co-operativeness, social service, and other forms of altruistic conduct disclose no close connection, the coefficients of correlation ranging from minus .1 to plus .23. Numerous studies of mutual friends yield similar results: their friendship is determined little by economic conditions. Studies of happy marriages present the

---

[15] See *Calamity,* chaps. 9-15.

same picture: happiness in this relationship depends little upon economic conditions (provided they are above the subsistence level). Observations on the conduct of the richer and poorer classes fail to demonstrate that the former are more altruistic than the latter, or vice versa. If we measure their respective charitable proclivities by the amount of voluntary donations for social well-being in proportion to their wealth and income, the richer classes prove in no way more altruistic than the poorer classes. If we measure their altruism and egoism by the pressure they apply for the protection of their selfish interests, the evidence is again negative. If we compare the richer and the poorer nations in respect to their intragroup and extragroup altruism, no definite conclusion in favor of either richer or poorer nations is warranted.

If, instead of comparative richness, we compare pastoral, agri-cultural, and industrial economic régimes, we find no valid evidence that any one of these régimes is particularly egoistic or altruistic. On the other hand, as we shall see, a marked contrast in poverty and wealth between the poor and the rich generates antagonism between these classes.

The same result is obtained when we measure egoism in terms of wars, revolutions, and crimes. As we have already noted, industrial nations, as well as prosperous nations and periods, do not prove any less belligerent, turbulent, or criminal than the pastoral or agricultural peoples and less prosperous peoples and periods.

Taken alone, then, economic conditions, whether in the sense of prosperity and poverty (above the subsistence level) or in the sense of pastoral, agricultural, and industrial systems, do not exert any tangible uniform altruistic or egoistic effects; although, in conjunction with other social and cultural conditions, they may operate in either of these directions or they may constitute neutral factors.

VII. SIMILARITY AND DISSIMILARITY

Having failed to find significant factors of altruism among various somatic and psychological traits, many thinkers of the past and present have sought for them not in this or that single somatic or psychological characteristic but in the similarity or dissimilarity of the interacting individuals and groups. Three different theories have been advanced in this field. The first of these theories claims that similarity of individuals or groups produces a solidary or altruistic relationship. The second theory contends that on the contrary it is the opposite poles, the dissimilarity, that attracts individuals and groups toward one another and establishes friendly relationships. The third theory states the existence of two different kinds of friendship: one based on the similarity of the interacting individuals and groups; the other, on their dissimilarity. One is the solidarity of similar and like-minded persons and groups; the other is the solidarity due to the lack of self-sufficiency on the part of individuals or groups and to their mutual supplementation.[16]

When tested, each of these theories is found to be untenable. A large number of studies of pairs of friends show that the friends are similar in a number of traits and dissimilar in a number of others. Thus, in three hundred pairs of friends studied, their behavior was found to be similar in 2962 traits and dissimilar in 1484 traits. Eighty-eight per cent of their standards and ideals were similar, whereas only fifty per cent of their hobbies, reading habits, shopping habits, and the like were similar. This means that not all similar or dissimilar traits are equally important in generation of friendship, some are effective, some are not; some similarities lead to friendship while others to animosity. Many other studies of friends reveal no preponderance of similarities over dissimilarities as compared with similarities and dissimilarities among nonfriends.

A large number of studies of choice of marriage mates and of happy and unhappy marriages yield a similar conclusion. In many countries like ours there seems to be a slight prevalence of certain similarities among those who fall in love and in happy marriages: to some extent the tall attract the tall, the blond gravitate to the blond, the intelligent to the intelligent, the

---

[16] See *Society*, chap. 4.

deaf-mute to the deaf-mute. The same is true of their similarities in nationality, religion, economic status, standards and ideals, hobbies, and other factors. However, side by side with such similarities there are many more dissimilarities. The coefficents of correlation in all similarities of pairs are comparatively low, ranging from negative to positive, from zero to .5. In most cases they remain around .2 or .3, and are hence far from being significant. Moreover, even the observed similarities of sweethearts and married couples hardly mean a specific attraction of like to like, but are ordinarily the result of unequal opportunities of the parties to meet and interact with similar and dissimilar persons. If in a given city from 67 to 76 per cent of the marriages studied are between persons living within twenty blocks of one another, the reason is not the special attraction of spatial propinquity but the greater opportunities enjoyed by neighbors to meet, fall in love, and marry as compared with the opportunities of persons remote from one another. For the same reason, among the first generation of Italian, Polish, and Finnish Americans, Italians marry preponderantly Italians, Poles marry Poles, and Finns marry Finns. When in the second and subsequent generations they increasingly meet and interact with non-Italian, non-Polish, and non-Finnish Americans, they increasingly marry persons representing other national ingredients of the American melting pot. Similarly, we note the decreasing proportion of marriages among persons belonging to the same religion: whereas in New Haven, Connecticut, 91.2 per cent of marriages in 1870 were among persons belonging to the same religion (Jew with Jew, Catholic with Catholic, Protestant with Protestant), by 1940 this percentage had fallen to 63.6.

In countries in which so-called exogamic marriages prevail, even this external preponderance of similarities between bride and bridegroom is lacking: in law and in fact the parties must belong to different tribes, clans, families, communities, etc. Even in Western countries the prohibition of marriages among close relatives, within certain degrees of consaguinity, contradict the claim that the more similar the parties, the greater the likelihood of their falling in love and marrying — that since members of the same family and other close relatives show the greatest degree of similarity, they are bound to be most strongly attracted and to show the highest percentage of intermarriage. If this were true, it would preclude even the enactment of a law prohibiting such unions.

Finally, the very fact that it is the members of *different* sexes who fall violently in love with each other, and not members of the *same* sex, testifies against a universal uniformity that in love and friendship like attract like. (Homosexual love is confined to an insignificant percentage of human beings.)

For all these reasons the theory of similarity or dissimilarity of individuals and groups as the sole basis for friendship or altruism cannot be accepted.

The fact that there is some similarity between friends, lovers, and married couples refutes the opposite theory that in friendship and love the opposite poles attract: the tall attract the short, the fat attract the thin, the intelligent the stupid, and the rich the poor, or that the religious gravitate to the atheists, and so on.

Untenable likewise is the third theory, namely, that there are two quite different forms of solidarity or friendship, one based on similarity, the other on dissimilarity. For in all cases of friendship, love, and altruism there is always a certain combination of similar and dissimilar traits.

What, then, are the valid conclusions in this matter? In a summarized form they are as follows.[17]

Among the thousands of traits in respect to which persons or groups may be similar or dissimilar, not all are potent in generating either altruistic or egoistic relationships. The majority of such traits (for instance, similarity or dissimilarity in preference for Chesterfield cigarettes vs. Camels, or Beechnut chewing gum vs. Wrigley's, or brown vs. black shoes) do not exert either an altruistic or an antagonistic influence on their relationships.

Only those similar or dissimilar traits that are regarded as important by the parties exert such influence. If a given society ascribes a high value to racial or religious traits, then similarity

---

[17] For detailed analysis of these, see *Society*.

in race or religion generates more friendly relationships than dissimilarity in these respects.[18] If another society considers racial and religious traits unimportant, then in such a society racial and religious similarity or dissimilarity plays a negligible role as a determinant of altruistic or egoistic relationships.

Which of the traits of similarity and dissimilarity are important for given persons and groups depends not so much upon the inherent biological and physical nature of these traits as upon the system of values of the respective persons and groups. In the religiously minded medieval society, similarity in religion was a crucial factor; in a society of atheists it is irrelevant to the generation of friendly or antagonistic relationships. In America, in the scale of values of the Southern states racial similarity or dissimilarity occupies an important place; in the scale of values of the Russian people it is irrelevant. Hence the racial friction between the whites and the Negroes in the Southern states and its absence in Russia. In the scale of values of a loving mother her baby constitutes the most important value; therefore she loves it even though physically and psychologically it may be as different from her as possible. Another child may be very similar to her baby; yet it does not generate the same love that her own baby elicits.

If the sociocultural systems of values of the parties are similar, then an important similar trait may generate both altruistic and antagonistic relationships between the parties under the following conditions.

A. It generates solidarity: (a) When the values equally important for the interacting parties are abundant and sufficient for all; when each party can have its full share without decreasing that of the other parties. The grace of God for Christians; the national pride of patriots; the prestige of the family, party, or union for its members. All these are, for their members, virtually inexhaustible and lead to the solidarity of the members. (b) If the egos of the interacting parties are already fused together in one "we." In this oneness the

---

[18] Therefore the most effective way of reducing interracial and interreligious friction in such countries is to disseminate the ideas and attitudes of racial and religious equalitarianism. Otherwise propaganda against such friction is doomed to failure. A great deal of the current propaganda against it maintains (explicitly or implicitly) the superiority of a certain race or religion. No wonder it has proved ineffective!

more of the value a member has, the richer is the unified "we," and the greater becomes the share of every participating member. In the condition of such a "we" even a scarcity of the important value leads to a solidarity of the parties. The "we" may be a good family, a labor union, a religious body, a nation, a political party and what not.

B. It generates antagonism: (a) When the values regarded as important by all the parties are scarce. (b) When the nature of the important value does not permit any sharing between the parties, so that only one of them can have the value, for instance, marrying a girl or boy equally desired by all the parties. (c) When the parties are not fused into one "we." (d) The antagonism of the socioculturally similar parties, due to a scarcity of the important value, may be mitigated by a "fair" and "just" distribution of the value between the parties (according to the notion of "fairness" and "justice" of the parties). In some cases this "fairness" means an arithmetically equal share for each party; in others, a "proportional" share to each party according to its merits.

An important sociocultural dissimilarity may generate both solidarity and antagonism between the parties with different systems of values:

A. If the values (or traits) of the parties are *quite dissimilar*, having no common ground and containing no value equally regarded as important by the parties, such values do not generate either solidarity or antagonism. The values of the other party are regarded as unimportant hobbies that provoke neither positive nor negative reactions. The same is true when some of the values of the parties are opposite but are considered unimportant and negligible.

B. When each party regards its values as important and when these values are opposite, one party denying what the other party affirms, such a dissimilarity (mixed with similarity in that all parties regard the values as important) generates antagonism between the parties. When an atheist and a believer, a communist and an anticommunist, regard their own values as important and assign a negative importance to the values of their opponents, they become antagonistic.

C. When the main values and norms of the parties are similar but their secondary values are diverse and mutually neutral, and especially when the other values are mutually supplementary, such a combination of similarity and dissimilarity facilitates the solidarity of the parties involved. Heterosexual marriage between parties having their main values as common and differing only in secondary values; a society made up of different racial or ethnic groups, each possessing its own values or traits, but all possessing a common system of values, thus constituting a multicolored united whole; a society with a well developed social division of labor but with the main system of values common to all groups and segments, these are concrete types of such solidarity. On the other hand, if such a group is made up of persons and subgroups with discordant values and norms, each person (in marriage) or subgroup (in society) having values different from one another, such a society constitutes an antagonistic body, in which the diverse values clash, or at best a neutral body, in which persons and subgroups are indifferent to one another. Such a "unity" is exceedingly loose and may disintegrate because of the slightest adversity. A society composed of a majority and a minority having no common system of values and many contradictory values cannot fail to become antagonistic. An explicit or implicit antagonism (or indifferentism) between the majority and minority becomes inevitable in such a situation. This antagonism may be mitigated through the introduction of common norms of a "fair and just" distribution (or limitation) of the clashing values according to the principles of "live and let live," "up to this point your values are legitimate," and "from here to there is the area of my values." Such mitigation and tolerance can occur only when the parties have a common fund of values, at least in the form of a recognition of these norms of "fair play." Otherwise even this minimum of mutual tolerance, as the lowest form of solidarity, is impossible in such a society.

From the above it follows that the combination of a basic similarity in the main values of the parties with a supplementary diversity in their secondary values is the most conducive to solidary relationships, provided that the main values are abundant or are distributed by all the parties according to their concordant norms.

An opposite and diverse character of the values and norms of the parties, when they are considered important (positively or negatively) and when the parties have no common system of values and norms, is the most conducive to the generation of intense antagonisms. Just such a combination of the dissimilar with the similar has uniformly been the cause of the sharpest antagonisms — wars, revolutions, riots, and interpersonal crimes and conflicts.[19]

These conclusions indicate that although the factors of similarity and dissimilarity play an important part in generating altruistic and egoistic relationships in interpersonal and intergroup reactions, their role is more complex than any of the three foregoing theories claims.

VIII. GENERAL CONCLUSION

In order to understand these roles we have had to consider the broadest possible scope of the values of persons and groups. These values embrace practically the totality of their social and cultural values. Thus we face the necessity of seeking the factors of altruism and egoism not in this or that single factor (somatic, biophysical, psychological, or mental similarities and dissimilarities), but in the total systems of values of persons and groups, that is, in their entire cultural and social environment and in the entire make-up of their own personalities. Each of the single factors considered, and the same is true of any other single factor, is found to be utterly inadequate to explain why persons and groups differ so widely in their altruistic and egoistic behavior, why this behavior changes, and why now altruistic and now egoistic tendencies increase or decrease.

Even such a comparatively simple fact as the health of an organism cannot be explained by any single factor, such as heredity, food or drink, vitamins or drugs, physical exercise, or climate. Its heredity, its manner of living and its total environment must all be considered. Only an organism with a sound heredity, properly satisfying all its vital needs, possessing healthful habits, and living in a wholesome milieu enjoys good health. This multiplicity of factors is still more true of the generation and maintenance of altruism. No single factor can account for it. Only the proper (inherited and acquired) make-up of the persons, functioning in a certain total cultural and social environment, can ensure this. Hence, in our search for the adequate

---

[19] See *Society*, chaps. 31-33.

factors of peace and altruism, we must now turn to a consideration of what kinds of persons and groups, what kinds of cultural and social institutions generate peace, harmony, and altruistic relationships.

PART THREE

Cultural Factors of

Altruism and Egoism

CHAPTER SIX

TWO BASIC PRINCIPLES

I. INDIVISIBLE SOCIOCULTURAL TRINITY

The fundamental shortcomings of the proposed cures for war and of the factors of altruism consist not only in the fact that they analyze single isolated factors, but also in their complete disregard for the indivisible unity of the three aspects of socio-cultural phenomena: *cultural, social, and personal.* Whatever social group we take, whether the family, the state, the church, a labor union, a business firm, or a scientific society, in every such group we find these three aspects. *A given culture is the sum total of the values for whose realization, use, and enjoyment the group is organized and functions.* The culture of a business firm is made up of economic values of certain kinds; that of a religious or scientific group consists respectively of religious or scientific values; that of the family consists of such values as love, procreation, and the education of children. The cultural values of a group are the *raison d'être* of its existence. It is established and exists for the realization, enjoyment, and diffusion of these values.

Every group exhibits, moreover, *a social aspect made up of all the social relationships occurring among its members. These relationships define the members' rights and duties, their functions and role in the group, their position and status.* In the state they embrace the rights and duties, functions, and positions of the president or monarch, the cabinet ministers, and the various ranks of the governmental hierarchy, as well as of the ordinary citizen. In the Roman Catholic Church these social relationships determine the rights and duties of the Pope, cardinals, bishops, priests, and plain parishioners. A similar network of social relationships is found in every organized group.

93

Finally, *every group is made up of the human individuals embedded in its culture and the network of its social relationships, each member having certain roles and functions and a certain position assigned him in the group.*

These three aspects are inseparable from one another. The cultural values of the Roman Catholic Church (clearly outlined in its Credo and in the totality of its religious beliefs, rituals, and material vehicles) are reflected in its network of social relationships, its social structure, and in the mentality and actions of its members: their beliefs, their prayers, their attendance at religious services, their contributions to the Church, their political voting as advised by the Church leaders, and so on. Conversely, the mentality and beliefs, actions, and functions of members of the Church are reflected in its social organization and cultural values.

Its social structure and cultural values could not be maintained by atheists or Buddhists. Nor could Catholics create or maintain a Confucian or Mohammedan religious organization or atheistic institution. The same inseparableness of the cultural, social, and personal aspects is exhibited by every other organized group. These three aspects constitute an indivisible trinity bound together by the ties of causal and meaningful interdependence.[1]

Hence any important change in one of these aspects of a group is usually followed, sooner or later, by a corresponding change in its other two aspects. Otherwise the group becomes morbid: an acute internal friction between its changed and its unchanged factors sets in, and, if not arrested in time, leads to a serious crisis and to the eventual disintegration of the group. If, for example, in the United States the majority of the citizens should become converted to nazism or communism, and if the Federal Constitution and the cultural values of American democracy were not correspondingly modified, the whole "organism" of the United States would suffer: friction and civil war between the converted and unconverted elements of its citizens would ensue; the legislative, judicial, and executive branches of the government would

---

[1] For a detailed development and demonstration of this basic principle, see *Society, passim.*

progressively degenerate in their functions; confusion and anarchy would grow apace; and the entire country would eventually find itself in a state of chaos. The same would be true if
the Constitution and values of the United States were radically
altered without corresponding change in the mental outlook and
conduct of its citizens.

For our problem this inseparable trinity of cultural, social, and
personal aspects of a group means that *altruistic individuals cannot be reared in a milieu of egoistic culture and social institutions.*
Conversely, *an altruistic culture and altruistic social institutions
are incompatible with egoistic members.* If such a discrepancy
arises, the group will be confronted by a grave crisis in which
either altruistic individuals will transform egoistic social institutions and cultural values into altruistic ones or else egoistic
institutions and cultural values will transform altruistic members
into egoistic ones.

Thus, *if we wish to eliminate wars and establish a creative
altruistic order, we must modify simultaneously our culture, our
social institutions, and the personality of our citizenry in an altruistic direction.* All attempts, such as the proposed social prescriptions, that aim to change only a segment of one of these
aspects are doomed to failure. Nay, more. They can merely
accentuate friction, bloodshed, and destruction instead of pro-
ducing peace, good will, and constructive creativity. One cannot
maintain the health and harmony of either a biological organism
or a sociocultural system through the application of a mere
specific, the superficial treatment of a single small area.

Such paramount values as external peace, peace of mind, and a
harmonious, creative social order cannot be bought so cheaply.
Such "bargains" do not occur in the world of trade and commerce. Still less do they apply to the greatest transactions of
human history. If we desire to eliminate war and to establish a
harmonious world order, we must pay the fullest price for this
value: we must transform in a creatively altruistic direction all
human beings, all social institutions, and the entire culture of
mankind in all its main compartments, including science, religion, law and ethics, the fine arts, economics, and politics.

Otherwise all attempts are doomed to be abortive and to prove harmful rather than beneficial.

II. Sociocultural Integration

Besides neglecting this principle of the indivisibility of the social, cultural, and personal aspects of the sociocultural universe, the fallacious theories which we have considered disregard another basic principle, namely, that of sociocultural integration. Implicitly or explicitly they assume that the total culture of any group or of humanity as a whole is nothing but a congeries of diverse social and cultural phenomena unrelated to one another either causally or meaningfully, each cultural value or social institution existing for itself alone, articulating its own values independently of those of other cultural and social phenomena. Only from such an "atomistic" standpoint can one propose a modification of this or that economic, political, or personal value as a sufficient remedy for war or as the means for creating a noble social order, without a corresponding modification of the rest of the cultural, social, or personal aspects of humanity. Many businessmen, politicians, and privileged persons who endorse the United Nations or a world government as a sufficient means for peace, suggest gravely sick patients who for the sake of recovering their health are prepared to give up smoking, without any other change in the diet or manner of living responsible for their illness.

A major culture, with its social institutions, is not a mere conglomeration of diverse cultural and social phenomena, unrelated to one another causally and meaningfully, but in its greater and most important part it represents a unity or major system whose components are permeated by the same fundamental principle and articulate the same basic value. The dominant part of its fine arts, science, philosophy and religion, its family mores, its mentality and way of life, each articulate, each in its own way, this basic principle and value. This value serves as its major premise and foundation. For this reason the important parts of such an integrated culture and society are also interdependent causally: if one important part changes, the rest of its important parts are bound to be similarly transformed.

Take, for instance, Western medieval culture. Its major principle, or the true-reality value, was God. All the important sectors of medieval culture articulated this fundamental principle-value as formulated in the Christian Credo. Its architecture and sculpture were the "Bible in stone." Its literature, again, was religious and Christian through and through. Its painting articulated the same Bible in line and color. Its music was almost exclusively religious: *Alleluia, Gloria, Kyrie eleison, Credo, Agnus Dei,* and so on. Its philosophy was almost identical with religion and theology and was centered around the same basic value-principle: God. Its science was a mere handmaid of Christion religion. Its ethics and law were but an elaboration of the absolute commandments of Christian ethics. Its political organization, its spiritual and secular powers, were predominantly theocratic and based upon God and religion. Its family, as a sacred religious union, was indissoluble and articulated the same fundamental value. Even its economic organization was controlled by a religion prohibiting many forms of economic relationships, otherwise expedient and profitable, and stimulating many forms of economic activity, otherwise inexpedient from a purely utilitarian standpoint. Its dominant mores, ways of life, and mental outlook stressed the union with God as the only supreme end, and a negative or indifferent attitude toward this sensory world, with all its wealth, pleasures, and values. The sensory world was considered a mere temporary "city of man" in which a Christian was but a pilgrim aspiring to reach the eternal City of God and seeking to render himself worthy to enter it. In brief, the integrated part of medieval culture was not a conglomeration of various cultural objects, phenomena, and values, but a unified system, a whole whose parts articulated the same supreme principle of true reality and value: an infinite, supersensory, and superrational God, omnipresent, omnipotent, omniscient, absolutely just, good, and beautiful, creator of the world and of man. Such a unified system of culture based upon the principle of a supersensory and superrational God as the only true reality and value may be called *ideational*. A basically similar major premise respecting the superrational and supersensory reality of God though differently perceived in its properties, underlay also the integrated culture of Brahmanic India, the Buddhist and Taoist cultures, Greek culture from the eighth to the end of the sixth century B.C., and some other cultures. They have all been predominantly ideational.

The decline of medieval culture consisted precisely in the disintegration of this ideational system. It began at the end of the twelfth century, when there emerged the germ of a new, and profoundly different major principle, namely, that *the true reality and value is sensory*. Only what we see, hear, smell, touch, and otherwise perceive through our sense organs is real and has value. Beyond such a sensory reality, either there is nothing, or, if there is something, we cannot sense it; therefore it is equivalent to the nonreal and the nonexistent. As such it may be neglected. Such was this new principle, one entirely different from the major principle of the medieval system of culture.

Beginning roughly with the sixteenth century, the new principle became dominant, and with it the new form of culture that was based upon it. In this way the modern form of our culture emerged, the sensory, empirical, secular, and "this-worldly" culture. It may be called *sensate*. It is based upon, and is integrated around, this new principle-value: *the true reality and value is sensory*. It is precisely this principle that is articulated by our modern sensate culture in all its main compartments: in its arts and sciences, philosophy and pseudo-religion, ethics and law; in its social, economic, and political organization; in its dominant ways of life and mentality.[2]

---

[2] See *Dynamics* and *Crisis, passim.* All the important recent works on culture recognize the integration of a major culture into a single system based on a major premise and articulating it in all its main compartments. Spengler's *Decline of the West* (New York, 1926-1928), A. J. Toynbee's *A Study of History* (New York, 1934-1937), A. J. Kroeber's *Configurations of Culture Growth* (Berkeley, 1945), and F. S. C. Northrop's *The Meeting of East and West* (New York, 1946) afford examples of such works. The main differences between their theories and mine are as follows. First, their analysis of what part of a given total culture is integrated into one system and what is not, is not carried far enough. They hold that the sum total of the phenomena of the Chinese, Hindu, Egyptian, Greco-Roman, Western, or any other great culture

As has already been said, since every great culture is integrated in its main part into one causal and meaningful system, one cannot alter any essential part of such a culture, its social institutions, or its members without the necessity of a corresponding change in the rest of the system. Otherwise the attempt is doomed either to fail or to produce a serious tension in the whole system.

Since the superstructure of such a sociocultural system is built upon its major premise, a rational change of the entire system in a desirable direction must concentrate first upon this major premise. This is the most effective and strategic method of transforming the whole superstructure.

While a modification of some superficial part of the system

---

is integrated into one system. My contention is that not all cultures are notably integrated. Even in great cultures only the central part is integrated into a single dominant meaningful-causal system; the rest either is not integrated or else is integrated into various minor cultural systems existing side by side with the dominant system. Second, Spengler-Toynbee's organic theory according to which each notable culture is supposed to arise, grow, and decline is fundamentally wrong. Major cultures do not follow the bio-organismic course indicated. Instead, after their emergence they continue for an indefinite period, shifting from one dominant cultural system to another, from the ideational to the idealistic or sensate and then in turn to a different ideational, sensate, or idealistic type. Such shifts constitute the chief turning points in the life history of important cultures. (Cf. my article on "A. J. Toynbee's Philosophy of History," *Journal of Modern History*, 1940). Third, in my work I have attempted to discover the most general major premises of leading cultures and the most generalized types of cultural systems found in all periods of human history among different societies. Spengler, Toynbee, and Northrop have endeavored to determine the specific major premise of a given unique culture, Mexican or American, German or Russian, Chinese or Hindu. Their types of culture are merely species of my generic types. Fourth, they ascribe an unchangeable character to each culture in its essential trait; for instance, the religious or intuitive or "aesthetic" character to the Oriental, and scientific to the Occidental cultures. Meanwhile, the Western culture of the Middle Ages was unquestionably religious or intuitive or "aesthetic," and after the thirteenth century it became scientific or "theoretic." On the other hand, the Oriental cultures have also had periods when they were scientific or "theoretic." In taking each culture as essentially static in this respect, they make a gross factual blunder. However, there is a surprisingly large measure of agreement between my theory and theirs when the latter are put into the larger and more adequate conceptual framework of my own. Where we differ, my analysis seems to be based upon a much more solid factual basis and fits the historical realities better than any of the other theories. The subsequent sketch of the culture that is to replace the decaying sensate culture of our time appears to be more adequate than, for instance, Northrop's "aesthetic and theoretic components." These are but a variation of my sensate. idealistic, and ideational cultural systems. Cf. *Society*, chap. 43.

may not effect a corresponding change in the rest of it, the replacement of the major premise by a more desirable one leads automatically to a corresponding transmutation of the entire system. With reference to our sensate system of society and culture, this means the advisability of replacing its major premise with a more altruistic one, thereby rendering the rest of the Western sociocultural system and its members more altruistic.

The *second strategic step in the change of a given sociocultural system (including its members) in the desired direction is the transformation of its next most important values and institutions, those of its subsystems. When the very foundation (the major premise) and the principal values and institutions of an integrated system are transformed, its secondary components and superficial features will change automatically.*

Such is the rational, most strategic, most efficient, and least painful mode of substituting for an unsatisfactory sociocultural system a better one, in our case a system that will not generate wars and other grave conflicts and which will yield the maximum of creative solidarity and ennobling altruism.

The fallacious cures that have been proposed proceed in the opposite direction. Ignoring the integration of most of our cultural values, social institutions, and forms of conduct and mentality into a single unified causal and meaningful system, and disregarding the fact that this huge structure rests upon the major premise of the sensate principle, these alleged cures attempt to solve the problem by applying this or that patch (political, economic, or educational) to the least seriously affected spot and through such patches to rejuvenate the system, evolving a peace-loving, warless culture and society devoid of conflicts. No competent architect, engineer, or physician would recommend such a procedure in renovating a dilapidated building, in rehabilitating a worn-out mechanism, or in rejuvenating an old and infirm body. Similarly, no competent social scientist and engineer can expect a peaceful or creative social order to result from the operation of such a method!

CHAPTER SEVEN

WHAT NEEDS TO BE CHANGED IN
CONTEMPORARY CULTURE — AND WHY

I. WHAT IS PATHOLOGICAL IN ITS GENERAL NATURE

If a simultaneous change of the major premises and basic values of a culture, of its major social institutions, and of the mind and behavior of its members is required in order to eliminate serious conflicts and to produce a creative order, the questions arise whether our principal sociocultural system needs such a change; if so, why; precisely what has to be changed in it; and what sort of new sociocultural system is to be substituted for it.

The answers to these questions are at hand. If, after investigation, we find that our present culture and social institutions generate mainly the egoistic forces of war and other grave forms of strife, that they produce predominantly selfish, avaricious, and uncreative personalities, and that they breed crime, then they require a radical change if we desire a peaceful, harmonious, cooperative, and creative social order — indeed, if humanity is to survive. Otherwise further world wars will be inevitable, and one or more of these will spell the end of human civilization.

The answer to the third question is this: we must eliminate precisely those elements of our contemporary culture which breed war, hatred, and other ultimately suicidal tendencies. The components of the cultural system that generate forces of mutual aid and love must be supplemented by components of the same character. Out of this combination a new harmonious cultural system is to be built, the semi-rotten sociocultural structure being thus replaced by a healthy, ennobling, and invigorating structure designed in its own altruistic style, markedly different from the old one.

Let us now see whether contemporary Western culture is in

need of such a radical reconstruction. We shall begin our examination with its basic characteristics.

In accordance with its major premise, namely, that *the true reality value is sensory and that there is no supersensory reality value,* the scale of values of our culture is fundamentally materialistic, hedonistic, and utilitarian. Good food and drink, comfortable clothing and shelter, sexual gratification, wealth and power, popularity and fame — such are its main values. The supersensory values of the Kingdom of God and the like are either denied as superstitions or rendered mere lip service. These reality-values, remnants of the medieval ideational culture, are, at best, regarded as childish fantasies. Fullness and richness of life is measured by the maximum of sensory reality-values, appropriated, possessed, enjoyed, and used by an individual or group. And the greater the share of wealth, comfort, power, fame, etc., one acquires, the happier and greater one is considered to be.

From birth to death everyone is molded by this ethos. The family, the nursery school, the group of children one plays with, the elementary school, high school, and college, the persons and groups one meets, the papers and books one reads, the movies and plays one attends, the business one is engaged in, all these agencies incessantly induce a person to strive to become rich, powerful, and famous. Greatness and leadership are measured in quantitative terms. If one acquires only a small share of these values, he is considered a failure and is relegated to the bottom rung of the social ladder. If he refuses to fight for as large a share as possible, he is regarded as devoid of ambition, perhaps as queer, maladjusted, mentally or morally abnormal.

This philosophy of sensate values produces primarily egoistic individuals and groups, all the more so owing to *the scarcity of the sensate values in comparison with the demand for them.* Moreover, the more of these values one has, the more he craves.

Only a few can become multimillionaires; only a few can possess ostentatious palaces and retinues of servants or be capable of conspicuous consumption; only a fraction can enjoy "wine, women, and song" in unlimited quantities; only a small minority can wield the power of dominion over many. The relative

scarcity of sensate values generates a relentless and often ferocious struggle. This proceeds now silently and inconspicuously;
now it assumes a beastly and bloody form, accompanied by the
triumphal shouts of the victors and by the cries or sighs of the
victims or frustrated competitors. By its very nature the sensate
scale of values pits individual against individual, group against
group, as rivals and enemies. In this sense it is essentially a culture of enmity and war rather than of love and peace.

Contemporary Western culture generates egoistic forces and
conflicts through another general trait: the *degradation of all
cultural and social values and the value of man himself to the
level of mere sensory material things.* In accordance with its
major premise it asserts that culture, social institutions, and man
are nothing but variations of the same sensory reality, mere
mechanisms of electrons and protons, mere concatenations of
sense data, mere complexes of inorganic and organic matter.
Progressively developing this principle, sensate pseudo science
interprets sociocultural phenomena in mechanistic, materialistic,
reflexological, biological, endocrinological, sexual, psychoanalytical, or economic terms. In its interpretation of man contemporary psychology denies the existence of conscience, or even
of consciousness, "mind stuff," or thought as something supersensory and nonmaterial. At best, it regards these as mere by-
products of the nervous system. When such "scientists" develop
their formulas, they depict man as an animal predominantly
controlled by his digestive and sex organs; or in terms of the
Freudian "id," consisting of oral, anal, and genital sex instincts,
plus destructive sadistic and masochistic instincts and the desire
to rape one's mother or seduce one's father (the Oedipus complex), masked by a thin and empty "ego" and by a cruel and
repressive "superego" leading to insanity when it seeks to stifle
the unbridled sexual and destructive instincts; or, according to
Adler, as an animal drunk with the lust for power; or as a
complicated and perverted reflex mechanism. Such are the
"scientific" conceptions of man, culture, and society created and
propagated by sensate culture, especially in its later stages, when
the medieval ideational concepts of man as a son of God, and of

cultural and social institutions as the realization of the Divine on this planet, have ceased to be operative.

The conflict-breeding consequences of such a degradation of man, culture, and society are all too evident. If man is a mere complex of electrons and protons, or a mere perverted animal, then why should we show any regard for him? Why not exterminate him if he happens to prove an obstacle to the realization of our desires? We do not hesitate to destroy inanimate things when they are impediments; and we crush a mosquito or scotch a snake that annoys us. Why should we behave differently toward a man under similar circumstances? If cultural and social institutions are simply a concatenation of sense data or a mere complex of matter, why stand on ceremony with them when they hinder the satisfaction of our lust for power, for sexual indulgence, or for destruction?

Moreover, when one thinks of himself (or of others) as a perverted animal, or in terms of an "id" surcharged with the libido and with destructive sadistic instincts, one can hardly fail to behave like a perverted animal. With such a "scientific ideology" one's conduct calls for no inhibitions, compunctions, remorse, or repentance.

Need we wonder, then, that when our culture reached this stage of manifest self-degradation, it dragged down into the social sewers all its values, all social institutions, and man himself? Finally, with ever-increasing bestiality, men started to kill or mutilate one another in steadily mounting wars, revolutions, and other conflicts, including crimes in individual relationships. Whereas all the international wars from the eleventh to the nineteenth century inclusive accounted for some fifteen million killed and wounded, the First World War alone took a toll of about twenty million, and the Second World War one of approximately fifty million!

The same homicidal conflicts are generated by sensate culture through the *excessive "relativizing" of its values and norms.* By their very nature, sensory realities and values are relative, as evinced by explicit scientific propositions and by the conventional norms of law, the fine arts, and manners and mores. Even the boundary line between what is sensorily true and false, right and wrong, beautiful and ugly, pleasant and unpleasant, is wholly relative. This relativity of all standards, values, and norms is definitely avowed by sensate culture in its deliberate repudiation of absolutes in every field. From the twelfth to the twentieth century the percentage of relativism in values and norms rose from 0 to 48.6, while that of absolutism declined from 100 to 51.4 per cent.[1]

As long as the absolute values, standards, and norms of the medieval ideational culture still lingered in the background of the rising sensate culture, from the thirteenth to the seventeenth century, this relativity of sensate values was held in check. The difference between the true and the false, right and wrong, the noble and the ignoble, beauty and ugliness, positive and negative values, was still clearcut. The approved modes of conduct were still sharply distinguished from criminal and dishonest ones. Though such values and norms were often transgressed, their validity and their binding power were never explicitly denied.

With the progressive decline of the medieval absolute values and norms in later centuries, sensory values became increasingly relative. They grew more and more conventional and conditional, less and less binding, until in the present century they virtually disintegrated. We live in an age in which no value, from God to private property, is universally accepted. There is no norm, from the Ten Commandments to contractual rules and those of etiquette, that is universally binding upon Hitlerites and anti-Hitlerites, Communists and Catholics, the rich and the poor, Negroes and white people, atheists and believers, monarchists and republicans, monogamists and polygamists. What one person or group affirms, another denies; what one pressure group extols, another vilifies. All values and norms have become mere playthings whose acceptance or nonacceptance depends entirely upon the whims of a given person or group. Hence the mental, moral, religious, social, economic, and political anarchy that pervades our life and culture. Hence, the reliance upon

---

[1] See *Dynamics,* II, chap. 14.

brute force, or upon fraud as the supreme arbiter of any conflict — upon the rule that might makes right.

Owing to this degradation of values, our contemporary culture generates incessant antagonism and powerful egoistic forces. When every individual and group regards itself as the supreme judge of values and standards, there inevitably arises the Hobbesian *bellum omnium contra omnes,* with no agency to arbitrate conflicts except sheer physical force assisted by fraud.

Persons born and reared in this atmosphere cannot be indoctrinated with universally approved values and norms. One moment they hear of "God and religion"; next they are told "God is a superstition, and religion is the opiate of the people's mind." Now they are told, "private property is sacred," now that it is a "theft." At one turn they are taught, "The marriage vow is inviolable"; at the next, "It is a hypocritical and harmful repression of the legitimate sex instinct by the stupid 'superego': one is entitled to satisfy it with any person of the opposite sex to whom one feels attracted." And so on. Children reared in such a contradictory atmosphere have no chance of being imbued with any universal standard or norm that becomes their second nature and controls their behavior from within. They are like rudderless boats driven hither and thither by every wind of temptation and circumstance. When they grow up, there is no uniform public opinion to control their conduct. Instead, they live amidst multitudes of different and even contradictory pressure groups and are subjected to divergent opinions. Such an atmosphere breeds, for the most part, a cynical, nihilistic, amoral, and asocial horde. Not controlled from within by universal standards, the members of the horde incessantly clash in their struggle for sensate values; and this clash, not inhibited by any deeply inculcated norms, becomes increasingly savage and bloody.

Under such conditions we should not be surprised at the upsurge of juvenile delinquency; at the failure of criminality in general to decline; at the upward trend of wars and revolutions, which, like criminality, are growing progressively more bestial, unrestrained by any law, divine or human. All this is but the natural fruit of the contemporary cultural tree!

II. Suggested Changes

If we desire to foster altruism and to suppress egoism, to do away with or markedly reduce interpersonal and intergroup conflicts, the foregoing properties of our contemporary culture must be eliminated. Their elimination calls for the following substitutions.

The major premise of sensate culture must be replaced by the broader, deeper, richer, and more valid premise that the *true reality and value is an infinite manifold possessing not only sensory but also supersensory, rational, and superrational aspects, all harmoniously reflecting its infinity.* As we shall see, such a premise is incomparably more adequate than the purely sensate premise of our present culture. The scale of values of such a premise contains not only sensory values but also the rational values of mathematical and logical thought in science and philosophy, fine arts, law and ethics; in rational living and acting; and above all, the sublimest values of the supersensory, superrational, and superconscious intuition. These values are the most creative and fruitful. They open to us the Kingdom of God, the pure forms of Plato, the ultimate reality and value in its infinite richness and sublimity. Taken together, in their unity, the three orders of reality and value, the empirical, rational, and superrational, unfold a universe immeasurably more ample, happier, and nobler than that of the merely sensory reality-values.

A culture built upon such a premise effectively mitigates the ferocity of the struggle for a greater share of material values, because material values occupy in it only a limited place and not the highest one. A large proportion of human aspirations tend to be channeled in the direction of the rational or the superrational perennial values of the Kingdom of God, of fuller truth, nobler goodness, and sublimer beauty. The very nature of these values is impersonal and universal, altruistic and ennobling. As these values are infinite and inexhaustible, the quest for them does not lead to egoistic conflicts. Hence, the replacement of the major premise of sensate culture by the fundamen-

tally different one which I designate as the idealistic premise, is
the most fundamental step toward the establishment of a creative, harmonious human order.

The proposed substitution means, in contradistinction to the
debasement of man, society and culture, *their elevation* to the
heights of the *Infinite Manifold*. The new idealistic culture
does not deny that man is composed of electrons and protons, or
that he is an organism with biological drives; but it asserts that
he is also an incarnation of the conscious mind and superconscious essence of the Infinite Manifold, God; that culture and
social institutions are a realization on this planet of the superorganic mind and superconscious creative genius; that as such
they are end values and cannot be degraded to the pseudo values
of mere means to an end, or to mere complexes of organic and
inorganic matter. This ennoblement of man's conception of
himself and of his cultural and social institutions inspires an
attitude of reverence, respect, admiration, and love toward his
fellow men, toward culture and society, toward the Infinite
Manifold, and even toward the whole universe as a part of the
Infinite Manifold. Working incessantly in this subtle way, an
ennobling culture exerts an immeasurably greater altruistic influence than all the altruistic preachings of our present culture.

Further on, *the excessively relativized values and norms of our
culture must be replaced by a set of fundamental values and
norms universally valid and unconditionally binding upon everyone; many negative or empty values and norms must be dis-
carded; sound relative values and norms should be preserved as
relative, but with a definite indication of the time and space
limits in which they are valid.* The establishment of a set of
universal values and norms puts an end to mental, moral, and
social anarchy. Their unconditionality clearly demarcates the
true from the false, right from wrong, and abolishes physical
force and fraud as arbiters of human conflicts and disagree-
ments. Their universality and unconditionality provide man
with an inner force for the control of human relations. They
make possible a sound and universal public opinion, a true
world conscience, a valid guide for human conduct and rela-

tionships. Backed by a universal world opinion and its pressure, these values and norms are freely obeyed and lead to the subsidence of lusts and conflicts.

Such, in brief, would be the consequences of the prescribed substitutions. They would usher humanity into a new era, perhaps the noblest and most creative in its history.

CHAPTER EIGHT

WHAT IS PATHOLOGICAL IN THE MAIN COMPARTMENTS OF OUR CULTURE

I. Science and Technology

In accordance with the major premise of sensate culture that the true reality value is sensory, it tends to reduce all cognition to sensory knowledge. It proclaims that only through sense perception, through what we see, hear, smell, touch, and so on, can we apprehend reality. It assures us that there is nothing in our mind that has not previously been perceived through our sense organs. Even mind itself is conceived as a mere concatenation of sense data. Since there is only sensory reality, there is no possibly of cognition of a (nonexistent) supersensory reality. The rational discipline of mathematical and syllogistic logic is admitted by the sensate theory of knowledge as a subsidiary means for the ordering of sense data, but this logic is viewed as a mere by-product of sense experience. Consistently with these premises, our sensate culture developed *science as a sensory, or empirical, system of knowledge of chemical, physical, and biological phenomena.* Quite logically it concentrated the cognitive efforts of humanity on a study of the empirical world through observational, experimental, statistical, and similar techniques, assisted by mathematical and syllogistic logic as a handmaid of sense perceptions. Quite naturally it focused man's inventive efforts on physical, chemical, biological discoveries and technological inventions. No less logically it denied any religious, theological, or metaphysical cognition of some supersensory reality (God; the soul; the ultimate reality; the mysteries of the fall of man, redemption, salvation, immortality, etc.). Accordingly it successfully relegated medieval religious and theological revelations to the limbo of ignorant superstitions, and it repudiated metaphysics of the nonsensory type as an unscientific fabric of fantastic and meaningless words, divorced from any reality. Explicitly or implicitly it divorced science, as a system of sensory knowledge, from religious, philosophical, ethical, and aesthetic cognition. In fact, it discredited all unconditional and universal standards.

With the progressive fading of the medieval universalistic standards, the moral, religious, and social irresponsibility of sensate science and technology has grown apace. Inventors have produced not only gadgets beneficial to humanity but also those that have brought death and destruction, beginning with gunpowder and ending with atomic bombs, poisonous gases, and means of bacteriological warfare. All the degrading theories of man and his sociocultural world discussed in the preceding chapter, all the physical, reflexological, biological, endocrinological, psychoanalytic, economic and similar desocializing and demoralizing interpretations of man and his sociocultural universe, have been elaborated in the name of science and technology, which have thus contributed much to the barbarization of man and the generation of disastrous interindividual and intergroup conflicts.

The irresponsible misuse of contemporary science and technology constitutes the gravest menace to the future of humanity. If they are left in this irresponsible position, in the hands of egoistic individuals and groups, they may easily destroy the very tree of life of mankind itself. If we wish to prevent such a catastrophe, science and technology must undergo a radical change.

In accordance with the major premise of the new culture that the true reality value is an Infinite Manifold with sensory, rational, and metasensory and metarational aspects, sensory cognition must be supplemented by adding to it rational and intuitive cognitions. These three modes of true knowledge are to be united into a single integral system of truth. The empirical aspect of the Infinite Manifold should be investigated primarily by empirical science through sensory observation in all its forms (experimental, clinical, etc.). Its rational aspects should be studied by means of the rational disciplines of logic, mathe-

matics, and the like. Its supersensory and metarational aspect is
to be apprehended through the superconscious, superrational intuition of charismatic religious prophets and ethical seers, of
great thinkers like Plato, of great artists like Beethoven and
Shakespeare.[1] Alone, none of the three modes of cognition gives
us the whole of truth. The history of human knowledge is replete with wrong empirical observations, false logical reasoning,
and misleading intuitions. Taken separately, each of these
modes is fallible. Blended, co-operating, and correcting one another, they yield a more valid, more adequate, and better tested
truth than one-sided sensory, rational, or intuitive cognition can
reveal.

Through this integration of all three modes of cognition, science will not lose anything of its essential value: it will remain
a system of empirical and rational investigation of the sensory
aspects of the basic reality. But it will free itself from its one-
sidedness; from its partial truths; and from its social, moral,
and even intellectual purblindness. As a result, the present war
between science and philosophy, science and religion, religion
and philosophy, will cease. Instead of offering humanity discordant, competitive partial truths, in this wholehearted co-
operation they will reveal a single integral truth, richer and
more valid than the one-sided truth of either science or philosophy or religion or arts.

The cessation of warfare between partial truths will lead to a

---

[1] By intuition is meant "an immediate awareness by a subject of some particular entity, without such an aid from the senses or from reason as would
account for that awareness. It gives us insight into reality as opposed to, or
supplementing, appearance." K. W. Wild, *Intuition* (Cambridge, England,
1938), p. 226 ff. As a superconscious mode of cognition and creativeness
intuition played an exceptionally important role in science, philosophy, religion,
ethics, and in all fields of creativeness and cognition. It lies at the foundation
of all scientific and other cognitions: their ultimate bases are intuitive. It has
been the first, real starter of almost all great discoveries, inventions, and creations in all fields of culture. It has been the source of certainty and ultimate
validity and value of such creations. Psychologically, intuition is a function
of the superconscious self in human personality (cf. chapters 13 and 14).
For the facts, evidence, and literature on intuition, see *Dynamics*, IV, chap.
16; and *Crisis*, p. 80 ff. I. Sikorsky calls it "the sixth sense"; F. S. C. Northrop,
"the aesthetic component."

replacement of our attitude of uncertainty by one of certitude. In its turn this will bring genuine peace of mind to a humanity now lost in the jungle of relative hypotheses and contradictory half-truths.

This fundamental reorientation of science and technology will render each individual religiously, morally, and socially responsible. Scientists and inventors will refrain from discoveries and inventions destructive or harmful to mankind, such as the atomic bomb; otherwise they will be unanimously branded as murderers or evildoers. Similarly, politicians will refrain from the abuse of science and technology. Thus these agencies will cease to serve the forces of egoism, enmity, antagonism, and destruction.

The science and technology of such a culture will pay much more attention to social, humanistic, and personality problems. In this new culture they will concentrate on the study of man and the social world as the least known and most urgent field of investigation. They are bound to make their greatest discoveries and inventions in precisely that field. The importance of such revelations is likely to far outweigh that of all the chemical, physical, and biological discoveries. They will give us, among other things, technical devices for probing, understanding, and controlling the human mind and human conduct, now so little known and still less controlled. They will open to us the secrets of the creativity of genius, of the intuition of prophets, of the insight of mystics, of founders of major religions. Psychology will then attain a real knowledge of the mind, instead of treating it merely in terms of the anatomy and physiology of the nervous system. The social sciences will then grasp the very essence of the city of man as well as of the City of God, instead of contenting themselves with an inchoate and superficial catalogue of incidental sociocultural objects, events and phenomena. Philosophy and religion will then achieve the highest wisdom respecting the ultimate reality-value instead of being a Tower of Babel of discordant beliefs, uncertain dogmas, questionable rituals, and congeries of meaningless words. These new discoveries and inventions will offer man the most effective techniques of self-control and self-development, making possible the attainment of an unprecedentedly high social and cultural level. Thus will dawn an era in which man apprehends and controls the inorganic and the organic, achieves self-control, and penetrates even the superorganic realm. He will become an incarnation of the highest creative forces of the universe, attuned to the Godhead. Deep peace of mind and good will toward one's fellows will prevail.

II. Religion and Philosophy

Being irreligious and essentially empirical and materialistic, our sensate culture has produced no major religion and hardly any notable idealistic philosophy. Christianity was created before the emergence of this culture after the thirteenth century. Only various dubious sects, short-lived, often eccentric, and now and then atrocious, have arisen during the past five centuries of the domination of this sensate culture. Christianity itself has been split by it into a multitude of sects and denominations quarrelling with and undermining one another. The external shell of Christianity, its funds and buildings, its rituals and dogmas, its administrative machinery and hierarchy, has grown during these centuries at the expense of its spirituality, ethical efficiency, and transfiguring power. Hence the increase of non-Christian and even anti-Christian behavior on the part of Western Christendom during this period. While paying lip service to their faith, in their overt actions Christians have violated its commandments even more than the pagans. *Fides sine operibus mortua est.*

A similar fate has attended the integral and idealistic systems of philosophy. The climate of sensate culture has been distinctly unfavorable to them. The integral and idealistic systems of metaphysics created during the sensate era have been primarily variations of, or extended "footnotes" to, the Platonic, Aristotelian, Plotinian, Christian, Augustinian, Erigenian, and Thomistic systems of philosophy. If a few great systems, such as that of Kant, have emerged, they have been a mixture of skepticism and agnosticism with idealism and integralism. Only materialistic, mechanistic, empirical, positivistic, instrumental, pragmatic, skeptical, and quasi-rationalistic systems of philosophy have flourished in the atmosphere of sensate culture.[2]

Constituting a secondhand version of the materialistic and mechanistic tendencies of science, without its creative discoveries or inventions, these philosophies have accentuated the demoralizing influences of sensate science without any of its advantages. In this sense the subtle, but all-pervading effects of such philosophies have been highly disastrous, having contributed notably to the release of egoistic and antagonistic forces.

As long as religion and philosophy remain in this deplorable state, they can contribute little to the cause of solidarity and the elimination of conflict. To perform this mission, they must undergo a fundamental transmutation. Christianity or some other great religion must revive its heroic age. The new religion must be vitalized by all-giving and all-forgiving love, love of man for his fellow men, for God, and for the entire universe, love manifest in deeds as well as in words and aspirations. It must be capable of lifting man again to the infinite heights of the Godhead and of re-establishing the broken unity between humanity and the creative soul of the cosmos. It must reassert the divine origin of man, in order to counteract his degradation to the level of a mere biophysical mechanism controlled by his unconscious and conscious egos. It must inspire man with an unquenchable longing to transcend the subconscious and conscious phases of his personality in quest of the superconscious realm of immortal truth, goodness, and beauty.

The discharge of these functions fulfills its highest mission. The rest, its dogmas and ritual, organization and machinery, funds and buildings, is relatively unimportant. The less attention and energy given to these externals, so much the better. The dominant religions and denominations must cease their "imperialistic" struggle for superiority and "vested interests." Laying aside their rivalry, they must stress their common basic verities and their common moral imperatives. If a person strives

---

[2] For the statistical data of the rise and decline of various systems of philosophy, see *Dynamics,* II.

for and achieves union with the Absolute, and if he manifests his divinity through deeds expressing his love for God and
man, that is all that is important. Whether he does this under the
banner of Hinduism or Buddhism, Taoism or Confucianism,
Jainism or Judaism, Christianity or Mohammedanism, "human-
ism" or "the Religion of Progress," mysticism or atheism, is of
secondary consequence. Conversely, if one does not feel the immediate presence of the Godhead, does not reverently walk the
earth, and does not manifest his divinity through actions inspired by unbounded love for others, he remains irreligious, no
matter how faithfully he performs the prescribed rituals, how
often he repeats the name of the Lord, or how closely he adheres
to the approved dogmas.

These are the transmutations the existing religions must
undergo in order to fulfill effectively their mission of freeing
man's genius from the shackles of his biophysical nature, of
ennobling him by a sense of his kinship with God, and of impelling him to deeds of love. Such religions are the must powerful generators of the forces of love, peace, and harmony.

A similar transformation must take place in the prevailing
systems of philosophy if they are to promote co-operation and
mutual aid instead of hate and enmity; they must become increasingly idealistic and decreasingly materialistic. They may
remain materialistic and mechanistic within the legitimate limits of these aspects of the Infinite Manifold. In stressing these
aspects they should clearly emphasize their partial and subordinate role, that there are nonmaterial, monmechanistic, rational, and superrational aspects transcending the material appearance of sensory phenomena; that even the sensory world is
not confined to the materialistic, mechanistic, and deterministic
aspects.

They must abandon other forms of ideological degradation of
man and sociocultural reality. They must cease the illogical
relativizing of truth and other values that leads to the oblitera-
tion of the boundary line between truth and error, goodness and
evil, beauty and ugliness. The relative has meaning only when
contrasted with the absolute. Without any absolute the very

concept of the relative becomes empty and meaningless. Such philosophies may indulge as much as they like in an analysis of what is indeed relative so long as they do not forget the absolute standards and values. Otherwise they tend to undermine all values and to become a mere medley of meaningless words and phrases.

Such, in brief, is the transmutation that philosophy must undergo if it is to contribute to our apprehension of the true reality-value; if it desires to foster altruism and the brotherhood of man; if it wishes to co-operate with science, religion, and the fine arts in revealing the Infinite Manifold and in re-creating its semblance on this planet.

III. LAW AND ETHICS

The law norms governing human conduct are obligatory, two-sided norms, defining clearly the rights of one party (the subject of right) and the obligations of the other (the subject of duty). In every society the totality of its law norms precisely define the rights and duties of each member in relation to every other member, as well as to outsiders. Each of us lives and acts amidst a complex network of legal relationships that indicate exactly what we are entitled to from others, what we owe to them, within what limits, under what conditions, and so on. Being obligatory, law norms are enforced by punishment of the violator, by fining him, by compelling him to repair the damage, by voiding the legality of his actions, and the like.

Purely ethical norms of conduct, per contra, for instance, those of the Sermon on the Mount, are one-sided and are merely recommended, not enforced. They envisage only the subject of duty, not the subject of right. In recommending the ethical duty of turning the other cheek to the smiter, Jesus does not grant anybody the right of smiting; in advising one to love his enemies, he does not authorize anyone (including the enemy) to hate his fellows. Ethical norms usually envisage conduct that transcends the obligatory legal conduct. If one can voluntarily apply such norms, well and good. If he cannot or does not, nobody can compel him to do so.

The ethical and law norms of medieval Christianity were universal, eternal, and unconditional, respectively recommended and obligatory for everyone. As the recommendations and commandments of God they were absolute, free from any relativity. Only the norms that contradicted these absolute norms were regarded as relative and changeable. The boundary line between right and wrong in the law and ethics of the Middle Ages was perfectly clear. Even its violators did not deny its validity.

In conformity with its major premise modern sensate culture tends to regard all legal and ethical norms as purely man-made rules, devoid of any absolute, eternal, or divine principles. As human conventions, these norms are declared to be entirely relative and changeable. Their functions are considered to be purely utilitarian: the protection of human life, or property, or other sensory values of either the whole of society or of its dominant minority. Under these conditions they have frequently served as mere instruments for the subjugation and exploitation of one person or group by another.

While the universal medieval norms were still operative in the background of the sensate law and ethics, the conventionalizing, relativizing, and degrading tendencies of the latter were kept within reasonable limits. With the progressive disintegration of the universal norms, these tendencies rapidly gained the upper hand until the man-made sensate law and ethics had forfeited virtually all their prestige, their inner binding power, and their ability clearly to distinguish between what is right and what is wrong, what is just and what is unjust. Thus they have lost most of their efficacy in controlling human behavior from within. In other words they have, as it were, committed suicide, giving place to unrestrained force and fraud as their natural heirs and successors in the relationships of individual to individual and group to group, in both the national and the international field. Hence the unprecedented multiplicity of wars, revolutions, crimes, and other forms of conflict and antagonism that have characterized this century.

The extraordinary progress of relativization of these norms corresponds to the decrease of the ethics of absolute principles from

100 per cent in the Middle Ages to 57 per cent between 1900 and 1920, and to the increase of hedonistic and utilitarian ethical principles from zero between the fifth and fourteenth centuries to 43 per cent in the period 1900-1920. The virtually complete loss of prestige on the part of our legal and ethical norms is well attested by the prevalent denial of any divine or eternal or even natural law and by the dominant "scientific" conceptions of these norms, according to which they are simply an ideological screen for selfish economic interests (cf. Marxism *et. al.*); a camouflage assisting the unscrupulous minority to exploit the naïve majority (cf. the radical ideologists); unreasonable repressions of our sexual and suicidal drives by the stupid and cruel "superego" (cf. the Freudians); mere "derivations" masking the egoistic "residues" (cf. the Machiavellians, Paretians, and others); or "rationalizations" of the most sordid biological drives. In brief, these norms are conceived as a kind of hypocritical and "high-falutin'" smoke-screen hiding the egoistical drives of persons and groups and promoting the gratification of carnal lusts.

They have been similarly discredited by the "scientific demonstration" of their diversity and contradictory character among different persons and groups. In certain societies they prescribe polygamic or polyandric marriage; in others, monogamy. In some groups they protect communal property; in others, private property. Now they prescribe the monarchic form of government, now the republican. On the basis of such conflicting and frequently self-contradictory norms, our culture has proclaimed and stressed their relativity and conventionality, entirely overlooking the universality of the basic norms and values. Thus our sensate society has lost any clear sense of what is right and what is wrong, what is lawful and what is not. The result has been a progressive moral and legal anarchy, nihilism and cynicism. What one group declares to be lawful, another brands as sham justice. The law, ethics, court decisions, legal enforcements, all are regarded as mere power politics directed by the mightier pressure group against the weaker one. If to the Allies the Nuremberg trial was an exemplification of justice, to the majority of Germans it was but an act of revenge on the part of the victors.

Those who are criminals in the eyes of one group are heroes in the estimation of others. Judges appointed by one party are deemed rascals by the opposition. This insidious devitalization of legal and moral norms has stripped humanity of everything but the law of the jungle, in which conflicts are decided by brute force.

Since these beggarly shreds of discredited and chaotic norms cannot guide human conduct, since they cannot effectively control it from within, they cannot generate the forces of just and harmonious relationships between persons and groups. Like the Gospel's salt that lost its savor, they are "good for nothing but to be cast out and to be trodden under foot." These sham norms must be replaced by a system of universal legal norms permeated by the true justice of the Golden Rule and the natural law. Likewise, our pseudo ethics must be replaced by the eternal moral imperatives of the Sermon on the Mount and by similar norms of all the great religions. We cannot build such a law and ethics on the basis of the existing lawyers' law, politicians' enactments, or decrees of dictators. In their bulk these are too contradictory, savor too much of expediency, and are frequently too unjust or egoistic. A new body of law can be built only on the basic principles of the natural law and the highest moral norms. Only such a law and ethics can become universal and binding upon all. Only such norms can become end values in their own right and effectively control human actions and relationships from within. Permeated by the principle of the Golden Rule, of unbounded love, they will re-establish themselves as the inexhaustible fountainhead of altruistic forces.

Side by side with these universal norms there will remain secondary, relative rules suitable for one group and unsuitable for others. Though diverse and incessantly shifting, they will not impair the validity of the universal legal and moral principles.

The proposed change of law and ethics means a fundamental reorganization of the codes of official law, of the character of legal sanctions, of legislative and judicial machinery, of the courts, and so on, in the interest of erecting a universal system of law and ethics. It means the end of the purely utilitarian and hedonistic conception of legal and ethical values. Animated by justice and love, the new law and ethics will lift to a higher plane the confused, disillusioned, demoralized humanity of the present time. In closest co-operation with a reintegrated science, philosophy, and religion, this new system of law and ethics will participate in creating a more exalted type of humanity on this planet.

IV. THE FINE ARTS

Medieval art was an articulation of the Christian Credo as the major premise of the medieval culture. Its greatest architecture was the cathedrals dedicated to God; its sculpture and painting were the Bible in stone and color; its music and literature were religious reiterations of the same Credo; ritual and mystery plays were its dramas. It was an art devoted to God and to the union of man with the Creator. It was a "visible or audible sign of the invisible kingdom of God," uplifting the soul of man to this exalted sphere. Its heroes were God, the angels, and the saints; its "plots" were the mysteries of the incarnation, crucifixion, resurrection, and redemption. Its artists wrought for the greater glory of God and for the salvation of the human soul. Such an art was the most powerful force for ennobling man and propagating the brotherhood of humanity.

The art of the period from the twelfth to the fifteenth century broadened its basis: besides the Kingdom of God it began to reflect the empirical world of the senses, but only at its noblest and best. Besides God its heroes included semi-divine heroes. Nothing ugly, debased, or pathological was portrayed by it. It remained a value-laden art, not yet divorced from religion, knowledge, or virtue. It ennobled the ignoble, beautified the ugly, immortalized the mortals; educated, inspired, purified, and uplifted man to the realm of great ideals.

With the growth of our sensate culture in later centuries, art also grew increasingly sensate; secular in its subject matter, visual or natural in its forms. It progressively abandoned its religious and ethical mission. It was devoted to art for art's sake, divorced from religion and philosophy, science, and ethics.

Eventually it became predominantly a refined instrument for sensory, if not sensual, gratification.

While the medieval art values were still operating in the background, they served to minimize the many pitfalls and fatal diseases of sensate art. At this prepathological stage it created its greatest values in literature and drama, painting and sculpture, architecture and music. But with the decline of the medieval art values it began rapidly to develop its morbid inherent traits, growing progressively less creative and more and more pathological, degrading, negativistic, and incoherent. From the lofty height of medieval art and from the idealistic summits of the art of the thirteenth to the fifteenth century it descended into the muck of the social sewers. Instead of God, its heroes and principal personages were hypocrites, gangsters and criminals, prostitutes, the insane or mentally defective, human derelicts, and the like. Its favorite settings were a criminal's hideout, a police morgue, an insane asylum, the bedroom of a mistress, adulteress, prostitute, or seducer; a night club, bar, or saloon; an office of plotters and hypocrites; or a city street featuring a sensational murder or other crime. Its principal topics were two Freudian instincts: those of homicide or suicide and — especially — of sex, in all its possible forms: in the caveman and "romantic" styles; in heterosexual and homosexual relations; in normal and perverted forms; and so forth. Art degraded itself to the role of a stimulant of homicidal and carnal appetites; to an instrument of relaxation and amusement, to excitation of jaded nerves, or to a mere handmaiden of advertised market commodities: laxatives, rubber, beer, soap, razor blades, etc. It sank to the level of "strip-tease dancers" and of clandestine photographs exhibiting the act of copulation.

In this role it has become a mere market commodity, to be sold and bought as any other commodity. To enjoy good sales it has been forced to cater to vulgar demands, because the volume of vulgar demands is always larger than that of refined ones. As a market commodity it has naturally become dependent upon commercial dealers and conditions. Hence it has sunk lower and lower in its standards. Degenerating in quality, it has attempted to compensate for this by quantity ("the bigger, the better!")

and incoherent diversity, by sensational "hits" and stunning techniques. The best-seller has thus replaced the classic; the commercial dealer the *arbiter elegantiarum;* the "cocktail aesthetician" the true real art connoisseur; the newspaper reporter the competent art critic. Picture-makers, show-makers, and music-makers are substituted for creative artists; glittering appearances for inner worth; technique for genius; imitation for creativity, market "hits" for lasting values; the commercial rackets of "art guilds" and "a-book-a-day clubs" for academies of art and associations of creative artists.

Divorced from science and philosophy, religion and ethics, art has grown increasingly vacuous and sterile.[3] It has ceased to stimulate artistic creative genius; instead, it stultifies and suffocates it. Likewise it has ceased to elevate its patrons morally or to integrate them mentally. Rather, it demoralizes and enervates them, dragging them down with it into the social sewers. It no longer serves the cause of human brotherhood and cooperation; instead, it disseminates the germs of egoism, enmity, strife, and criminality.

Its stultifying effects are clearly evinced by the contemporary decline in the production of great works in practically all fields of art with the possible exception of architecture, which is beginning to show some signs of real creativity. The Shakespeares, Dantes, Cervantes', Goethes, Schillers, Hugos, Tolstoys and Dostoievskys all belong to earlier centuries. So also do the Bachs, Mozarts, Beethovens, Wagners, Tchaikovskys and Brahmses. The same is true of the Raphaels, Rembrandts, and Michelangelos. The twentieth century has not produced a single genius in any field of art comparable to the greatest creative geniuses of the preceding centuries or even to the foremost masters of the nineteenth century. We live in an age of "midgets" in art. Their "best-sellers" come, enjoy sales of a million copies, and within a few months or years are "gone with the wind" into eternal oblivion.

The demoralizing effects of our art, especially of the movies,

---

[3] For the factual evidence and many details of these summary conclusions, *see Dynamics,* I, chaps. 6-13.

jazz, crooning, and detective stories, have been demonstrated by a number of investigations. The more frequently children attend the movies, the less altruistic and co-operative and the more demoralized they become.[4] Most of the movies play a tangible role in generating delinquency and other antisocial traits. With a slight variation the same may be said of the bulk of our literature (especially the yellow press and "pulp" magazines), jazz and crooning, plays and shows.

Decadent sensate art obviously cannot regain its former creativity, nor can it serve the purpose of breeding altruistic human beings or an altruistic social order. Hence it must give place to a new art based on the major premise of the future idealistic culture. Like the Greek art of the fifth century b.c. or the European art of the thirteenth century a.d., this new idealistic art must disavow the empty role of art for art's sake. Beauty must again be united with truth and goodness, not in the sense of becoming a mere instrument for the service of science and philosophy, law and ethics, or religion, but as an equal partner in an alliance of the highest values. The beauty of such an art is a value-laden beauty, not a specious veneer. Only such a value-laden art has survived and proved immortal. Only under such conditions can art regain its creativity. Only then does it become an end value rather than a mere marketable commodity, or a plaything for sensual gratification. With its elevation to the rank of an end value, its servants once more enrich human culture in the guise of seers, prophets, and educators, new Homers and Shakespeares, new Bachs and Beethovens, new Phidias' and Michelangelos. Liberated from the thraldom of commercialism, of vulgar demands, of stultifying and vacuous art criticism, and divorced from the role of a handmaid of eroticism, sensationalism, and negativism, artists can again fully unfold their creative genius and can again create *nec humanae laudis amore, nec temporalis*

---

[4] Among the considerable number of studies that demonstrated such results, see H. Hartshorne, M. May, and J. Maller, *Studies in the Nature of Character* (New York, 1929), II, 269 ff.; F. Eastman, *The Menace of Movies* (Chicago, 1927); and the fourteen-volume series *Motion Pictures and Youth* (The Payne Fund Studies, W. W. Charters, general editor, (New York, 1930-1934).

premii cupiditate . . . sed in augmentum honoris et gloriae nominis Dei.

Such an art, needless to say, is free from pathology and demoralizing negativism. Instead of debunking the immortals, it immortalizes the mortals; instead of ignobling the noble, it ennobles the ignoble; instead of rendering ugly the beautiful, it beautifies the ugly. From the level of social sewers it 'soars again into the pure atmosphere of the mountain peaks, attaining even the lofty sphere of the transcendental values. It becomes once more an enlightening, inspiring, and ennobling force, unfolding a vision of divine beauty, purifying man by its catharsis, and tending to unite the whole of humanity in a single intimate brotherhood.

V. General Conclusions on the Transformation of our Culture

The preceding discussion concisely indicates what aspects of our contemporary culture are decadent; what elements in it generate the forces of enmity; by what these pathological factors are to be replaced; and for what reasons. The basic conclusion reached is that the very roots, the major premise, of the tree of sensate culture are now hopelessly unsound. The longer the rotting roots of sensate culture remain, the more withered becomes the entire tree and the weaker tends to be its creative power. Under such conditions there is no possibility of rearing creative and noble human beings, nor of establishing a harmonious cultural order. Our moribund culture breeds germs of hatred, envy, and antagonism which engender endless wars, revolutions, and other bloody conflicts.

In its younger days it was vitalized by creative genius. Its hate-breeding forces were counterbalanced by the forces of sober self-interest and rational solidarity. Now it is exhausted and decadent. What is worth preserving in it will be incorporated in the richer and more comprehensive body of the new culture. The time has come to remove the rest of it from the stage of living history to a historical "museum" or "funeral chapel." For the sake of the very survival of humanity, the continuation of its creative mission, and the establishment of a noble and harmonious social order, we must set about the task of rearing the temple of the new culture. *Vivos voco, mortuos malo!*

PART FOUR

Social Factors of Altruism and Egoism

CHAPTER NINE

WHAT MUST BE CHANGED
IN ALL SOCIAL INSTITUTIONS – AND WHY

I. Molding Power of Organized Groups and Institutions

A newborn biological organism is molded into a human personality not only by incessant cultural forces but no less effectively by the ceaseless actions and reactions of other human beings organized into the social institutions amidst which one is born and lives. Being concrete and tangible, human beings and their actions mold our mind and conduct from the moment of birth to death. Moreover, they influence our destiny even before our birth: the prohibition of marriage between those belonging to different races, castes, and strata, or legalized infanticide in the case of a certain class of babies, inhibits the procreation of one kind of children and facilitates the multiplication of another kind. Similar results are obtained through the regulation of abortion and contraceptive methods and through the legal control of sexual life prescribing under what conditions sex relations are permitted or prohibited. Likewise, the totality of organized groups or institutions controls our destiny even after our death: they determine whether our name shall suffer oblivion or shall survive (as famous or infamous).

From the cradle to the grave we breathe the atmosphere of organized groups, and the incessant impact of actions and reactions shapes our body, mind, personality, and conduct. If this complex of social institutions is saturated with the poisons of egoism, we tend to become egoistic; if it is permeated with invigorating altruism, we are molded along altruistic lines. Let us glance at the entire constellation of our social institutions from this standpoint. Do they breed predominantly altruistic or egoistic persons? Can we abolish at least the gravest forms of intergroup and interpersonal conflict without changing the nature of

our institutions? If a change is needed, what parts are to be abolished or modified?

II. THREE CONFLICT-BREEDING PROPERTIES OF OUR INSTITUTIONS

Pronounced social differentiation and stratification; the competition of egoistic men and groups with other men and groups;
and the contractual and compulsory fibers of which the network
of our institutional relationships is composed; such are three
fundamental traits of all our institutions. These forces generate
primarily egoism and conflicts.

A. *Overdeveloped Social Differentiation and Stratification.*
Within a given city there are thousands of different groups: family, race, sex, and age groups; various nationality, political,
economic, occupational, artistic, ethical, religious, educational,
scientific, philosophical, philanthropic, recreational, and other
groups, cliques, factions, sects, and parties. Within the confines
of a state the number of such groups and strata is still greater,
and taking humanity as a whole their number is to be counted
by millions. As a result of this vast differentiation and stratification, each of us belongs not to one group or society but to many.

If the values and norms of conduct of all these groups and
strata were mutually harmonious and reconcilable, these groups
would be solidary with one another, their relationships would
be peaceful, and their members would be impelled to practice
altruism. The norms of conduct would be rooted deeply in their
members, effectively controlling their actions and relationships
from within. Under these conditions social differentiation of
mankind into different groups and strata would generate altruistic rather than egoistic forces.

Unfortunately, we have seen that the actual situation is
quite otherwise. Through the excessive relativizing of all values
and norms in our sensate culture, these are very different, indeed,
often contradictory, in different groups and strata. The values
and norms of conduct of a given family, race, creed, state, or
occupational group are frequently irreconcilable with those of

other groups of the same category. What one group affirms, another denies; the "Thou shalt" of one stratum is countered by the "Thou shalt not" of another stratum. The values and norms of the privileged white group in the Southern states clash with those of the organized Negro groups, as do those of the Association of Manufacturers with those of the labor unions, those of Catholics with those of atheists, those of communists with those of the advocates of "free enterprise," and so on. The values and norms of the family often clash with those of the state; those of the state with those of religion; those of religion with those of occupational groups; and so forth. During the Second World War and other wars the Christian religion recommended loving the enemy; yet the state demanded wholesale slaughter of the foe. Special occupational interests dictated labor strikes; but the state required uninterrupted work as a patriotic duty. The family desired to keep its breadwinner; but the state drafted him for military service. Objectively considered, the interests and values of almost any of the existing groups irreconcilably clash with those of other groups. And such a clash is not mere "prejudice and superstition": it is an objective irreconcilability of the respective values and norms of Bilbos and Negro leaders; of Jews and anti-Semites; of communists and Catholics; of conscientious objectors and glorifiers of war; and the like. As such it cannot be eliminated merely by debunking it as "prejudice and superstition." [1]

Thus our overdeveloped differentiation and stratification into a multitude of groups and strata, with their contradictory values and norms, inevitably generates incessant interindividual and intergroup conflicts. It leads to the mental, moral, and social disorganization of persons embedded in such a matrix of groups. Being a member of many conflicting groups and strata, an individual receives from them opposing commands, norms, and values. He is placed in the position of a ball pushed and pulled in

---

[1] This is the reason for the impotency of all the otherwise commendable propaganda against racial and religious tensions. In spite of a flood of such propaganda during the last few decades, neither racial nor religious tensions have decreased. In fact, they have sharply increased.

opposite directions. His family imbues him with values and often demands from him actions irreconcilable with those inculcated or demanded by his state citizenship; these in turn, frequently conflict with the values and demands of his occupational, economic, or religious affiliations. As a result of this incessant pressure he has little chance to develop an integrated self, with a single harmonious set of values and norms of conduct. His soul becomes parceled and divided into many mutually contradictory selves. He becomes a rudderless boat, a house divided against itself.

His situation may be summed up as follows. Amidst the jungle of contradictory norms and values, an individual lacks a consistent set of standards. His personality thus remains unintegrated. He is the victim of endless conflicts, worries, and unhappiness, which render him an irritable psychoneurotic whose irreconcilable selves incessantly war with one another, with other persons and groups, with God and the world at large.[2] Under these circumstances he cannot develop a sense of true altruism or consistently obey the commands of Christianity or any other moral norms.

These inner conflicts are responsible for unhappiness, deterioration of one's physical health, growing cynicism, outbursts of rage, violence, and destructive tendencies, criminality, and even suicide. If one is subjected from birth to mutually contradictory

---

[2] The real cause of most contemporary psychoneuroses and mental illness is not the fantastic Freudian repression by the superego of man's libido and destructive instincts, but, rather, the disparity of the pressures (values, norms, and demands) of the multitude of groups to which he belongs. They give him no chance to be at peace with himself, with others, and with the world at large. Growing differentiation and stratification is the cause of the increase of psychoneuroses during the last few decades. Among other evidence pointing to this conclusion is the fact that, in spite of an enormous multiplication of psychoanalysts and psychiatrists during these decades, mental functional disorders have increased rather than diminished. This means that the diagnosis and treatment of the factors of psychoneuroses has been faulty. In the case of physical maladies, such as infectious diseases, where the diagnosis and treatment have been accurate an expansion of medical and sanitary services has markedly reduced such sicknesses. This is not the case with psychoneuroses. (For a systematic development of the ideas of this section, see *Society*, chaps. 12-15, 19 and 48.)

norms of conduct, one group teaching that property or the marriage vow is sacred, another group declaring that possession of property is theft and the marriage vow a bourgeois hypocrisy, he can scarcely believe that any value is sacred or any norm is binding. The slightest biological or other stimulus is sufficient to induce him to violate his norms and standards. Such violations multiply, leading to ever-growing interpersonal and intergroup conflicts. Brute force and fraud raise their ugly heads as the supreme arbiters.

Individuals placed in this situation are bound progressively to transgress even their *contractual obligations and loyalties.* Like an investor who puts his money into too many banks, an individual attached to a multitude of contradictory groups exhibits only scant loyalty to any and is unconditionally loyal to none. His "freely accepted obligation" becomes in his eyes superfluous; he unhesitatingly repudiates it at the first temptation, the more so since if he attempts to be loyal to the values and norms of one group, such a loyalty means disloyalty to other groups, with opposite sets of standards.

So long as this situation persists, there is no hope of avoiding its disastrous consequences. Hence arises the necessity of modifying this breeder of egoism, conflict, unhappiness, and mental disease.

The first remedy consists in canceling one's membership in the less important organizations with mutually conflicting norms. If one believes that the values of group B are less significant than those of group A, he can relieve his situation by dropping his affiliation with group B. If he does the same with regard to all his irreconcilable groups and finally remains a member of only those organizations whose standards and norms are harmonious, he frees himself from conflicting values and norms; from inner conflicts and worries; from egoism, cynicism, and disintegration; from psychoneuroses; and the like. Controlled by the harmoniously directed forces of mutually concordant groups, he is like a ball pushed by many forces in the same direction. He regains 'is inner integrity, his peace of mind, his sense of a clear conscience, his determination and will power. His duties are regarded as sacred and are gladly fulfilled. His conduct is both consistent and resolute.[3]

Unfortunately, the prescribed remedy is limited in its application. An individual cannot terminate his membership in many groups. Thus, his citizenship in the state group or membership in the family group cannot be terminated, as a rule, by his own decision. Likewise his occupational or economic position cannot often be changed through his own volition. It is hardly possible for most of us freely to rearrange our affiliations with all the groups and strata to which we belong. Hence the necessity for a more radical modification of our group structure. This consists in *such a rearrangement of groups and strata that their antagonism is eliminated, that they do not impose mutually contradictory commands upon the individual and impel him to conflicting actions.* The groups and strata may be diverse; but so long as their basic values and norms are not contradictory, most of their conflicts are eliminated and the individual is freed from internal conflicts, attaining unity in diversity. We cannot eliminate the division of functions among groups, nor their diversity, but we can abolish most of their antagonistic values and standards. This can be done when *all groups and strata subordinate their values and standards to a set of universal values and of concordant norms of conduct.* The essence of such values and norms for interpersonal and intergroup relationships has been sublimely formulated in the Sermon on the Mount, in the Golden Rule, and in similar injunctions on the part of all world religions and all real ethical systems. If all groups and strata, no matter how

___
[3] It is precisely this operation of freeing an individual from his connections with mutually contradictory groups, values, norms, and standards that lies at the basis of the reorientation, reintegration, "transference," and "sublimation" of his standards and norms whereby he is relieved of his functional mental disorders, psychoneuroses, confusion, and disintegration. Success in the treatment of these mental disorders is due mainly to this therapeutic operation, and not to the alleged liberation of the libido or death instincts from repression by the superego or to a mysterious sublimation of these instincts in conformity to the demands of the superego. As we shall see (chapters 12-15), the Freudian and other psychoanalytic theories are fantastic. When psychoanalysts do not disorganize but actually help their patients, they do this contrary to their own theories!

diverse they may be, apply these norms in their ideology and their overt actions, if most of their standards and norms contradictory to these supreme norms are eliminated, then humanity will achieve real unity in diversity, most clashes will be eliminated, and the individual will regain his integrity, happiness and peace of mind, and kindly and warm-hearted attitude toward his fellow men, the world at large, and God.

B. *The Glorified Competition of Men and Groups.* The second general characteristic of our social institutions is represented by egoistic men and groups indefatigably competing with other men and groups for success, and superiority in all fields of activity, beginning with the football field and ending with the battlefield. Egoistic competition explicitly lies at the basis of our economic and political institutions. In the opening chapters of our texts in economics and politics this principle is stressed and overstressed. In thousands of forms it is daily repeated and glorified. It is declared to represent the very nature of men and groups, constituting the basic motive of all human activities, the source of all inventions and achievements, the driving force of social progress and order. Competition, success, and victory are alleged to be the heart and soul of our social system. Our paramount ethos centers around them. From the cradle to the grave everyone is imbued with a sense of the glory of victory over his competitors and opponents; with the fighting spirit; with the cult of power; with the sweet intoxication of prize-winning in sports, business, politics, science, religion, ethics, the fine arts, and what not. Our heroes and supermen are invariably militant persons who successfully subjugate their rivals in activities ranging all the way from innocent sports to murder and other crimes. Our very institutions are, first and foremost, instruments for subduing rivals.

By the very nature of this principle, it breeds incessant interindividual, intergroup, and international conflicts. If egoistic competition in respect to insignificant values does not engender jealousy, enmity, hatred, ruthlessness, and destructive conflicts, competition involving important values generates all such forces. Other conditions being equal, the greater the values involved in the competition, the more profound, unquenchable, and destructive the antagonism. As long as selfish competition remains the foundation of our social life, there is little hope of eliminating enmity and grave conflicts. Hence the necessity for limiting and supplementing this principle.

In the field of ideology the conception of man as a purely egoistic creature controlled by egoistic motives should be dispelled. There hardly ever existed a purely egoistic person. If human beings have been controlled by the egoistic factor of the struggle for existence, no less have they been motivated by the need for mutual aid and co-operation. The helplessness of a newborn babe and the non-self-sufficiency of man in general have made co-operation, mutual aid, sympathy, and sacrifice an indispensable condition of the survival of the human species. For these reasons alone, altruism is as much a part of man's second nature as egoism. The natural man as a purely egoistic person is a fiction invented by modern pseudo science. It confuses the egoism due to the specific traits of sensate culture with man's inherent nature. So far as such a myth has influenced human beings, justifying their selfish propensities, it has been destructive and antisocial. As an invalid and degrading conception it should be replaced by a more scientific conception of man as a creature possessing altruistic as well as egoist propensities.

The false glorification of egoistic competition as the dominant motive for industry and creative activities must be replaced by sounder theories, more adequate scientifically and less destructive socially. The discoveries, inventions, and major achievements in religion and ethics, law, philosophy, the fine arts, science and technology, as well as in practical life, that have enriched human culture have not been due primarily to egoistic motives, that is, considerations of personal advantage. The extreme egoists, the antisocial Scrooges, criminals, and the like, have contributed scarcely anything to the enrichment and ennoblement of human life and culture. They have been parasites and destroyers rather than creators. On the other hand, almost every important discovery, invention, and creation has been the product of the collective, co-operative effort of many persons and of many generations.

In the personal motivation of the real builders of human culture purely egoistic considerations have played a very modest role — often none at all. Creators of notable religious and ethical values have acted contrary to or in disregard of egoistic considerations, most of them deliberately sacrificing many personal advantages, sometimes even their life, for the sake of their creative activities. They have acted in the interest of the well-being of humanity or for the greater glory of God rather than for the sake of wealth, fame, sensual gratification, and the like. In a slightly less degree the same is true of the overwhelming majority of all other creators, inventors, and discoverers, eminent scientists, philosophers, lawgivers, artists, and so on. Many of these were so little motivated by egoistic considerations that they did not trouble even to attach their names to their creations or achievements, which hence remained anonymous. Homer and Dante, Bach and Mozart, Michelangelo and Phidias, Plato and Kant, Archimedes and Newton, were motivated primarily by a sense of the needs of their fellow men or by the irresistible *élan* of their creative genius ("divine madness," "superconscious inspiration," etc.). From the standpoint of the egoistic theory such creators were guilty of stupidity; for they profited little from their activities in a material or practical sense. Many of them were penniless and died in poverty. They enjoyed few physical comforts, few privileges, scant power, in short, a minimum of sensate values. Many of them suffered persecution for their creative activities. To declare that egoism and egoistic competition are the only source of human progress and culture may suit the interests of unscrupulous exploiters of creative forces, be they slaveowners, sterile potentates, destructive politicians, or what not; but science is entitled to state the facts as they really are. By dispelling such fictions science may serve the cause of altruism, good will, and creativity, helping to prepare the ground for the cultivation of more co-operative human relationships.

Deflated ideologically, egoistic competition must, moreover, *actually* be reduced in all social institutions and in the relationships of individuals and groups. It is hardly possible to eliminate it entirely from the conduct of the majority of people and from all social groups and institutions. But it should and can be limited, being replaced in part by the opposite principle of noncompetitive co-operation and service. The cult of victory and success can be mitigated and partially supplanted by the ethos of humility, love, and sacrifice.

That such a limitation and such a replacement are feasible is well attested by the multitude of family groups and groups of true friends and by the millions of altruistic actions performed daily by even allegedly egoistic men and groups. The relationships between the members of even the average family or group of friends are determined only in part by selfish interests. In their greater part they consist of noncompetitive co-operation, service, and sacrifice inspired by love or sympathy, each member striving to do his best to promote the welfare of the other members, regardless of his own personal advantage. The joys and sorrows of one member are shared by the family as a whole. The achievement of one member becomes the achievement of the rest of the family. Ordinary mothers and fathers gladly sacrifice their time, strength, comfort, and even health and life to help a sick child; and a similar sacrifice is cheerfully made by the children for their parents.

In the same way are motivated the relationships between real friends. Less pure but similar is the motive force determining the relations of the members of many preliterate tribes, of some pastoral and agricultural peoples, of monastic and religious sects, and even of a regiment on the battlefield, where everyone fights for the other members, and the whole regiment stands behind every soldier, without any meticulous calculation of personal advantages and disadvantages. Nonegoistic motivation is daily evinced by a host of unselfish acts, as when a stranger rushes into a burning house and at the risk of his life attempts to rescue persons unknown to him, or when, in a drive for a community fund, people contribute anonymously a large portion of their means for the welfare of others.

The existence of such groups, persons, and actions eloquently attests the possibility of a marked limitation of egoism and selfish competition, of the cult of success and victory, and the feasibility of their partial replacement by noncompetitive co-operation, generosity, and willing sacrifice. Moreover, if the organization of a group or institution is deliberately aimed at a release of altruistic forces, the group morale becomes particularly powerful in propelling its members in the direction of co-operative and unselfish actions. This has been demonstrated by experimental studies of school children undertaken by several investigators (especially by H. Hartshorne and M. May, whose works are cited above).

A notable reduction of egoism and egoistic competition among groups and individuals is possible without any corresponding reduction of their industry and creativeness. In a number of cases achievement is actually promoted by a restriction of the fighting spirit and of the cult of success obtained at the cost of the defeat of rivals.

For a small fraction of humanity, its foremost creators and altruists, the motive of egoistic competition can be eliminated completely without detriment to their creativity. If geniuses are assured the minimum of subsistence requirements, they will continue to create for the greater glory of God or the edification of man.

The specific forms of the limitation of egoistic competition are many, depending upon conditions, including the nature of the prevailing institutions. Competitive successes are frequently a matter of sheer good luck. It is only reasonable not to credit the full fruits of such luck to the chance victors. Moreover, a considerable proportion of competitive victories in all fields are the result of questionable politics, machinations, favoritism, or outright dishonesty. Such victors are not entitled to their prizes. Most genuine achievements are the result of the collective activity of many known and unknown workers. The credit should be given to the aggregate of the contributors. Scarcely any of the major successes in such fields as business, economics, and politics are actually due to the superhuman efforts of this or that captain of industry and finance or the leader of this or that political faction. It is only just to assure the highest possible minimum of economic and political values to everyone before gigantic fortunes, conspicuous luxuries, or dictatorial powers are granted to any individual or faction.

On the other hand, *the burden of sacrifice, suffering, grief, and sorrow is distributed, under the egoistic competitive system, out of all proportion to the merits or demerits of individuals and groups.* The nobler part of humanity is generally allotted a far larger proportion of these burdens than its more callous part. A more equitable distribution is both desirable and possible. The cross of Calvary should be borne not simply by Jesus and a small fraction of humanity but by everyone. Thus the sufferer would become a member of one suffering collectivity instead of bearing his bitter cross alone and forsaken. The problem of a more equitable distribution of burdens and sorrows is even more important than that of advantages, privileges, and pleasures. Oneness in sorrow binds human beings by stronger and nobler ties than community of privilege, power, or vice.

The limitation and replacement of the egoism and self-centered competition of our institutions along these lines will markedly reduce envy and hatred, wars and other conflicts, engendering a spirit of good will among men and mitigating even the sorrows of the innocent victims of misfortune.

c. *Predominant Contractual and Compulsory Relationships.* However diverse, all human relationship can be grouped into three main classes: familistic, contractual, and compulsory. *Familistic* relationships are permeated by mutual love, devotion, and sacrifice. They are exemplified by the relationships between the members of a devoted family. The ego of a member is there merged in a single "we" with common values, joys, and sorrows. Help is gladly given and gladly accepted. The group is a solidary entity.

Contractual relationships are marked by a voluntary agreement of the parties for their common advantage. Such relations are devoid of love as well as enmity. The parties remain self-centered and seek their own advantage, but through the free exchange of services or values they reconcile their advantage with that of the other parties.

Compulsory relations involve coercion of the weaker party by the stronger. Such relationships are inherently inimical and antagonistic. They are the worst form of interpersonal and intergroup relationship, frequently resulting in grave conflicts.

The bulk of the interpersonal and intergroup relationships of the Western population of the nineteenth and early twentieth century was made up of contractual fibers. Economic relations between employer and employees, buyer and seller, and producer and consumer in the capitalist economy have been mainly contractual, the parties voluntarily entering into an agreement to exchange wages for services or money for merchandise. In contrast to the economy of slavery or serfdom, coercion has played a minor role; in contradistinction to the familistic economy, labor and capitalists, employer and employees, buyers and sellers, have not been perceptibly attached to one another by a sense of love or devotion. They have merely pursued their own interests. Similarly, our political relationships have also been predominantly contractual, with the rights and duties of the government and the citizens freely agreed upon and definitely limited, the government being elected by the citizens, everyone being assured the minimum of his inalienable rights, and the duties of each being clearly defined by covenant. The family and marriage have likewise been contractual, the parties voluntarily entering into the marriage contract. The same applies to religious, scientific, artistic, professional, educational, and other groups and associations.

The contractual structure of Western society has thus been fully developed. While less noble than the familistic type of relations, it has been incomparably better than the coercive system of foreign conquerors, autocratic governments, slave-owners, and the oppressive nobles of the feudal age.

Though contractual relations are implicitly egoistic, each party trying to get as much as possible for as little as possible, nevertheless, so long as the parties entered into the contract voluntarily, so long as they fulfilled their obligations, so long as they did not attempt to use the agreement to the detriment of the other party, their egoistic interests were compatible with their common advantage, their relationships remained free from enmity, and internal and international peace was tolerably well preserved throughout the century from 1815 to 1914.

Unfortunately, in the course of their development these contractual relationships degenerated. Their implicit egoism progressively led to abuse of the contract at the expense of the other parties. The growing relativization of legal and moral obligations impaired the binding power of contracts and resulted in ever-increasing violation of their contractual obligations by individuals, groups, and governments. Economic and other conditions, such as depression and unemployment, deprived many parties of contractual freedom on an equal basis and converted many agreements into compulsory contracts made under duress. Finally, as a result of general demoralization, certain parties, such as gangs of criminal racketeers, unscrupulous politicians, and commercial cynics, began to conclude contracts detrimental to the rest of the population.

This degeneration of contractual relations naturally resulted in the dislocation and eventual crumbling of the whole contractual structure. The delicately balanced egoistic forces finally lost their equilibrium and exploded in a series of unparalleled conflicts, wars, revolutions, and other intergroup clashes, as well as interpersonal conflicts. Contractual capitalism and democratic governments were swept away, being supplanted partly by paternalistic régimes but principally by coercive economic régimes and political dictatorships. Contractual freedom of thought, speech, the press, association, religion, and occupation has been steadily replaced by authoritarianism. The contemporary world exhibits a notable decrease of true contractual relationships in interpersonal and intergroup action; a considerable increase of purely compulsory relationships; and a slight accretion of familistic relations.[4] It is evident that as long as degenerate contractual relations or compulsory relations persist, there is no hope of lasting internal or international peace. The very nature of pseudo

---

[4] For a detailed analysis of these problems, see *Dynamics*, III, chaps. 1-4; *Crisis*, chaps. 5-7; *Society*, chaps. 29-33.

contractual and compulsory relations generates incessant brutal conflicts.

In the texture of our institutions and groups (1) the compulsory fibers should be reduced to the very minimum; (2) pseudo contractual relations formed under duress must be replaced by true contractual ones freely entered into, faithfully sustained by all the parties and not used to the detriment of the other parties to the contract, and devoid of prejudice to the public at large; (3) the familistic relations should be increased as much as possible, extending far beyond one's own family, friends, or faction, potentially over the whole of humanity.

How to accomplish this is a technical question to be discussed later. Here it suffices to indicate clearly what should be done with the fibers of our human relationships in order that they may produce peace and harmony instead of enmity and conflict.

This chapter has singled out three general properties of our social institutions. It has demonstrated their conflict-breeding functions and has indicated how to render our institutions peace-generating centers instead of hatred-breeding foci. We are now prepared to undertake a diagnosis of our dominant institutions in order to see what their role is in generating altruistic and egoistic forces.

CHAPTER TEN

WHAT MUST BE CHANGED IN THE FAMILY, SCHOOL, AND RELIGIOUS INSTITUTIONS — AND WHY

I. The Family

Of all social institutions the good family has possibly been the most effective agency of altruism and familistic relationships. Within the limited circle of the family and kinship group it has fused husbands and wives, parents and children, into one familistic "we." More successfully than any other group it has transformed its members into a single entity, with a common fund of values, with common joys and sorrows, spontaneous co-operation and willing sacrifice. This altruization of its members and the transmutation of their egos into one collective "we" has been its main role, unrivaled by that of any other institution or group. It is true that the altruism has often been confined to the small family-kinship circle. It is true also that some families have failed in the discharge of this function; yet even with these limitations, the family has done more to engender altruism than any other group.

Viewed from this standpoint, the contemporary Western family leaves much to be desired. It has increasingly failed in its main task; has increasingly generated the forces of egoism and demoralization.

The principal reason for this is to be found in the growing transformation of the family from a familistic union of husband and wife into an implicitly egoistic contractual association of a male and female in the interest of pleasure and utility. Some sociologists assign this "modern family" relation the "high-falutin'" name of "companionship." In such a family as in any contractual association, the egos of the parties are not merged in a single collective "we." Each ego seeks to preserve its freedom and independence. They remain intact in their bargaining, calculating, pleasure-seeking and utility-hunting. And the pleasures and utilities themselves tend, in accordance with the sensate nature of our culture, to grow more and more physiological, materialistic, and hedonistic. Under these conditions, when the union yields less sexual or hedonistic pleasure than was expected, or affords a smaller amount of material utility, home comforts, dresses, furs, jewels, cars, food and drink, etc., then as soon as the sex or property appeal of another male or female proves more tempting, the value of such a marriage union declines, and the bond of "companionship" weakens and easily disintegrates. The divorced or deserted party speedily forms a new sex or marriage relationship. In some cases people change partners almost each season, with side-line sex excursions in between. With each subsequent change of partners the egoistic nature of the "marriage bond" becomes increasingly palpable, until the marriage becomes scarcely distinguishable from the "sex companionship" of a prostitute and her customer, of a mistress and her paramour, of a gigolo and his patroness. "Marriages" among leading heirs and heiresses and some of the Hollywood "aristocracy" are notoriously of this type. The mounting curve of extramarital relations, divorce, and desertions, and of premarital sex relations which have made the assumed chastity of unmarried girls largely a myth, points clearly to the increasing diffusion of this sort of "marriage" among all classes.

It goes without saying that this traffic in sex partners develops not a sense of devotion and loyalty but rather an attitude of extreme sensate selfishness. It frequently produces nervous wrecks incapable of maintaining even the basic integrity of their personality, to say nothing of radiating happiness and good will. It degrades marriage from the lofty plane of a sacred union for life to the low level of casual sex relations with constantly shifting partners.

Such "bedroom companionship" cannot inculcate self-discipline, a sense of duty, or the capacity for self-sacrifice. Instead it merely inflates the role of the libido, the partners feeling perfectly justified in their quest for its full satisfaction, untrammeled by any "repression by the stupid superego." Under the benediction of the Freudian theories and similar fantastic ideologies, they become convinced that, like all human beings, they are but an incarnation of the "oral, anal, and genital libidos" which urge one to seduce his or her parent of the opposite sex (the Oedipus complex), and of the instinct of destruction, death, and suicide which fatally impels one to sadistic and masochistic actions (the Thanatos complex). Finding such a conception of human nature perfectly normal, they think and act accordingly, without any sense of remorse or compunction. The result of such a type of "marriage" is a multiplication of masochistic and sadistic psychoneurotics and antisocial wrecks who constitute a profitable clientele for Freudian practitioners.

Another of its consequences is an increase of childless marriages, on the one hand, and, on the other, an atrophy of parental love and a growing indisposition to bestow the proper care upon children. From the standpoint of these roving "libido-death bags" children are a nuisance, an obstacle to their happiness. Hence they try to prevent conception. Frequently, as a consequence of sexual excess, they are sterile. In either case the companionate marriage generally remains childless. If, inadvertently, a child is born, the parents increasingly tend to get rid of it, sending it to some school or nursery or giving it to a state institution or to some foster parents. In recent years such "offerings" have become so numerous that not only are the state institutions overcrowded but even remotely satisfactory foster homes cannot be found to meet the rapidly mounting demand.

Even a *normal* family is today a poor school for the socialization of children. With both parents working outside in order to meet their subsistence requirements, as is the case with millions of low-income families, or, in the well-to-do classes, with the father spending his time at his business office and the mother devoting herself to various "society" activities, the children are left largely to themselves, enjoying little parental control or guidance. They are allowed to give free rein to their caprices and fancies, growing up for the most part in an environment of city streets and spending much of their time at the movies or even in bars and saloons. Their "pals" are casual street-corner acquaintances or neighborhood "gangs." At home (and home is ordinarily a mere overnight lodging place) they often witness prevarication, hypocrisy, lying, recriminations, quarrels, enmity and hatred, or worse, on the part of their parents. Such a family, needless to say, is a poor school for developing a sense of altruism among children. Indeed, it makes for their demoralization and disintegration.

Need we wonder, therefore, that in spite of the boasted increase of nurseries, schools, and intellectual development, juvenile delinquency is on the increase; that the proportionate share of youthful criminality is mounting; that the incidence of juvenile vandalism, the desecration of cemeteries and churches, the damaging of street lights, telephone poles, fire and police signal boxes, automobile tires, and so on, is rapidly rising? This is only to be expected. Society should not blame any one but itself for these fruits of its family and marriage system. As long as this system remains what it is, there is little hope of an appreciable decrease of juvenile delinquency, or of molding unselfish, well-integrated, responsible citizens out of the unloved, unwelcome, and neglected children of our Freudian, hedonistic, "companionate" marriage and family.

The ideologies of Freudianism, "companionate marriage," unrestrained sex freedom, and so on, should be discredited, not only because of their demoralizing influence but as pseudoscientific, fantastic nonsense. In the light of our existing knowledge, there is no difficulty in demonstrating their utter fallaciousness as pathological products of a disintegrating sensate culture. Deflation of such ideologies strips the roving "libido bags" and their pseudo marriages of the glamour with which they are invested by these ideologies. The traits of such sexually morbid persons, with their Oedipus, Thanatos, and Narcissus complexes, are revealed as a blend of mental aberration, sensuality, parasitic egoism, and social irresponsibility. Thus exposed, most of the devotees of this cult of libido and sadism will be brought to their senses, leaving only a small fraction of incurables to wallow in the muck of their "ids" and mental aberrations.

A similar deflation must be applied to our vulgar and salacious novels, films, plays, and songs, to erotic dancing, and to the exploitation of sex for commercial purposes by the yellow and the high-brow press, the radio, and other means of entertainment, propaganda, and indoctrination. This does not mean a taboo on sex as such: sex and erotic love have always been counted among the basic values of true art and life. Deflation concerns only the sordid and degrading abuse of these values for commercial and similar purposes, resulting in the mass production of aesthetically worthless novels, cinemas, plays, and songs; in high-brow magazines serving as a stimulus for the resuscitation of the sexual potency of their enervated and debilitated readers; in yellow journals filled with sordid sex scandals; and the like. These should all be relegated to the category of social sewers; their producers and agents, to that of panderers; their patrons to that of consumers of muck. Through concerted public opinion most of these vulgarities can be removed from the public stage of social life.

Marriage and the family must be restored to their place of dignity among the greatest values in human life, not to be trifled with. As a socially sanctioned union of husband and wife, of parents and children, the family is to be radically differentiated from all unsanctioned sex associations. It should become again a union of bodies, souls, hearts, and minds in a single collective "we." Its basic function, that of inculcating deep sympathy, compassion, love, and loyalty in its members, not only in relation to one another but toward humanity at large, must be restored and fully developed. This extension of altruism far beyond the limits of the family, to embrace all creeds, races, nations, classes, and strata, will be a new distinction of the family as compared with its old form. Thus the ennobled family will become a true *consortium omnis vitae, divini et humani juris communicatio.* This is necessary because no other agency can perform this function as well as the average good family. This type of family will become the cornerstone of a new creative social order.

The technical means of rebuilding this kind of family are many. First, each individual must make an effort to achieve it in his individual life. Second, when public opinion in this matter becomes united, its pressure will exert an enormous and decisive influence. Third, sound legislation fostering such a type of family, discriminating against mock marriages and pseudo families; limiting freedom of marriage and divorce; discrediting panderers in all their high-brow and low-brow forms; and depriving irresponsible parents of certain privileges, including the right to neglect and demoralize their children, such legislation, supported by the conscience of society, can accomplish a great deal in this direction. It will be ineffective if it runs counter to genuine public opinion. It will be powerful if it is supported by the unofficial law convictions of the public. In that case it will not need to be severe in its sanctions and penalties.

II. The School

The family is the first and most decisive molder of the personality and conduct of children. School institutions are their next molder, especially in modern societies, where nursery schools and kindergartens share this task with the family at the early age of two or three years. As one passes to the elementary school, high school, and college or university, their formative role increases.

In addition to this educational function our schools perform a selective role as an agency that tests and selects individuals, assigning them to their proper social positions. It bars incapable pupils from the higher professional, governmental, and big-business positions, assigning to these mainly its capable pupils. Most of these positions are closed to persons without college diplomas. Pupils whose education is limited to the elementary schools are doomed, for the most part, to occupy positions of unskilled, semiskilled, or skilled labor. This selective role of the schools is as important as their educational function.[1]

If school education is well organized, it can reinforce sound family education to such a degree that the combined effects are indelibly stamped upon the pupils for the rest of their lives. If

---

[1] See P. A. Sorokin, *Social Mobility* (New York, 1927), chaps. 8 and 9.

the family education is defective, a sound school education may correct, to a considerable extent, its shortcomings. If the school system is defective, it can do an untold amount of harm to its pupils. It can misshape their minds, distort their souls, demoralize their conduct. Likewise, when the school as a selective agency operates properly, it distributes persons on the basis of the principle: to everyone according to his ability. The whole of society profits from such an allotment of its members. The aristocracy, as well as the lower strata, successfully discharge their functions; everyone is satisfied with his work; and society enjoys a harmonious and creative life. If a school system is defective in this respect, it places the incapable persons in positions of leadership, and the capable ones in the ranks of unskilled or semiskilled labor. Persons so placed discharge their functions inadequately; dissatisfaction pervades society; and in hundreds of other ways society suffers from such a maldistribution of its members.

Our contemporary school system is grossly defective in both respects. *As an educational agency it fails to develop character and a sense of altruism, especially in the high schools and colleges.* The schools of our sensate culture limit their educational function chiefly to training the intellect. They pay scant attention to engendering a social outlook. If a pupil receives the prescribed quota of high marks in his courses, he is graduated with honors, though his conduct may be on the borderline between the legal and the criminal. It is not necessary for honor students to be altruistic or even ethical. Aside from a perfunctory enforcement of formal discipline, our schools have no curriculum or technique of inculcating moral strength or unselfishness. Virtually the only devices for molding character, various sports, competitions, prizes, etc., are based on an explicitly competitive principle, animated by the ethos of rivalry, by the spirit of subduing one's rivals in football, oratorical contests, and the like. There is little competition in humility, sacrifice, social service, and so forth.

The ideals inculcated by our school system are those of becoming a wealthy businessman, a powerful politician, a successful professional man, and the like. Thus our sensate schools breed egoists rather than altruists, and fighters rather than peacemakers. The same result they achieve, especially on the high school and college levels, through the sophistication of the ideology and conduct of their students, whose minds are filled with a host of pseudoscientific, mostly animalistic theories of man, his culture and values, embracing God and religion, ethics, marriage, property, and what not. "Traditional" values are corroded by the acids of so-called scientific criticism. The distinction between right and wrong is shattered by a barrage of positivistic, materialistic, relativistic, and mechanistic artillery. Students are "liberated" from their "superstitions and prejudices" without having these replaced by any genuine set of real values. For these are substituted pitiful odds and ends of debunking, seminihilistic, and degrading sensate ideologies. The result is a sort of moral trauma. A pervading attitude of nihilism and cynicism divests students of their moral armament, making them sophisticated flotsam and jetsam or else rampant egoists, ambitious fighters free from the restraint of ethical conventions, religious "prejudices," and other "superstitions," devotees of the cult of unlimited power and success, followers of the principle that "everything is permitted if you can get away with it."

Is it surprising that no close correlation has been found between school education and school success, on the one hand, and altruism, morality, social service and ethical ennoblement? Should we be puzzled by the fact that the tremendous increase of schools of all levels since the thirteenth century has not been followed by a decline of war and other conflicts? Is it any wonder that the twentieth century is the most highly schooled, most technological, and most scientific century in all history and at the same time the most selfish, inhuman, and bloody?

No wonder that our upper classes, recruited predominantly from the most successful graduates of our universities, have not shown any moral superiority to the lower classes, recruited mainly from either the illiterate or the semiliterate pupils of the first grades of the elementary schools!

Even as *an agency of purely intellectual training, our contemporary schools leave much to be desired, especially on the college level.* They tend to cram the minds of the students with miscellaneous bits of information rather than to develop their powers of logical thought except in such departments as mathematics, physics, and chemistry. They produce chiefly standardized specialists, picture-maker's, music-makers, fiction-makers, show-makers, and mediocre technicians, physicians, architects, preachers, teachers, officials, and businessmen, rather than original creators. Their organization inhibits rather than stimulates original genius sharply divergent from the prevalent patterns. In the field of the social and humanistic sciences this tendency has gone so far that Plato's *Republic* would unquestionably be rejected by many departments if it were written now for the first time and submitted as a doctoral dissertation. The aridity and all-pervading sterility in the field of the social and humanistic studies and in that of the fine arts is the nemesis for this concentration on technique instead of on substance, on incidental details instead of on important phenomena, on a narrow approach to a subject instead of on depth and breadth of insight, on a misleading preciseness instead of approximate validity, on conventional standards instead of on the free initiative of original, creative genius.

Defective also is the contemporary school system as a selective agency. To say nothing of the notorious lack of opportunity for poor children to even enter the high schools and colleges, the very selective criteria of our schools are defective. Owing to their aforesaid shortcomings in respect to character training, our institutions do not sift persons with highly socialized character from those with egoistic, cynical, and weak characters. Indeed, they tend to promote the latter type to the upper strata of society. Likewise they favor the standardized technicians (known as "competent researchers," "precise scholars," "excellent organizers," "popular leaders of public opinion," etc.) rather than creative geniuses; pretentious mediocrities rather than modest but competent persons; cynical go-getters rather than sincere and honest "solitudinarians." Such persons may enjoy a short-lived success; but as mediocrities rather than a real aristocracy of mind and heart, they cannot enjoy any lasting prestige or influence.

For a time they may fool others (even themselves) but they cannot cheat history. Finally, such "leaders" possess no capacity for coping with the crucial social problems of the age, as is suggested by the mounting curve of crises and catastrophies.

This defective selection on the part of our schools leaves within the lower strata many an inborn leader, creative genius, and strong moral character. These real aristocrats cannot fail to percieve the vacuity of our so-called aristocracies, their egoism, their glittering sham. Hence they naturally challenge the upper classes — if need be, revolt against them and, with the help of the lower classes, often dethrone them. This explains the brief duration of our aristocracies: today bosses, tomorrow nobodies; from shirtsleeves to shirtsleeves in three generations.

As long as these defects of our school system persist, it will continue to generate selfish and destructive rather than altruistic or creative forces.

As educational agencies the schools must establish a carefully elaborated system for developing altruism in their pupils. They must instill in them a set of universal values and norms, free from superstition and ignorance as well as from the degrading, cynical, nihilistic, and pseudoscientific theories of our time. This task should be deemed as important as intellectual training.

Intellectual training must be reconstructed in the interest of developing logical thinking and a passionate search for the truth rather than of cramming the mind with fragments of this or that knowledge or of imparting a superficial acquaintance with the fashionable intellectual currents of the day. Instead of the prevalent vogue of short-sighted "practicality" they must imbue the students with a sense of true wisdom, which is infinitely more practical in the long run than most of the so-called "practical" theories of our time. Specialization must be supplemented by a broad general education making students the inheritors, users, and guardians of the immortal values of human culture in all its fields. Obsession with techniques must be supplanted by a deep insight into the essence, or substance, of the phenomena studied. The cult of misleading precision should be corrected by the quest for approximate validity. Cultivation of the conventional needs to be supplemented by a strong stimulation of creative genius. Standardized requirements for students (especially for university students) must be freed from their rigidity, permitting the maximum of freedom for young scholars in developing their particular aptitudes.

Along similar lines the school must be remade as a selective agency. So long as a certain degree of stratification is inevitable in any society, its aristocracy should be recruited from those of real creative genius be it intellectual, artistic, moral, or social. Only such an aristocracy can be truly beneficial for humanity. It is not the master but the servant of the people. Its leadership is based not upon external coercion, machination, or wealth but upon its creativity and beneficence. It is not the "dominant minority," but merely a *primus inter pares.*

Thus transformed, the school will be one of the mainsprings of the altruistic and constructive forces which make for peace, happiness, and genius.

III. RELIGIOUS INSTITUTIONS

Religion is a system of ultimate values and norms of conduct derived principally through superconscious intuition, supplemented by rational cognition and sensory experience. As such it tends to constitute the supreme synthesis of the dominant values and norms of conduct. Its superconscious intuition makes us aware of, and puts us in contact with, the superconscious aspect of the ultimate reality value, the Infinite Manifold, God, or the Holy. Herein religion is little dependent upon logic and sensory experience. In so far as it attempts to give a rational and empirically correct synthesis of the superconscious, the rational, and the empirical aspects of the Infinite Manifold, it draws upon syllogistic and mathematical logic and upon empirical science.

Virtually all the major religions and all genuine religious experiences have apprehended the ultimate reality value in a very similar way so far as its superconscious aspect is concerned. The differences between the Tao of Taoism, the "Heaven" of Confucianism, the Brahman of Hinduism and Buddhism, the Jehovah of Judaism, the God of Christianity, and "the Inexpressible" of mystics consist mainly in differences of terminology, in the accentuation of this or that aspect of the Infinite Manifold, and in the even more subsidiary differences of rationalized dogmas and cults. In these secondary traits religions vary and undergo change; in their intuition of the ultimate reality value as an Infinite Manifold, as in their basic values and norms of conduct, they remain essentially unchangeable. The scale of values of all genuine religions unanimously puts at the top the supreme value of the Infinite Manifold itself (God, Brahman, Tao, the Holy, the Sacred), and then, in descending order, the highest values of truth, goodness, and beauty, their inferior and less pure varieties, and finally the sensory and sensate values. Likewise, the moral commandments of all genuine religions are fundamentally identical. Their ethics is the ethics of unbounded love of man for God, for his fellow men, for all living creatures, and for the entire universe. In brief, in their intuitive system of reality — values and norms of conduct, religions remain true to themselves, undergoing little change, and depending little upon logic and empirical knowledge.

In their rational and empirical ideologies religions, as has been said, naturally depend upon logic and empirical science. Since these are incessantly changing, religions change also in these respects: in their theological rationalizations, in their cult and ritual, in their empirical activities and organizations. If a religion does not modify these logical and empirical elements in conformity with changes in logical and sensory knowledge (mathematics, logic, and science), it becomes obsolescent in these components and is eventually supplanted by a religion whose logical and empirical values and norms are up to date. The superconscious essence of the supplanting and the supplanted religion remains, however, essentially the same. Religion as a superconscious intuition of the Infinite Manifold is perennial and eternal; as a rationalized system of theology, as an empirical system of cult, ritual, and technical activities, it is incessantly changing.

There has been scarcely any great culture without a great religion as its foundation. The emergence of virtually all notable cultures has been either simultaneous with or preceded by the emergence of a notable religion which has constituted its most valuable component. The decline of any major culture or the end of one era and the beginning of a new era in its life history has again been marked by either the decline of its religion, or by a replacement of one religion by another. Only eclectic cultural congeries have been devoid of an integrated system of religion. Such cultural congeries have functioned mainly as material to be used by creative cultures. Without Confucianism and Taoism the Chinese culture is unthinkable; without Hinduism and Buddhism there would have been no great Hindu culture; without the Greek religion and philosophy Greek culture would have been impossible; without Mohammedanism there would have been no notable Islamic-Arabic culture; without Zoroastrianism the Iranic culture could not have achieved a high level. The same relationship applies to the Egyptian, Babylonian, Judaistic, and Western Christian cultures and religions.

If we wish to build a truly great culture, we must create or recreate one or several great systems of ultimate reality — values and norms of conduct for the various parts of the human race. Like different languages, each denoting the same objects in its own words and idioms, humanity may have different "religious languages," each in its own way conveying the experience of the Holy, putting men in touch with the Infinite Manifold, and constituting the indispensable condition of the creativity of their culture and of a peaceful, altruistic social system.

Viewed in this light, the existing major religions, Christianity, Judaism, Hinduism, Buddhism, Taoism, Confucianism, Mohammedanism, Jainism and others, do not urgently need to be replaced by new religions or to be drastically modified. Their intuitive system of reality value (God, Brahman, Tao, etc. as an Infinite Manifold) and their conception of man as an end value, as a son of God, as a divine soul, as a bearer of the Absolute; these intuitions and conceptions are essentially valid and supremely edifying (in varying degrees for the different religions).

Similarly, their ethical imperatives, enjoining a union of man with the Absolute and an unconditional love of man for his fellows and for all living creatures, call for no radical change. Some of these norms, such as those of the Sermon on the Mount, are, indeed, incapable of improvement.

What is needed, therefore, concerns not the essence of the great religions but its revitalization and the modification of their secondary traits.

It is essential to recover a vital sense of the living presence of God, of union with the Infinite Manifold, such as has been experienced by the mystics and other deeply religious persons. This experience should not be attended by the emotional outbursts and bodily convulsions typical of many present-day "revivals." A large proportion of contemporary believers hardly ever enjoy such an experience. Their religiosity is chiefly a formal adherence to the prescribed ritual and cult, a mechanical repetition of traditional formulas, the mere outer shell of religion without its living flame. Hence their religious ideologies scarcely influence their overt conduct.

This reawakening of intense religious experience is inextricably connected with the actual application, in overt behavior, of the ethical norms of religion. *The transformation of overt conduct in the direction of practicing what one preaches is another fundamental change that must be effected by the leading religions.* We have seen that in modern times there has appeared an unbridgeable chasm between avowed beliefs and standards, on the one hand, and their embodiment in actual practice on the other. Thus the adherents of Christianity overtly behave, as a rule, in the most un-Christian manner. Since they retain but the formal shells of their religion, devoid of its real substance, such a chasm is inevitable.

The revitalization of religion consists precisely in these two essential tasks: (1) *re-creation of a genuine religious experience;* (2) *realization of ethical norms in the overt behavior of the believers.* A truly religious person, feeling vividly the presence of God, walks humbly and reverently on this earth and loves the other children of God and all living creatures to his utmost capacity.

These are the paramount needs of religious transmutation. Believers, especially religious leaders, must concentrate their efforts on these tasks instead of devoting most of their energy to the external shells of religiosity; their cult and ritual, their institutional property and hierarchy, their rational theology and dogmas, their politics and their claims for the superiority of their own brand of religion over the others.

The sacredness of man as an end value and the ethical commandments enjoining love are limited in several religions to the circle of their own believers. This tribal provincialism, with its double standard of morality, should cease. *Any true religion of the future must be universal in the sense that everyone, regardless of his race or nationality, creed, age, sex, or status, is regarded as a sacred end value.*

Its logical and empirical aspects, which are incessantly changing and whose validity depends upon logical and empirical science, *religions must bring into harmony with existing science and logic, dropping what is obsolescent.* This concerns theological speculation and dogma, cult and ritual, and the technique of man's spiritualization and moralization. Keeping abreast with logic and science in these subsidiary features, religion enters into harmonious co-operation with science, logic, and philosophy without sacrificing any of its intuitive truth revealed through the superconscious of its seers, prophets, and charismatic leaders. On the other hand, in its turn it supplements science, logic, and philosophy through its system of ultimate reality — values. In this way religion, logic, science unite to form a single harmonious team dedicated to the discovery of the perennial values and to the proper shaping of man's mind and conduct.

For the realization of these objectives *religions need not only to be familiar with existing techniques but also to create new, more fruitful, and more adequate techniques of religious and ethical transformation.* (Cf. the next section of this work for an elaboration of this topic.)

If the foregoing tasks are successfully performed, religion will contribute as never before to the creation of a society characterized by peace and harmony, happiness, and a sense of kinship with the Infinite Manifold.

CHAPTER ELEVEN

WHAT MUST BE CHANGED IN OUR POLITICAL, ECONOMIC, AND OTHER INSTITUTIONS— AND WHY

I. POLITICAL INSTITUTIONS

A. *The State.* There have been good and bad monarchies and republics; aristocracies, and democracies; régimes of one, of the few, and of the many. In themselves none of these forms guarantee that the government will function for the benefit of the citizens rather than for that of the few exploiting the many. Everything depends upon the content put into each of these forms and upon the personnel of the state machine.

If the content of each of these régimes is indeed aimed at and actually makes for the mental, moral, and material benefit of the citizens, and if the state machine is operated by wise, competent, and altruistic social servants, then the state is good and functions well, no matter what may be its formal designation. If, on the contrary, the state machine functions for the benefit of a selfish minority, and the rulers are incompetent, rapacious or corrupt, the state is bad and functions poorly.

But even the good states of the past, and especially those of the present, are among the most egoistic, cynical, and Machiavellian of all institutions. Being the power machine *par excellence,* the state is designed first of all for defensive and offensive warfare with all the groups whose interests conflict with its own. Being a sovereign power machine, it cannot fail to experience the lust for power. For the same reason its policies cannot avoid the naked power politics of the *raison d'état,* unrestrained by any of the ethical norms obligatory for private conduct. As a coercive apparatus (having at its disposal the army and navy, the police force, gallows and firing squads, prisons and concentration camps) in relation to all who violate its official laws,

159

which are often unjust and ethically untenable (like the laws establishing slavery and serfdom or decreeing mass extermination of its opponents) the state inevitably becomes callous, cruel, tyrannical, and cynical, and now and then corrupt. Ordering thousands or even millions to kill or be killed, imprisoning or executing all kinds of violators (including saintly martyrs and altruistic opponents of its unjust laws), eulogized and perhaps glorified in its sovereignty and power, the state has been the most militant and power-drunk of all social institutions, incessantly generating internal and international conflicts in their bloodiest and most inhuman forms. The sovereign states, especially the big empires and their governments, have probably slain more people, in their international and civil wars, than any other social institution. As long as cynical, Machiavellian, power-drunk sovereign states remain, even a single world state of the same cynical type, no durable peace is possible. Hence the institution of the state must be drastically remodeled.

A genuine ennoblement of the state will be possible only when the citizens and the officials become wiser, more competent, more altruistic. Only then will the state be the true servant of humanity instead of its master. All the preceding and subsequent suggestions, aimed at rendering men and their cultural institutions more altruistic and creative, tend to bring about just such an ennoblement of the state. When this basic reform is achieved, all the other necessary improvements will be relatively easy.

The states, including the world state, and their governments should be subjected to the same universal ethical and legal commandments as apply to private organizations and persons. They should not be above these universal moral and legal imperatives. Their cynical policy of the naked Machiavellian *raison d'état* must be terminated.

Negatively this means that they should be stripped of their sovereignty, especially of their right to wage war. It means also the limitation of the power of the state to coerce, suppress, punish, and execute its citizens, specifically, of the misuse of capital punishment and firing squads. All armed forces must be disbanded and reduced to a police force sufficient for the maintenance of domestic law and order. Within a few decades, through such demobilization and disarmament, a state could benefit its citizens economically to a far greater extent than it could through dozens of victorious wars. If the funds required merely for the maintenance of huge armed forces and armaments were used for a few decades for productive purposes, the profits would far exceed the dubious gains derived from military ventures. This disarmament would preclude the invention and manufacture of atomic bombs and similar satanic instruments of destruction.

The aforesaid prohibitions apply also to the world state to be created for the discharge of limited functions on behalf of mankind as a whole. Its legislative, judicial, and executive bodies should be composed of not only the representatives of the states as such but also of representatives of industry and agriculture, science, religion, and the fine arts. The presence of these leaders as full-fledged members of the world government would tend to mitigate the militancy of the state representatives and would markedly increase the competence, moral sense, impartiality, and prestige of the world government. Its enforcing apparatus should be limited to the necessary minimum of police power. Like the individual state, it must be denied the privilege of inventing, manufacturing, or using atomic bombs and similar means of destruction. It should likewise be subjected to the universal moral and legal imperatives and be forbidden to pursue the power politics of the nihilistic *raison d'état.*

In order to ensure the mutual interdependence of the states (which should constitute mere territorial regions) it would be advisable carefully to rearrange their boundaries, detaching a portion of a given state and exchanging it for a portion of an adjacent state. In this way the "sacredness" of the territorial boundaries of the states, together with their chauvinistic patriotism, would lose its prestige. Traveling, communication, and circulation of ideas among the disarmed states should be as free as possible.

As a positive measure, a universal bill of rights, inalienable and inviolable for every human being, should be promulgated and enforced as the basic principle of the constitution of every state, including the world state. These inalienable rights must embrace not only the "four freedoms" but all the necessary conditions for decent material, educational, and moral standards which the available resources permit. Such rights naturally presuppose corresponding duties and responsibilities.

The government of the states must consist of a combination of the elected representatives of the citizens of the electoral districts and of those of agriculture, industrial management and labor, religion, science, the fine arts, and the professions. A sufficient proportion of representatives of labor, management, agriculture, science, religion, and the professions, elected by their respective groups, independently of the territorial electoral districts, would weaken the vested interests of a given territorial district and immeasurably heighten the competence, impartiality, morality, and prestige of the government. The representatives (as well as the experts employed by the government) should be genuine social servants, competent and responsible managers of the functions entrusted to them rather than potentates, masters, or dictators. An extension of the city-manager plan to the state government might be desirable in many cases.

Since the function of the state government should be social service, its representatives should not enjoy any special privileges or particularly high salaries. Persons who are eager to serve others will be perfectly satisfied with such conditions. Conversely, greedy, selfish persons, looking to government positions as a means for realizing their rapacious ambitions and lust for power, will be discouraged by these conditions.

Since the state government must be a government of the people, by the people, and for the people, and since existing technical methods make it possible quickly to obtain the opinion of the citizens on any essential matter, it should not pass any important law or measure without a preliminary determination of the opinion of the citizens in the form of either the old-fashioned referendum or adequately organized polls. The legislative body would not be entitled to enact any legislation contrary to the majority vote of the citizens, no matter how large may be the majority vote of the legislature in favor of the measure. Thus direct democracy, or the town hall system of government, would be restored in lieu of indirect representation, with its many short-comings.

As to the sphere of government management and control, no rigid universal rule can be laid down. It would depend on the special conditions prevalent in the various states. As a general principle the state government should discharge only those functions which cannot be administered well by nonstate organizations (or are not so administered). In this sense its field should be residual, taking care of the needs not satisfied by any other agencies, or satisfied by them more poorly than they could be fulfilled by the state. (Cf. the next section of this chapter.)

The foregoing discussion gives an idea of the reorganization of the state necessary to terminate its role as the principal breeding ground of sanguinary strife, lust for power, and corrupt politics. Thus remodeled, it would become one of the most beneficent of human institutions, a true social servant instead of a callous master.

B. *Political Parties and Other Institutions.* The same principles apply, with corresponding modifications, to other political institutions — municipal and local governments and political parties. At present, political parties are predominantly militant machines animated by the lust for power and booty. As intermediaries between the voters and the state governments, they have usurped the role of agencies for ascertaining the opinions and wishes of the electorate. They have monopolized elections, depriving the citizens of the possibility of freely choosing whom they wish, since there is no possibility of voting for candidates not nominated by the parties. To a considerable extent they have converted the citizenry into a mere instrument for serving the selfish interests of the bosses or party caucus. Through various tricks and other dubious practices they have corrupted the basic principle of elective democracy, degrading the functions of statesmanship to the sordid quest of politicians for spoils, or booty. In these and many other ways they have robbed the citizens of much of their freedom and have become one of the chief foci for generating forces of strife and enmity. In countries with a single dictatorial party, such as Communist Russia or Nazi Germany, the insidious effects of the system are all too evident. To a lesser degree the same evil effects are apparent also in countries with a two-party or multi-party system. The foregoing and many other disastrous effects of contemporary political parties on democracy and the political, social, economic, and moral life of the citizens have been amply demonstrated not only by ideological anarchists, syndicalists, and other radical theorizers but by the most impartial, conservative investigators, such as M. Ostrogorsky, J. Bryce, G. Mosca, R. Michels, and C. E. Merriam.

It is evident that such political parties cannot serve the purposes of a peaceful and creative society. They need to be radically transformed along the lines recommended by the foregoing investigators. First, the changes suggested for the state organization, particularly the decentralization of the election of representatives from territorial districts, and their supplementation by representatives of industry, agriculture, science, religion, etc, would render the monopoly of elections by political parties impossible. The corporative bodies elect their representatives themselves, without undue influence being exerted by political parties. This decentralization would drastically limit the monopolistic power of political parties, would reduce their autocracy, and would restore to the citizens a portion of their electoral freedom. The suggested modesty of the remuneration and privileges of the members of the state government would discourage self-seeking persons with the lust for power and booty from engaging in the activities of political parties as a means to these ends. Furthermore, the technical facilities for obtaining a poll of public opinion on any problem or candidate render the existence of our rigid political parties, with their encyclopedic platforms, largely superfluous. Instead, on any question special leagues *ad hoc* could be organized for and against a given measure, paralleled by an intelligent discussion of the problem by the citizens and by experts. Such a change would eliminate the inevitable confusion in the minds of the voters arising from the long-winded platforms of the parties, with their hundreds of points which no citizen is competent to judge and intelligently vote upon, as well as from the irresponsible promises and generalities of the candidates during the campaign and from blind party devotion. Assisted by experts, the citizens could easily grasp the single problem under consideration by the league and could cast their votes intelligently.

Such leagues, being temporary organizations, would be essentially free from the permanent vested interests of the encyclopedic parties and their preoccupation with sinecures, booty, and the like.

Again, the increasing complexity of social questions makes party politicians more and more incompetent to handle these problems intelligently. Instead, the competence of experts is required, combined with an alert sense of responsibility. This factor operates in favor of the progressive elimination of contemporary political parties.

Finally, a heightened sense of duty and social service would tend to free political leagues and associations from the selfishness, corruption, and irresponsibility typical of present-day political parties.

These and similar measures would transform political parties from belligerent machines employing the spoils system, bribery, deceit, corruption, vituperation, and even murder and civil war, into genuine agencies of social service.

II. Economic and Occupational Institutions

A. *Economic Inequality.* Experimental studies of young children between the ages of three and four, six to nine, and nine to twelve years show that a conspicuous inequality in economic or other privileges generates strife and enmity among them at an age when they are as yet hardly imbued with the ideas of equality and inequality.[1] Still more true is this of adults. It

---

[1] See P. A. Sorokin, "Experimental Study of Efficiency of Work," *American Journal of Sociology* (1930); J. Piaget, *The Moral Judgment of the Child* (London, 1930), p. 312 ff.; and J. B. Maller, *Co-operation and Competition* (New York, 1929).

was stressed by thinkers and observers even in ancient times. Plato says that with a sharp division between the poor and the rich "a state is not one but two states, the one of poor men, the other of the rich; and they are . . . always conspiring against one another."[2]

The validity of this generalization is well corroborated by human history and by present-day observation. The antagonism between the poor and the rich is especially sharp when the contrast between riches and poverty is most marked; when the wealth is acquired not through meritorious efforts but through inheritance, luck, manipulation, various dubious devices; and when the rich ignore the existence of *noblesse oblige* and misuse their wealth and power for antisocial purposes.

In contemporary populations the economic chasm between the multimillionaires and the poverty-stricken strata is as wide as it has ever been in any country. The consequence is an ever-increasing class war between the rich and the poor strata. Strikes, lockouts, riots, revolts, and revolutions have made this century more turbulent than any of the twenty-four preceding centuries. As long as this gulf persists, especially under the conditions of a decadent sensate culture, enmity and strife between the haves and the have-nots are bound to continue.

This antagonism can be substantially mitigated by (1) securing to every person a decent economic standard of living; (2) limiting the amount of wealth possessed by any individual; (3) reducing the chasm between the standards of living of the rich and the poor; (4) making every rich person a trustee of the wealth entrusted to him rather than an arbitrary agent in its disposition, thus depriving parasitic, demoralized, irresponsible heirs and heiresses of the possibility of a scandalous misuse of their riches; (5) responsible, socially constructive, and morally exemplary conduct on the part of the rich as genuine leaders; (6) deflation of the value of pecuniary wealth in the total scale of human values by means of scientific, ethical, and religious demonstration that excessive riches do not make human life nobler or happier than a decent, moderate income sufficient to

2 Plato, *Republic,* viii.

meet all the real physical, mental, moral, and cultural needs of man.

These measures would not only mitigate the enmity between the paupers and the millionaires but would exert a multitude of other influences beneficial to the cultural life and creativity of humanity in general. Ethically, from the standpoint of the natural law, not to mention the Golden Rule and the Sermon on the Mount, such measures would be fully justified. Economically they would leave a sufficiently wide margin for the operation of economic incentives. Through equitable distribution, through economic security for all, through remuneration of the real creators of wealth and penalization of its parasitic and irresponsible squanderers, through social stability and harmony, these measures would stimulate the production of wealth infinitely more than they would inhibit it through a slight limitation of so-called "economic incentives." Socially and politically they would limit the autocratic, and therefore irresponsible and often selfish, misuse of the power of wealth for destructive and antisocial purposes. Likewise they would inhibit the degradation of the highest values to the level of marketable commodities worth so many dollars; the debasement of the arts and sciences, religion, and politics as mere merchandise bought and sold and obliged to adapt themselves to the whims and market demands of the rich. Finally, they would introduce peace and harmony into our interpersonal and intergroup relationships. Otherwise the rich are doomed to lose their wealth through revolutions and wars, confiscation and nationalization, which might deprive them also of their health and bodily security and even of their very lives. *Sapienti satis.*

B. *Competition and Co-operation, Pecuniary and Nonpecuniary Incentives.* The suggested changes imply that the role of selfish, unrestrained competition in economic activities must be rigorously curtailed, being replaced as far as possible by noncompetitive co-operation vs. the competitive co-operation of groups for their own interests irrespective of those of other groups. This is possible only if one is motivated not merely by egoistic considerations of economic advantage but also by enjoyment of one's work and a desire faithfully to perform one's moral and social duties.

It is scarcely possible for the rank and file of humanity to abolish selfish competition and pecuniary motivation entirely. But in an idealistic culture and society it is quite feasible to minimize their role and to promote noncompetitive co-operation and nonprofit motivation. Even in contemporary society the part played by economic competition and pecuniary motivation is unduly exaggerated, as has been shown in Chapter Nine. If we were to assume that all persons occupationally engaged are actuated only by competitive economic incentives, and that the enjoyment of their work, the creative urge, sympathy, and a sense of social duty do not play any part, we should be unable to explain a large proportion of past and present economic and occupational activities.

In the first place, the bulk of the activities of the members of the family, cheerfully helping one another in multitudes of ways without any pecuniary reward, would be a complete mystery. And these activities constitute the lion's share of human activities. The same is true of the economic and other activities of friends assisting one another without any material profit, and of all the purely philanthropic activities.

No less mysterious would be the activities of an overwhelming majority of major and minor creators: Christs and Buddhas, Mozarts and Beethovens, Platos and Kants, Hesiods and Dantes, Galileos and Newtons, Machiavellis and Vicos, and the host of lesser creators. Since many of these lived and died in poverty, and most of them enjoyed a very modest income and standard of living, they should be regarded, under the presupposition, either as utter failures, incapable of securing a good income through better remunerated work, or as fools or pathological types. The explanation lies in the fact that their creative activities have been motivated almost entirely by the creative urge, by the enjoyment of their work, and by their sense of duty to God and humanity. The medieval craftsman and the majority of teachers, preachers, doctors, poets, artists, and so on, have done their work not simply for its meager economic returns but primarily for the sake of nonpecuniary motives.

Still more true is this with respect to soldiers who voluntarily enlist in the army, fight, and, if need be, die, for their country or group with practically no pecuniary reward, and to the martyrs and all others who sacrifice themselves for nonpecuniary values.

Even captains of industry and finance are actuated by many nonpecuniary motives. If it were not for the enjoyment of their organizational and economically creative activities, their prestige, and their occasional sense of social service, many of them either would not have entered upon a business career or would soon abandon it. They would be even less disposed to bequeath a large part of their fortunes to various scientific, philanthropic, and social institutions.

This means that even for our society the role of competition and pecuniary incentives is highly exaggerated. This is still more true with respect to the ideational and idealistic societies and cultures of both primitive and historical peoples. There have been and are countless preliterate tribes, as well as religious, occupational, national, and other groups, in which these factors have played a very insignificant part. The overwhelming majority of their activities, including the economic ones, have been determined by nonpecuniary, nonegoistic motives. In an idealistic culture, pervaded by the spirit of altruism and affording a decent minimum of economic security for all, people are bound to discharge faithfully their occupational functions owing to the sheer enjoyment of their work, from a sense of duty and self-respect, and in the interest of improving the economic conditions of others, especially when an equitable distribution of wealth is achieved, when the highest possible standards are secured for all, when each person engages in the occupational activities most congenial to him, when unhygienic and monotonous working conditions are minimized, and when everyone is assured that in working for all he is working for himself and that all are working for him. Even the least attractive occupation in such a society, if socially necessary, may become an honor occupation, like that of a soldier on the battlefield. If need be, such occupations may be remunerated more highly than the more attractive ones. But even this may not be necessary: a society with an alert sense of duty and social service may develop an intense competition for even such occupational work among socially minded persons.

To sum up: The widely accepted opinion that competition and selfish pecuniary incentives are the only motives determining economic activities is largely a fiction of sensate society. When put to the test, it is found to be highly exaggerated even with respect to sensate man, to say nothing of idealistic and other more altruistic societies.

c. *Occupational Changes.* Parasitic and antisocial occupations must be eliminated. The distribution of persons among various occupations must conform as far as possible to their special aptitudes, tastes, abilities, and preferences. The principle of equality of opportunity in this respect should be fully realized. Each child should be given the maximum opportunity to discover and train his abilities through a general and then specialized school education and through a period of apprenticeship with craftsmen, masters, or specialists. Such equality of opportunity exists at present in only a rudimentary form.

The aptitudes and capacities of each individual are further tested by the occupation itself. Successful persons are promoted, the unsuccessful ones being demoted or else forced to seek another field of work. This acid test will continue to operate in the future, since the aptitude and intelligence tests prescribed by contemporary science are notably fallible. In case of a mistaken choice, one should shift to other occupations until he finds the one which is best adapted to his abilities and tastes. All socially necessary occupations should be regarded as true vocations, as merely different ways of serving the needs of humanity. The existing sharp gradation of occupations into "superior" and "inferior," "high-brow" and "low-brow," should gradually disappear. Likewise, the striking and often quite unjustifiable contrasts in the economic remuneration of various occupational pursuits should be mitigated or eliminated. More attractive and responsible pursuits offer their own reward in their very attractiveness and responsibility. Less attractive, more unpleasant occupations deserve at least as high a remuneration as the more enjoyable ones.

III. PRIVATELY MANAGED AND GOVERNMENTALLY MANAGED ECONOMY

If the foregoing changes are carried out, and if the real causes of privately and governmentally managed economy are properly understood, then the hotly debated problem of these two types of economy resolves itself into a purely technical question rather than one of principle, one of necessity rather than of choice or preference. The proponents of so-called "free enterprise," as well as of governmentally managed (communist, socialist, Fascist, Nazi, and other totalitarian) economies, represent their favorite economy in the most idealized terms and that of their opponents in an equally distorted form. Similarly fallacious is the manner in which they depict the history, and especially the causes of the emergence and domination, of each of these types of economy.

The basic facts in this field are as follows. First, *both types of economy are as old as human history itself, and each type has been about as common as the other.* Contrary to the prevalent opinion that the governmentally managed economy, in all its totalitarian and semi-totalitarian forms, is something new and exceptional, initiated by the Russian communist revolution, it has been, in fact, the prevalent system of many preliterate tribes. In ancient Egypt, even in normal times, governmental management and control of economic activities applied to the larger part of production, distribution, and consumption of economic goods, and in some periods, such as the Ptolemaic period, became almost completely totalitarian. A similar system existed in Sparta, Lipara, and several other ancient Greek states; in ancient Rome after 301 A.D.; in Byzantium throughout its entire history; in China during certain periods, including the beginning of our era and the eleventh century (with Wang-an-Shi as the totalitarian prime minister); in ancient Peru and Mexico; and in many other countries and periods. Hence the governmentally managed type of economy cannot be regarded as something new, exceptional, or wholly abnormal. Similar generalizations apply to the form of economy managed by private individuals and groups. In its long history mankind has employed both types.

Second, *neither of these types possesses as many or as great virtues as are ascribed to it by its overenthusiastic proponents, nor as numerous or egregious vices as are claimed by its opponents.* The very fact that each of these economies has existed for centuries in several major historical cultures is sufficient evidence that neither is as bad as its opponents contend. No wholly bad and unworkable economy can survive for even a few decades.

Third, *the identification of each type with either equality or freedom is utterly unwarranted.* For instance, it is commonly assumed that a governmentally managed economy is one of equality, devoid of contrast between riches and poverty, or exhibiting less marked economic inequality than privately managed systems. As a matter of fact, the actual situation has been very different. There was no equality in the earlier totalitarian régimes between the slaves, serfs, and lower classes, with their submarginal standard of living, on the one hand, and the aristocratic classes, with their luxurious manner of living, on the other. The same is true of the recent or contemporary communist and Nazi totalitarian systems. If in some cases there has been less inequality in the totalitarian economies than in the privately managed ones, this has been by no means the rule, and vice versa.

Similarly, the belief that a privately managed economy invariably yields a greater amount of freedom than a governmentally managed economy is another myth contradicted by the facts of history and current reality. Yes, to the beneficiaries of privately controlled slavery and serfdom it affords a measure of freedom; but not to the masses of slaves and serfs. To the captains of industry and finance such a system has indeed afforded a great deal of freedom; but not to the colonial semi-slaves, to the unemployed, or even to the wage earning proletariat, especially during periods of fully developed *free enterprise,* before the state began to curb the economic absolutism of capitalists, employers, and owners, and before the proletariat created labor unions and political parties for the protection of its minimum freedom and rights.

Conversely, in some of the totalitarian economies the rank and file of the people have felt about as free as they feel in the most democratic and capitalistic of present-day economies, the only difference being that the conception of freedom in the two cases has been somewhat different.

Much the same may be said of the other virtues and vices ascribed to each type of economy by its respective proponents and opponents. Like the forms of government, each type may exhibit good and bad forms, which will depend upon how each type is organized, and under what conditions, for whose benefit, and by what kind of personnel it is operated.

The fourth, and most important, point is that the emergence and domination of each type are not a matter of wishful thinking but the inexorable consequences of definite causes. This point seems to be largely overlooked by almost all those who discuss the problem. The main causal formula here runs as follows: *When a given organized group faces a grave emergency menacing its existence or its basic values, the governmental control over it tends to become more rigid and severe and tends to expand to embrace many social relationships of its members hitherto free from such control. As the emergency passes and conditions become more nearly normal, the governmental controls tend to relax.* Great emergencies comprise wars, revolutions and other severe internal disturbances, famines and grave economic depressions, plagues and other epidemics, earthquakes, volcanic eruptions, floods, droughts, and so on, in general, all the conditions that menace the existence and the basic values of the groups. Therefore, *when a given group passes from a state of peace to that of war, from prosperity to impoverishment (with unemployment and other "satellites" of economic depression); when it tends to be disrupted by revolution, riots, dissensions, and anarchy; when earthquakes, floods, droughts, epidemics, or similar calamities assail it; or when it is menaced by other groups, in all such cases the governmental control over the group tends to increase in its extent and severity. And vice versa.*

This uniformity is well corroborated, first of all, by the fluctuation of governmental control in the state groups. Under conditions of grave emergency, from ancient times up to the present, governmental control in all state groups has invariably expanded, sometimes resulting in communistic, absolutist, or other varieties of the totalitarian state. The greater the emergency, the greater has been the increase of governmental control. *And vice versa.* Conspicuous examples of the operation of this rule have been afforded in the twentieth century by the First and the Second World Wars and by the depression of 1929 and the subsequent years. In all Western countries, including the United States and other democratic countries, governmental control and regimentation markedly expanded and became more exacting and severe during the two world wars and the great depression. In Russia, where the war factor was reinforced by revolution, famine, epidemics, and other calamities, governmental control began rapidly to expand during the First World War under the Czarist régime, continued to increase under the Kerensky régime, and reached its maximum possible limit under the Communist régime. The Communist régime itself, during the first years of its existence, with its unlimited regimentation, was essentially but a manifestation of the tendency toward unlimited governmental regimentation elicited by a multitude of grave emergencies, such as war, revolution, famine, and epidemics. When, after the First World War and the termination, in 1921, of the civil war, conditions began to improve, the control exercised by the Communist government began to relax, especially during the years between 1932 and 1939, prior to the outbreak of the Second World War. Owing to the First World War and its "satellites," in almost all Western countries there was a sharp increase of governmental regimentation after 1914. In many Western countries it manifested itself in a replacement of the liberal, democratic state, with its limited governmental control, by various totalitarian régimes and dictatorships; in others, by a marked increase of governmental regimentation, carried on under the name of the "New Deal" in the United States and under different names in other countries. During the Second World War the increase became especially rapid and spectacular. What has been said of war applies equally to other emergencies.[3]

When this uniformity is understood, most of the changes of the political and socioeconomic régimes in the same state and most of the differences between the political and economic régimes of different states become readily comprehensible. If, for instance, the United States, prior to the Second World War, had a political régime with a very modest governmental control of the life and relationships of its citizens, and with a minimum of autocracy and militarism, the main reason was that, being protected by two oceans, the country was relatively free from the danger of wars and invasions; that it was very rich in resources and very prosperous; and that it had suffered few major calamities. As a result it was democratic, liberal, and nontotalitarian in its political and socio-economic networks. With an increase of danger due to the less highly protective role of the oceans and to other conditions, governmental regimentation and autocracy began to increase.

On the other hand, Russia, occupying an open Euro-Asiatic plain incessantly invaded by Europeans as well as Asiatics throughout its whole history, had been exposed to the constant threat of war, had had to wage many wars, and hence could not fail to develop an autocratic and quasitotalitarian government, with much more rigid controls than those exercised by the United States. Russia could survive only by becoming more centralized, more militarized, and governmentally more autocratic than the United States.

When other emergencies, such as the famine, epidemics, and internal dissensions that have frequently befallen Russia, were added to the constant threat or reality of war, the relatively auto-

---

[3] For a factual corroboration of this law in the history of Egypt, Babylonia, Persia, Greece, the Hellenistic states, Rome, Byzantium, medieval and modern European states, ancient Peru, Mexico, and other states, see *Dynamics,* III, 192 ff., and *Calamity,* chap. 7. These works also contain copious bibliographical citations.

cratic political régime, beginning with the Tatar invasions of the thirteenth century and extending up to the present time, is easily comprehensible.

When applied to the economic régime, the law under discussion explains why certain countries have had a state-socialist, communistic, or totalitarian economic régime, largely managed and controlled by the government, with a meager development of "free enterprise," whereas other countries have possessed capitalistic and "free enterprise" economic systems directed predominantly by private individuals and organizations.

The law explains also why the economic régime of the same country fluctuates between the pole of free enterprise, with its *laissez faire, laissez passer,* and that of an economy managed and controlled principally by the government. Even the most capitalistic country, with virtually no governmental domination of economic relationships, tends to develop a communistic, state-socialist, or totalitarian system if for a decade or so it is subjected to such calamities as wars and famines. Conversely, the most communistic or totalitarian nation, with an economy entirely managed by the government, becomes progressively less totalitarian, with decreasing governmental control of economic relationships, when it enjoys for a few decades internal and international peace, prosperity, and freedom from grave calamities. Such fluctuations depend little upon the actions of this or that individual, be he a king, dictator, or president. Only the *details* of these sociocultural processes are determined by the wisdom, ability, and experience of the rulers.[4]

What has been said of the fluctuation of governmental control in the state groups may be said, with an appropriate modification, of the expansion and contraction, the hardening and softening, of governmental control in other organized groups. When a given local community is visited by a devastating flood or fire,

---

[4] This law of fluctuation of governmental control is evidently unknown to such scholars as F. A. Hayek, and to most chambers of commerce, and Senators and other public officials, who preach the virtues of capitalism and the vice of regimentation. No wonder they cannot forecast the increase or decrease of regimentation and are impotent to change its course!

a calamitous earthquake, or the like, the normal laws are replaced by martial law or a state of siege, with a sudden corresponding increase in the severity of the laws and their enforcement and with an expansion of governmental control of the community.

When a religious organization is menaced by heresies, dissensions, and internal conflicts, as in the case of the Christian Church in the thirteenth century and the period of the Reformation, the control exercised by the Church government tends to expand and to become much more rigid. The phenomenon is illustrated in the case of the Catholic Church by such measures as the Inquisition; the founding of the Society of Jesus; and the Counter Reformation, with its various reforms aimed at the cleansing of the Church and the centralizing of its control over the entire Catholic world.

Again, when a family or a business firm enters a period of adversity, it must tighten its controls or else disintegrate.

To sum up: The fluctuations under discussion are ever-repeated and universal processes. In large and well-organized groups like the state they manifest themselves unequivocally; in smaller groups, in a less definite form.

From this law may be deduced several practical suggestions.

If we do not desire a totalitarian type of economic or political régime, we must strive to make the world free from grave emergencies, especially from wars, revolutions, famines, and major depressions. In a society free from serious emergencies there is no need for any undue expansion of state control and regimentation, and this does not take place. The more successfully emergencies are prevented or combated by private groups and persons, the less occasion does the state have to intervene. Conversely, if capitalists and the other partisans of free enterprise cannot or do not successfully cope with emergencies, (if, for instance, they cannot prevent chronic depressions, with their army of unemployed, or competition for foreign markets and colonies, leading to war) — under such conditions the intervention of the state government and an expansion of its regimentation and control of economic and other affairs are inevitable.

If certain important needs of a society cannot be met by free enterprise, because their satisfaction is unprofitable for private interests, because the capital needed exceeds the resources of private persons or groups, or because the state or some other important group can perform these functions better than the free enterprise economy, then the state or some co-operative or other public organization should meet the needs in question. For instance, cathedrals and churches, schools and universities, research institutions, hospitals, large-scale means of communication, highways and other transportation systems, certain natural resources (including lands and forests), not to mention monetary systems, cannot be adequately managed by private persons or financed through private resources. Control of such economic institutions by the state or by some other public organization is accordingly both necessary and advisable.

When economic functions can be faithfully and competently discharged by both private persons or groups and the state government, both systems can harmoniously coexist, each specializing in the particular fields in which, under the given conditions, it meets the economic needs of society more successfully. But when the proponents of each system of economy are impelled mainly by their selfish interests and hence fail to meet successfully the requirements of society, each group attempts to achieve a monopoly, becomes intolerant in its claims and counterclaims, and resorts to coercion and even civil war, to the grave detriment of society as a whole. Such are the main lines of reconstruction of economic and occupational institutions dictated by the goal of peace and a creative social order.

IV. The Press, Radio, and Motion Pictures

Finally should be mentioned the press, radio, and motion pictures, as important instruments of indoctrination and education. Unfortunately, in their present form they release destructive as well as constructive forces. They not only ennoble but enervate and demoralize. They engender strife as much as they serve the cause of peace and creativity.

Like other phenomena in our decadent sensate culture they

are obsessed by negativistic and pathological exhibitionism. While a good deed is rarely mentioned on the front pages of a newspaper and is not regarded as news, sex scandals, murders, and other sensations and crimes fill page after page with text and pictures. Much the same is true of the cinema and radio. Whereas really important inventions and discoveries, theories, and events are hardly reflected in the press, on the screen, or in radio programs, these devote themselves to all kinds of vulgar "hits," short-lived sensations, and glittering vacuities. Concentration on sex, glamor, and eroticism (both coarse and refined) and on vulgar or fatuous stunts; such is the principal "educational" pabulum proffered!

Even in their ostensibly informative functions, represented by their news dispatches and editorials, their columnists and commentators, they often fail lamentably. A reporter wholly ignorant of a foreign country is regarded as competent to write about its problems after a three-day or one-week visit. A columnist or editorial writer, commentator, or movie potentate is considered a competent judge of anything he chooses to discuss or to stage. When we add the bias due to the vested interests of all such "free enterprises," the amount of misinformation and misinterpretation they purvey may be readily appreciated. As a result of these and similar traits it is uncertain whether they serve more the cause of peace and real education than that of enmity and miseducation.

In any case, in order to become a genuine constructive force they must be reformed. They must cease to propagate pathology, negativism, sensationalism, vulgarity, demoralization, misinformation, and miseducation. This concerns especially the yellow press, radio, and cinema. Dedicated to the service of truth, goodness, and beauty, all these agencies can become powerful constructive forces of peace and cultural uplift.

V. GENERAL CONCLUSION

The preceding sketch of the transmutation of social and cultural institutions gives a sufficient idea of the kind of transformation required. Surrounding every person from the cradle to the grave, these institutions incessantly mold his mind, character, and conduct. Properly transformed, they can release forces of altruism, good will, and creative energy hitherto little exploited.

If no single cultural or social factor can perform this task unaided, in their totality they can accomplish it successfully. The transmutation suggested is neither impossible nor exceedingly difficult. If it entails certain sensate losses for certain persons and groups, these losses would be merely temporary and more apparent than real. From a broader standpoint and in the long run, everyone would immeasurably enrich his values and ennoble his life, and humanity would thus be saved from catastrophe and suicide.

PART FIVE

PERSONAL FACTORS OF CREATIVE ALTRUISM

CHAPTER TWELVE

OUR INCOMPETENCE IN EFFECTING THE TRANSFORMATION OF MAN

I. THE ROLE OF PERSONAL EFFORT IN CREATIVE ALTRUISM

If it is difficult, indeed, virtually impossible, for a person or group to be altruistic in a thoroughly selfish environment, one does not become altruistic automatically even in an environment permeated by kindness and generosity. Though such a culture facilitates the development of these qualities, incessant personal effort is needed in order that they may take firm root in one's mind and actions.

The same is true of the development of creativity. Even in a stimulating sociocultural milieu a creator must incessantly strive in order that his potentialities may be realized. Achievement does not come automatically or ready-made. This applies alike to poets, artists, musicians, philosophers, prophets, scientists, and inventors. Edison rightly observed that "Genius is one per cent inspiration and ninety-nine per cent perspiration." Moreover, in the development of their genius eminent creators do not slacken their efforts but rather increase them, because whoever fails to progress suffers retrogression.

The same is true of altruism. It is a special kind of creativeness in the field of goodness, entailing principally ethical values in distinction from the cognitive values of truth, realized primarily by science, philosophy, and religion, and the values of beauty, realized predominantly by the fine arts. Famous altruists, such as Saint Francis of Assisi, are as truly creative giants in the field of goodness as are the foremost scientists, philosophers, founders of religions, and artists in their own particular fields. Since creativity in any form requires active effort, altruism requires it also. It demands it perhaps even more than the other forms; for genuine altruism has to be practiced incessantly.

Whereas achievement in other fields proceeds by spurts, with periods of relaxation in between, a true altruist needs to be continuously on the alert in order to remain faithful to his mission. The same is not true of other types of creators. Once a symphony or scientific discovery is achieved, it remains, even though its author entirely abandons his creative activities.

This need of effort, with its pains and frustrations, does not mean that altruistic or other creative activities are boring, joyless, or depressing. Quite the contrary. The most effortful creative moments are those of the purest, richest, and most intense happiness. No real creator would exchange them for any effortless and painless experience. Beethoven ecstatically describes this in the choral movement of his *Ninth Symphony*. Few, if any, persons could match the inexhaustible cheerfulness of Saint Francis, that singing "jester of God," who was happy under conditions of utmost hardship, poverty, hunger, and humiliation. The same is true of the ineffable joy of the true ascetics, mystics, and altruists in the moments of their union with the absolute or of the full performance of their duty. In spite of its incessant effort, fatigue, trials, frustrations, and even moments of black despair, the highest altruistic creativity, like any other, is a source of supreme gladness.

II. Inadequacy of Our Knowledge of Altruism and Its Techniques

Efforts to be altruistic or creative are adequate when they lead to the realization of the goal envisaged, and inadequate when they fall short of this purpose. Knowledge how to become truly altruistic or creative may be derived through science, philosophy, or religion, that is, through sensory experience, logical reasoning, or superconscious intuition, respectively, through trial and error, or through all these channels.

The question arises: How much do we know of the methods and techniques necessary to render ourselves and others less selfish and more altruistic, less heedless and more creative, less pathological and more healthy mentally and morally, less frustrated and more happy? At the present time this is the paramount problem of humanity. If the existing body of knowledge in this field were sufficient, humanity could make itself altruistic, creative, and happy. Such a transformation would eliminate wars, criminality, and all sociocultural and individual ills. Humanity would be able to recover the lost Garden of Eden. Otherwise these evils are bound to continue, culminating perhaps in the destruction of our civilization.

When we take account of the existing theoretical and practical knowledge and techniques for rendering individuals and groups altruistic, creative, happy, and sound in mind, we find that our knowledge in these fields is insignificant and our techniques are wholly inadequate. This conclusion may appear unduly pessimistic to many, especially to those devotees of science who equate it with an omniscient and omnipotent God. It may sound alarming to those who make their living by selling pseudoscientific concoctions, even poisons, to the gullible public as scientific panaceas. The evidence supporting the conclusion is, briefly, as follows.

If the necessary knowledge and techniques had been available, mankind would have been able to avoid wars, civil strife, and other sanguinary conflicts. Humanity does not desire such catastrophes, but does not know how to prevent them. Humanity prefers peace to a third world war; yet there is no assurance that it will not occur. Within two years after the armistice, the relations between the former allied nations had already markedly deteriorated. Evidently, we do not know the efficient means to prevent such a deterioration.

Judging by the increase of criminality and juvenile delinquency, we seem to be quite able to transform noncriminals into criminals and delinquents. The reverse transformation, however, is rarely achieved. In spite of all our boasted "scientific" measures, reformatories, juvenile courts, experts, and other means of preventing or curing criminality, some 90 per cent of the first juvenile offenders become hopeless "repeaters."

The same ignorance applies to the ways and means of increasing happiness. Suicide indicates a deliberate preference of death to life. Persons who commit it are presumably unhappy. Suicide in the West has shown an upward trend during the past century or two. Its increase is a barometer of growing unhappiness.

A similar generalization may be made with respect to mental health. When medical science discovered the nature and cause of certain infectious diseases, these diseases declined among populations that followed the scientific prescriptions. The same success has not attended the treatment of various mental disorders, in spite of the enormous multiplication of psychoanalysts, psychiatrists, mental hygienists, clinics, and other institutions devoted to psychotherapy. In fact, mental disorders have exhibited a sharp upward curve.

Virtually every family and school desires that its children shall be sound in mind and well integrated in conduct and shall become good citizens. Yet multitudes of these children go astray, turning into human derelicts, even in families and schools that command the services of the best educators, specialists, and experts.

The same inadequacy is demonstrated by the impotence of a host of otherwise commendable movements for the alleviation of various social evils. The ineffectiveness of these movements is attributable to the fact that they do not know efficient techniques for combating these evils and must rely principally upon propaganda and other speech-reactional techniques. During the past decade the United States has been flooded by propaganda against anti-Semitism and racial conflicts. Yet these tensions have not perceptibly abated. All these facts clearly show our ignorance in the fields discussed.

III. REASONS FOR THE PERSISTENCE OF OUR IGNORANCE

Among the many reasons for the failure of Western science in these fields the following deserve special note. First, *the greater complexity of mental phenomena as compared with biological and inorganic ones.* Our knowledge and techniques dealing with the physico-chemical world are far superior to those concerned with organic phenomena; and these, in turn, are more adequate than our knowledge and control of mental phenomena. The greatest puzzle for the human mind is the mind itself, especially as it functions on the highest plane. Its activities remain the most mysterious and the least controllable of all phenomena.[1] This is the chief reason why our knowledge and control of altruism and creativity have been so meager.

The second reason is *the concentration of Western sensate science during the past four centuries on the study of physical and vital phenomena, to the neglect of "mind stuff," especially in its highest manifestations.* Only a small fraction of Western thought has been devoted to mental, moral, and superorganic phenomena. Even at the present time the United States Congress and various foundations and individuals are devoting billions to the investigation of the physico-chemical world and to a less extent the biological world, but are unwilling to grant anything substantial for an investigation of man as a thinking or superorganic entity. Hence contemporary Western science knows little more about mind, personality, or the means for promoting altruism, creativity, and happiness than has been discovered through the past experience of the West or the East. We have made notable progress in increasing our knowledge of the anatomy and physiology of man's nervous system, but we have made scarcely any contribution to the understanding of mental phenomena and the techniques of their control.

The third reason for our ignorance in this field is to be found *in the sensate conception of man as a mere physical or vital phenomenon.* Man has been conceived and studied almost exclusively as a material mechanism, as a biological organism, as a concatenation of atoms and molecules, as an electromagnetic field of forces, or as a complex of sense data, of reflexes and instincts, of biological drives and propensities. The very existence of mind, consciousness, conscience, and will, to say nothing of the superconscious has been either flatly denied or, at best, granted mere lip service.

This attitude is still prevalent. Contemporary science still regards man as a mere physical mechanism, or as an organism conditioned by the "id," by "subconscious" or "unconscious" drives, reflexes, and instincts, screened by a mirage of what is

[1] Cf. H. Bergson, *The Creative Mind* (New York, 1946), p. 42 ff.

called "consciousness," "mind," "thought," "purpose," "ego," or "superego," factors which possess scarcely any objective existence and which play an insignificant role in conditioning men's conduct and relationships. Almost all the dominant currents in contemporary psychology, psychiatry, pedagogy, and other social and humanistic disciplines are but variations of this conception.

Quite consistently, the scientific disciplines of our sensate era have applied, for man's education and control, methods and techniques of the same mechanistic or materialistic nature, aimed to influence first and foremost one's reflexes, drives, instincts, "id," "subconscious," or "unconscious," hardly ever one's "conscious" mind, and never the superconscious.

J. B. Rhine appropriately stresses this point. "Our philosophy of government depends entirely upon our view of the nature of the governed. What is man? What is the human nature that must be dealt with by the functions of governing? Broadly speaking, there are two opposing conceptions of man. Simply stated, these two views of man represent him as either a *person* or a *thing*. The 'person' view . . . is concerned mainly with his *mind*. The other view lumps men off as the masses or classes, as manpower (like horsepower), in other words, as things. . . . One view takes for the center of man's control his experiencing *mind;* the other, his objective, physical *brain*. One is the psychocentric, mind-centered view of man; the other is the cerebrocentric, brain-centered standpoint. The psychocentric view takes the mental life of an individual as the really central part of him. It is this mind of man that we educate, build our institutions around, and this is what we govern. The cerebrocentric view sees the physical brain as the intricate control center of the individual's world and as the real basis of personality. Whatever psychical activity may be, whether a fiction, an epiphenomenon, or a reality of uncertain degree, it is not, in this view, the dominant force in a man."[2]

From this conception there follow two entirely different techniques of control, education, and transformation. One tends to

[2] J. B. Rhine, "Parapsychology and the Government of Men," *Journal of Parapsychology* (1944), pp. 247-249.

center on the mind, especially on its highest functions. The other aims to influence the body, especially the nervous system, and through these changes to modify the human machine in a desirable direction. The methods and techniques of "psycho-centric" control are subtle, only in part material, directed to a release of the conscious and superconscious forces of the mind. Those of "cerebrocentric" control are predominantly mechanical or material, designed to patch up the defects in human anatomy, operating through the "id," "subsconscious," or "unconscious," ignoring all "superconscious" factors, and paying scant attention even to the "conscious."

As has been said, Western science during the past few centuries has adhered principally, sometimes exclusively, to the animalistic conception of man and has employed largely the techniques consistent with this theory.

It is this conception and this technique that are predominantly applied by *psychology, psychiatry, and psychoanalysis for the treatment of mental disorders.* The psychoanalytic view of man is simple: he is an animal; his personality consists essentially of the unconscious "id," which represents oral, anal, and genital sex instincts, and a death instinct (Freud), the lust for domination (Adler), or a combination of these and other animal drives. From infancy we are supposed to be imbued with various sex drives, and especially with the lust to seduce our father or mother, (the Oedipus complex) and to inflict sadistic destruction upon ourselves and others! The "conscious" ego is something which strives to co-ordinate and adjust these all-powerful animal drives, but which is fickle and weak, a mere epiphenomenal by-product of the "subconscious." Then there is a "superego," which embodies society's conventions and norms. The chief function of the "superego" is to suppress, repress, and sublimate the powerful drives of the unconscious "id." When it represses, the result is mental disorder, sadism, masochism, psychoneurosis, suicide, destruction.

Of the same pattern is the psychoanalytic (Freudian) interpretation of the origin and functions of society and culture. The patriarch of a certain horde, suspicious of his mature sons' sex intentions toward their mother, expels them. Their unsatisfied lust binds them together into a homosexual "band of brothers." They eventually return, and slay and eat the patriarch. Overcome with remorse (though how such remorse could arise remains a mystery!), they renounce their incestuous spoil and form a community bound together by a common guilt, remorse, fear, superstition, and taboo of the dead ancestors. Such is this "ingenious" theory of the origin of society and social values!

In line with this theory of personality and society, the therapeutic technique of psychoanalysis for handling mental disorders consists essentially in liberating one from the repressions of the cruel "superego" by bringing to light and releasing the repressed libido and death impulses, and then in curing the malady either through the untrammeled satisfaction of these impulses, freed from the inhibitions of the "superego," or through "transference" and "sublimation" of their energies in the service of some high purpose. It is clear that this conception and this technique concentrate on man as a perverted animal; on his subconscious as the basic driving force; on an "adjustment" of his "ego" and "superego" to the "id," rather than on an adjustment of the "id" to the norms of a rational "ego" and a sociocultural "superego." Instead of lifting man and society to the higher levels of the conscious and superconscious, instead of sanctifying parenthood and childhood, Freudianism degrades them to the level of perverted animalism. If a person, by divesting himself of the repressions of the superego, finds "peace of mind," he is considered to be cured, especially if he succeeds in "sublimating" the energy of his libido and death drives in the interest of some higher purpose which attractively camouflages these drives through ideological rationalizations.

In spite of this incidental factor of "sublimation," the theory and practice in question are scientifically fantastic, with the exception of the technique of revealing and releasing hidden associations and impulses, a technique derived, as we shall see, from age-old religious and other practices. Morally they are degrading; socially, they are highly disastrous. Therapeutically they sometimes achieve trifling successes (through a technique borrowed from ancient practices), but for the most part prove ineffective and frequently, in the hands of ignorant practitioners, decidedly harmful. Freudianism, indeed, is one of the most insidious products of our decadent sensate culture. A certain disillusioned Freudian rightly declared that "the Freudian theory is itself a disease." [3] Its spread is a revealing symptom of the mental aberration of the society which it infects: in an insane asylum insane theories are bound to be more successful than sound ones.

Is it any wonder, then, that in spite of the successful diffusion of such theories and techniques, in spite of the vast increase of psychoanalysts, and of psychoanalytical institutions, research, and literature, mental disorders have not abated and the bulk of patients have not experienced any notable recovery from their mental ailments? The principal success of psychoanalytic therapy has been achieved in the case of patients who have suffered largely from imaginary ailments, have undergone treatment, and have been temporarily cured of slight mental disturbances. Even these trifling successes have been confined chiefly to wise psycho-analysts who—in their practice—did not follow theories of Freud.

Psychosomatic psychiatry is freer from the fantastic theories of Freud and his followers, but in its own way it regards man primarily as an organism or nervous system. Thus it attempts to cure his mental ailments through physical techniques applied to the body. Surgical operations on the nervous system or some other part of the body, electric shocks, the administering of certain drugs, and attention to food, exercise, and overt activities —these are the principal methods and techniques employed by

---

[3] J. D. Suttie, *The Origin of Love and Hatred* (London, 1935), chap. 13. See also, for the harmful effects of psychoanalytical treatment (when it follows the Freudian theory), P. Lecky, *Self-consistency* (New York, 1945), p. 98 ff. The critical literature on Freudianism is enormous, and in this work there is no need to cite it. It is enough to say that scientifically the Freudian theory of personality is phantasmagoric; his conception of the "id" and "subconscious" entirely one-sided; his theory of the "ego" and "superego" vague, undeveloped, and fantastic; and his conjectures on the origin of society and culture and the nature of civilization supremely ignorant. Indeed, from a scientific standpoint it is pathological, the product of a brilliant but distorted mind. Its successful diffusion would have been impossible save in a decadent sensate culture like that of the twentieth century. Cf. *Society*, chap. 19.

psychosomatic psychiatry. When the trouble is really due to the defects of the body, particularly of the nervous system, these measures now and then prove helpful, provided the "repairs" are skillfully performed. They take account, however, of only a fraction of the mental disorders, leaving a large proportion of serious psychoneuroses uncured. Hence the progressive increase in the number of permanent inmates of mental hospitals.

The same theories and techniques dominate *our treatment of alcoholics, juvenile delinquents, criminals, and other derelicts.* They are "cured" for the most part through extermination, through imprisonment or confinement in the appropriate institutions, or through the application of therapies directed chiefly toward physical changes, only slightly toward the transmutation of their conscious mind, and almost never toward their superconscious. No wonder that these techniques fall short of their purpose! More successful are such exceptions to the rule as the techniques practiced in such groups, as "We Are Not Alone" and "Alcoholics Anonymous"; for these employ some of the "psychocentric" techniques of mutual help and self-help.

Similar are the presuppositions of *the contemporary "art of governing men" and of social control in general.* Cavour once said that even morons can govern with a generous use of cannon, prisons, gallows, martial law, and unrestrained coercion. If we add to these overt forms of compulsion a host of less explicit techniques of material pressure, — those of bribery, sinecures, wining and dining, economic deprivations, intimidation and terror—the overt and concealed forms of coercion applied to the lowest impulses of man indeed constitute the basic foundations of the contemporary "art of governing" and of the ultimate authority of most governments. In dictatorial régimes the coercive nature of their "art of governing" is obvious; in others it is milder and somewhat camouflaged, but no less fundamental than in tyrannical régimes. The politicians of our time (who have replaced real statesmen) are an incarnation of this technique.

Again we must not be surprised at its failure. Governments and their sensate "expert advisers" have been unable to ensure even the elements of peace, order, and harmony in domestic or international relations. Notwithstanding the use of coercion in its crudest and bloodiest forms, they have been unable to prevent devastating wars, sanguinary revolutions, or other grave conflicts, to say nothing of their gross failure to procure for the mass of the citizens the necessary minimum of food, shelter, clothing, security, and peace of mind. And there are no signs that they can do so in the near future.

Even the plans of the United Nations, the world government, and other popular schemes for ensuring peace are based upon the same premise: physical force and coercion sufficient to crush all opposition. Even certain eminent scientists have carried this obsession so far as to assure us of the peacemaking effects of atomic bombs and similar lethal weapons. In their opinion the very destructiveness of these instruments affords the best guarantee of peace. Ignorant of the testimony of history that the invention of more efficient weapons has invariably served to produce more terrible wars, they voice the prevailing belief in physical force as the only effective means of controlling human relations.

The same obsession lies at the root of our theories of the education and modification of human beings and the reorganization of our social institutions. Their predominant techniques are likewise addressed mainly to the "unconscious," partly to the conscious, and hardly ever to the superconscious, and are essentially material, mechanical, and sensory. Sensation and perception, conditioned reflexes, pain and pleasure, are considered the principal sources of learning; sensory experience is viewed as virtually the only source of cognition. Reason, with its formal syllogistic and mathematical logic, is admitted, but is interpreted as a mere by-product of reflexes and instincts, of sensation and perception. It is regarded with suspicion, and its speculative propensity is constantly checked by the data of sensory experience. The superconscious is emphatically denied as a gross superstition.

The techniques of moral and social education are chiefly physical coercion, reward and punishment, unconscious suggestion and imitation (mimesis), conditioned response or habit (established through mechanical repetition), and persuasion, addressed mainly to the emotional and hedonistic propensities and partly to the calculating faculty of man. In other classifications these techniques are listed as follows: discipline (coercion), ordeal and vigil, ceremony, the story, play, exhortation, counseling and mental hygiene, propaganda, discussion, practice and participation.[4] In still other classifications[5] we find the techniques of reward, praise, flattery, persuasion, advertising, slogans, badges and symbols, propaganda, gossip, laughter, satire, invective, commands, threats, and punishment.

All these methods of education and control rely on coercion rather than on spontaneity; on egoistic self-interest rather than on disinterested social service; on a mechanically achieved balance of powers rather than on harmonious freedom. They rarely, if ever, seek to invoke or stimulate the energies of the superconscious. When they use those of the conscious, they play upon the motives of selfish calculation, the cult of "victory" and "success," egoistic ambition, and the like.

In indoctrination and propaganda, in advertising and publicity, these techniques attempt to achieve their effect by hypnotizing the public through the sheer impact of volume and repetition, the endless reiteration of the same slogan or other speech-reaction pattern. They almost invariably appeal to the lower nature, the basest and most primitive sensations, emotions and feelings.

Thus, whatever field of education we take we find that the Western sensate science of the last few centuries has viewed man primarily as a physical entity or biological organism governed predominantly by physical forces, biological drives, and the "subconscious," with only a slight participation of the conscious ego and with a complete exclusion of the superconscious. In accordance with this conception, the techniques of education and of mental and moral transformation have naturally been predominantly physical and mechanical, operating through the "uncon-

---

[4] H. Hartshorne, *Character in Human Relations* (New York, 1932).
[5] F. E. Lumley, *Means of Social Control* (New York, 1925).

scious" and only to a slight extent through the conscious phase of man's total personality. The full utilization of the conscious forces has been largely neglected. The release and exploitation of the profound, potent, and creative "fission forces" of the superconscious have been utterly ignored. In this neglect of the forces of the conscious and particularly of the superconscious lies one of the basic reasons of our ignorance and helplessness in these fields. Hence the striking incompetence of Western science in performing the task of rendering man's conduct altruistic, of teaching him self-control, of curing his mental and moral disorders, of making him competent and happy.

CHAPTER THIRTEEN

THREE REMEDIES

Since, besides the complexity of mental phenomena, the main reasons for our helplessness in rendering man creatively altruistic are the neglect of these phenomena by science during the past four centuries, the wrong conception of man and the sociocultural universe entertained by this science, and the disregard of the existing body of Oriental and Occidental experience in the field of the superconscious, the first remedial steps evidently consist in the correction of these grave defects.

I. INCREASING STUDY OF THE "ENERGIES OF MAN"

An incomparably greater proportion of scientific research and cognitive effort must be devoted from now on to the study of the superorganic "energies of man," as William James[1] called them, in all their personal, cultural, and social manifestations. If during the next fifty years no important discovery should be made in the field of natural science, this would not seriously matter. But if our knowledge and control of man's highest energies are not markedly expanded, this will mean a real catastrophe. For the sake of man's very survival, the governments, foundations, universities, private endowers of research funds, and science itself must shift the bulk of their resources and activities to this field. A series of research institutions should be established. The most productive minds should be dedicated to this purpose. With such a concentration of resources and cognitive activities a rapid multiplication of our knowledge and control of the phenomena in question would result.

Next comes the replacement of the prevalent conception of man's nature and of the structure of his personality by a more

---

[1] William James, "The Energies of Men," *Essays on Faith and Morals* (New York, 1943), pp. 216-237.

adequate conception, warranted by the existing body of evidence. In a tentative black-and-white sketch the essentials of this conception are as follows.

II. Structure of Personality

Four different forms or levels of energies and activities can be distinguished in our total personality and behavior. First are to be noted *the unconscious, purely biological energies, functions, and actions*. Breathing, the circulation of the blood, heart action, and digestion, controlled by the autonomic nervous system, involving simple reflexes and instincts, furnish clear-cut examples of these unconscious energies and actions. More complex and variable unconscious activities, with their driving forces, also belong to this class. These are represented by the energies impelling the organism to eat or drink; to perform certain actions to alleviate pain or excessive heat or cold; to satisfy sexual tension; to free from or resist dangerous objects inspiring fear; to relax when tired; to urinate or defecate; to seek the society of other human beings; to care for helpless offspring; to break away from obstacles hindering the freedom of motion; to cry, laugh, yell, or growl, according to circumstances; to pursue a certain animal; or to gaze at this or that object. The specific forms of these biological or unconscious energies are numerous, as are likewise the specific patterns of the respective activities.

As compared with Freud's subconscious "id," the unconscious energies are much more complex, consisting not only of the libido and death instincts but of many biological drives irreducible to these two Freudian energies. Moreover, virtually none of the unconscious, biological energies are sadistic or antisocial *per se,* or specifically social and altruistic. According to the sociocultural conditions and the degree of operation of the superconscious energies, they manifest themselves now as antisocial, now as social; now they lead to conflict, now to co-operation. Hence the unconscious, biolgical realm in man is neither an inferno, as conceived by Freud, nor a paradise of virtue, as it has sometimes been depicted by ideologists of "the natural man" and "the ideal human animal unspoiled by civilization."

Finally, contrary to Freud, these energies do not constitute a single closed hydraulic system, with a constant libido energy circulating through the various channels. The total quantity as well as the qualitative forms of these energies and activities vary according to the biological and sociocultural conditions.

Next to these unconscious energies and activities devoid of a conscious self or ego come bioconscious energies and activities associated with a set of biological egos in personality. When a person is aware of his biological tension, and the tension enters the field of consciousness, the biological energy becomes bioconscious and leads to bioconscious activities on the part of the corresponding biological ego. Thus, when one grows aware of a pain and consciously strives to alleviate it, or when he says, "I am hungry or thirsty or tired," and consciously seeks to allay his hunger, thirst, or fatigue, the purely unconscious energies and activities assume a bioconscious form and involve a set of corresponding conscious biological egos. These energies, activities, and egos constitute a second stratum of personality adjacent to the stratum of the unconscious. Like the latter, the total quantitative energies of this stratum vary; still more variable is the qualitative set of biological egos. It is incessantly changing, one biological ego appearing and, after its satisfaction, being replaced by another. When one is hungry, his "nutritional ego" emerges and occupies a large area of the field of consciousness and activities. When his hunger is satisfied, it recedes into the field of the subconscious, giving place to another biological "ego," for instance, the sex ego.

These bioconscious forces and egos are inherently neither antisocial nor social in character. If their propensities are sanctioned by the sociocultural egos, for instance, if hunger or the sex urge is satisfied in forms approved by the norms of law or religion or hospitality, they operate in harmony with the corresponding sociocultural egos. If such propensities are disapproved by the sociocultural egos, for instance, if satisfaction of hunger is achieved through theft, or that of the sex ego through rape, the biological egos conflict with the sociocultural egos. Biological egos and their energies may be harmonious with one another; for instance, when cold and hunger together impel one to seek food or warmth or both. They may also conflict with or act independently of one another; for instance, when hunger impels a person to actions inconsistent with those dictated by the sex drive, either weakening or inhibiting the sexual impulse or else, as in the case of prostitution, forcing one to perform certain actions in the absence of the sex impulse.

Above these bioconscious energies, activities, and egos lies the stratum of conscious sociocultural energies, activities, egos, and thought. They are derived from and generated by the conscious, meaningful interaction of thinking persons in their collective experience and learning. Through this collective experience they are accumulated and transmitted from person to person, group to group, generation to generation. In the process of this interaction they are patterned into the specific scientific, philosophical, religious, ethical, artistic, political, and technological forms of sociocultural thought, norms, values, activities, and institutions.

A person possesses as many sociocultural egos and activities as there are sociocultural groups to which he belongs. Most of us have our family ego and activities, our state-citizenship ego and activities, our nationality ego and activities, our political ego and activities, our local community ego and activities, our religious ego and activities (if we belong to an organized religion), our occupational ego and activities, and the lesser egos of the societies, clubs, and other associations to which we belong. Each of these egos and activities is different from the others. In the midst of our family our ego is that of a father, mother, brother, sister, son, or daughter; it is imbued with the appropriate ideas, emotions, and feelings; our activities assume certain definite forms; even our costume (such as a bathrobe and slippers) is of a typical kind. When we leave the home and reach the scene of our occupational work, the ascendancy of the family ego gives place to that of the occupational ego of a doctor, professor, pastor, engineer, businessman, farmer, clerk, or the like. Our occupational ego considers and discusses quite different things, in a different way, and with different emotions as compared with those of the family ego. In our occupational role we perform very different activities, in a different setting, with different co-actors (bosses, co-workers, and subordinates) in a different garb. If our occupational ego were to think, talk, and behave as our family ego does, we should be looked upon as "queer" and should probably soon lose our position. Our occupational ego frequently does things of which our family ego disapproves, and vice versa. These two egos are, in fact, as unlike in their mentality and activities as two different persons.

When we go to church, our religious ego replaces the family and occupational egos. This religious ego is quite different from both in its mentality and activities. It is concerned with God, sin, and salvation; it prays, sings hymns, kneels, and performs other acts of quite another character.

A similar transformation of our egos takes place when we attend a political rally. Our political ego may think, say, and do many things of which our family or religious ego is ashamed.

Each of these egos is a reflection of the meanings, values, and norms of the particular group which it represents, and, its activities are defined and prescribed accordingly. We can remain a member of a social group only as long as we fulfill its demands. One remains a citizen of the United States or a member of the Roman Catholic Church only as long as one performs the duties and maintains the values and standards (in thought and actions) prescribed by the United States government or the Catholic Church respectively. Otherwise he is penalized or else forfeits his group status for violation of his duties. The same is true of any organized group. Each seeks to impress upon a person its own image in the form of a particular ego; each attempts to mold a person after its own pattern; each demands a portion of our time and energy; each prescribes in detail our activities, functions, rights, and duties. The state does not accept church prayers in lieu of taxes; our occupational group does not accept the care of our children in lieu of occupational work; and vice versa.

Almost all our activities are merely the discharge of the functions and duties of the groups to which we belong. The purely biological activities alone are excepted, to some extent, from this rule. These groups incessantly subject us to various demands and stimuli, and we incessantly respond to these through the respective egos.

To sum up: *The diversity and multiplicity of the groups to which we belong account for the plurality and diversity of our sociocultural egos. The totality of one's sociocultural egos is a microcosm reflecting the sociocultural macrososm in which one is born and reared and in which one acts and interacts.*

If the groups to which we belong are mutually harmonious, if they impress upon us mutually harmonious ideas, beliefs, standards, and values, and impel us to mutually harmonious duties and activities, then our sociocultural egos are also harmoniously integrated into a single composite ego, free from inner conflicts and contradictions. In this case we resemble a ball pushed by many different forces in the same direction. Under these conditions our duties and purposes are definite; our conscience is clear; our peace of mind is undisturbed (unless biological egos interfere); our will power is unimpaired; our conduct is consistent. Fortunate indeed are such persons!

If, on the other hand, our groups are at war with one another, then our respective egos are also at war. If the state denies what our church affirms, or if our family demands from us activities prohibited by our occupational group, these antagonisms necessarily involve those of our respective egos. Under these conditions, particularly if the conflicting groups and their values are equally important for the individual, one becomes a house divided against itself. Incessant conflicts of duties and activities demanded by antagonistic groups are his lot. His will power is undermined, his vitality and energy are sapped, peace of mind becomes impossible, he grows hesitant and confused, and his conduct becomes inconsistent. His inner conflicts destroy his mental equilibrium and lead to serious mental disorders, psychoneuroses, melancholia and depressive moods, and sometimes suicide.[2]

---

[2] Pavlov's experiments with dogs clearly demonstrate the neurosis-producing role of more or less equal but contradictory stimuli. If a circle of light was

One way out of such a situation is for a person deliberately to sever his connection with some of the conflicting groups, eliminating their egos, values, and norms, thus making his own egos noncontradictory and in this way restoring his peace of mind and mental equilibrium. Still another escape is the path of complete skepticism, cynicism, and nihilism respecting all groups and their values. This is the path of despair, of desocialization and demoralization, the individual becoming controlled predominantly by his unconscious and bioconscious egos.

Finally, as was mentioned in chapter nine, some succeed in eliminating the contradiction of their egos by subordinating all of these, with their contradictory values, to one supreme ego and set of values in which all the lesser egos and values become secondary and relatively unimportant. This supremacy of the superconscious self, unfortunately, is rarely achieved nowadays. Contrary to Freud, most psychoneuroses are generated by the antagonism of various sociocultural egos with one another and not by the repression of biological egos by the Freudian "superego." Only a minor proportion of psychoneuroses are due to the conflict of biological egos with one another or with certain sociocultural egos.

The ideally integrated person is thus one whose bioconscious and sociocultural egos are in a state of mutual harmony. Such a person attains the highest level of mental stability and harmony on these empirical levels. The poorly integrated person, on the other hand, is one whose bioconscious egos are at war with one another, whose sociocultural egos conflict, and whose

---

thrown on the screen and the dog was then fed, and if at another time an oval of light was thrown on the screen without being followed by food, no neurosis occurred. The animal easily differentiated between the respective stimuli, responding appropriately with the secretion of saliva in the one case and without salivation in the other. But when the oval was gradually made more nearly circular until the ratio of its axes was 8:9, the dog became excited, showed its teeth, barked, and tried to smash the apparatus — in brief, developed an acute neurosis which lasted for several months. Since it was unable to differentiate the circle from the oval and was thus placed in a contradictory position by conflicting stimuli, its nervous system suffered a breakdown. Cf. Ivan Petrovich Pavlov, *Conditioned Reflexes* (New York, 1927), pp. 133, 290-292.

bioconscious and sociocultural egos are antagonistic and dishar-
monious. Such a person is likely to become an inmate of a
mental asylum.

*There is a still higher form of energies and activities, realized
in varying degrees by different persons, namely, the superconscious energies and activities.* These constitute the fourth, and
highest stratum of man's personality, representing the supreme
type of creative functioning. They are frequently designated
as "the divine in man," "the manifestation of the Godhead,"
"the creative genius," and so on. They manifest themselves in
the foremost achievements of human genius in the fine arts,
religion, law, ethics, philosophy, science and technology, and the
highest forms of social, economic, and political organization.

When the superconscious operates to a slight extent, its
principal function is to integrate the multitude of bioconscious
and conscious egos into some kind of unity, some sort of self
that lies behind and at the basis of complex of one's various
disunited egos and energies. When the superconscious is fully
operative, it acts as the supreme controller of one's biosocial
and sociocultural egos, energies, and activities. Even if it remains shackled and, as it were, "imprisoned," its existence is
nevertheless intuitively apprehended as a mysterious and immortal soul, self, spirit, or Godhead. Such expressions as "my
mind" presupposes this self as something that stands behind the
mind as its possessor and potential master. This superconscious,
or self, is "egoless," in the sense that when it operates one ceases
to be a mere bioconscious or sociocultural empirical ego. All
other egos lose their identity in the superconscious self as a
superpersonal Infinite Manifold, or Godhead, transcending the
limits of human personality and individuality. Those who are
controlled by the superconscious unanimously regard themselves
as mere instrumentalities operated by the Divine Soul, by God,
by "divine madness," by "divine genius," by "inspiration," by
"the creative *élan*," by "eros" (in the Platonic sense), and so
on. "Not me, but God working through me," "deliverance from
personal self" "by the grace of God," "union with the Absolute," "inspired and swayed by genius," "completely possessed

by the creative *élan,*" "attuned to eternity and infinity," these and similar expressions of great religious seers, genuine mystics, and creative giants attest this personal egolessness of the superconscious.

The egolessness of the superconscious differs radically from that of the unconscious in that it is the source of creative achievement. "When a man goes into a deep sleep, he enters a plane beneath consciousness. . . . When he returns from his (unconscious) sleep, he is the same man who went into it. The sum total of the knowledge he had before he went into the sleep remains the same. . . . No enlightenment does come. But when a man goes into Samâdhi (the superconscious union with the Absolute, with an attending deliverance from personal egos), if he goes into it a fool, he comes out a sage." [3]

As already observed, with the exception of a limited number of psychologists such as William James, philosophers like H. Bergson, inventors like I. Sikorsky, and astronomers like G. Stromberg, contemporary philosophers, psychologists, and scientists, as a rule, do not admit even the "mind stuff," and most of them flatly deny the superconscious. We may leave them to their errors! It takes a mind to deny the existence of mind. Any affirmation or denial, such as "A is B" or "A is not B," including the proposition "There is no mind and no thought," is in itself a mental phenomenon. When such "scientists" indulge in any thinking, any affirmation or denial, they contradict themselves and clearly demonstrate the existence of the "mind stuff," thought, and mental energy. The very sterility of their research in this field is additional evidence of the fallacy of their assumptions and conceptions.

As to the superconscious in the foregoing sense, its reality is demonstrated by its objective, sensory, or "operational" manifestations, above all, by the phenomenon of creativeness. Major discoveries or inventions cannot be achieved through the mere conscious, rational activities of our bioconscious and sociocultural egos. Teachers of English know the rules of English composition; yet none of them becomes a Shakespeare, and

---

[3] Swami Vivekananda, *Raja-Yoga* (Mayavati, 1930), p. 77.

few, if any, even second-rate poets or writers. Professors of music know the rules and techniques underlying great musical composition; yet none of them becomes a Bach, Mozart, Beethoven, Brahms, Wagner, or Tchaikovsky. Teachers of logic, scientific methodology, and research techniques know all the rules governing these disciplines. Nevertheless, few of them become eminent philosophers or scientific discoverers and inventors.

Professors of theology and religion, as well as bishops and priests, are rational experts in the field of religion. Yet few of them have founded any great religion. Genuine creativeness demands something more than the operation of our conscious egos. This "something more" is the inspiration or intuition of the superconscious. It is unimportant how we designate it, as "the superconscious," "genius," "the grace of God," "divine madness," or what not. Whatever the name, it is something irreducible to any "unconscious" factor or even rational consciousness. If the as yet largely unknown "fission forces" of the superconscious are revealed and fully exploited, they can become the most decisive agency of man's self-control, as well as of the control of others and of all the known and unknown forms of the inorganic, organic, and conscious energies in man and the universe. Their neglect by sensate science has been one of the chief reasons for its failure in the fields discussed. What is needed is a concentration of humanity's efforts on unlocking the secrets of the superconscious as the realm of the most powerful, most creative, and most ennobling forces in the entire universe. The more man becomes an instrument of the superconscious, the more creative, wiser, and nobler he grows; the more easily he controls himself and his unconscious and egoistic conscious energies; the more he comes to resemble God, as the supreme ideal. In the superconscious lies our main hope, the road to humanity's "promised land" of peace, wisdom, beauty, and goodness.[4]

---

[4] Cf. William James, *op. cit.*; A. K. Coomaraswamy, "What Is Civilization?" [Albert Schweitzer Jubilee Book] (Cambridge, Mass., 1946); and G. Stromberg, *The Soul of the Universe* (New York, 1940).

Such is the structure of human personality, its egos, energies, and activities. Beginning with the unconscious, they extend to the superconscious. This concept of man must be substituted for the fallacious conception entertained by contemporary pseudo science. Its "subman" and even "conscious man" demand, of course, a further study of their properties and a refinement of the techniques for their modification in the desired direction. But this is not the most important task. Much greater concentration on the nature of the superconscious, and on the methods and techniques of its unfolding and unhindered operation, is the central problem of science and religion and of humanity itself.

III. CONSTRUCTIVE USE OF THE EXISTING KNOWLEDGE OF MAN'S TRANSFORMATION

Preoccupation with the biological "subman" by Western sensate science naturally led it to ignore or neglect even the existing body of experience in relation to rendering man more altruistic and releasing in him the forces of superconscious creativity, especially those of moral creativeness.[5] Blinded by its materialistic, mechanistic, and empirical bias respecting anything "superconscious," "spiritual," or "religious," this pseudo science largely disregarded the techniques of Lao-tse and Buddha, Christ and Saint Paul, Saint Francis of Assisi and Ramakrishna, the yogis and ascetics, the mystics, the founders of monastic orders, and other eminent altruists and moral educators. In comparison with the altruizing of millions which these achieved, all the "socialization" accomplished by scientific educators counts for little. As compared with the sublime love practiced by the former, the kindness and good-neighborliness of utilitarian humanists are but pale shadows of altruism. When the degree of absorption in the superconscious which they attained is compared with the immersion in the "unconscious" and conscious fostered by pseudo science, the gulf between these two

---

[5] In this work I discuss specifically only moral creativity. The other forms of creativity, scientific, artistic, and so on, also urgently call for searching investigation.

attitudes becomes truly striking. When the facts of "conversion" in the sense of a sudden transfiguration of the mentality and overt conduct of the converts, the transmutation of their *tota substantia, renati in aeternum,* are compared with the slight improvement in the honesty and morality of pupils and juvenile delinquents now and then effected by "scientific means," the superficiality and inefficiency of these "scientifically engineered" transmutations become all too obvious.

If the major altruists and moral educators of humanity and the genuine converts from egoism to altruism succeeded in their difficult tasks, this means that somehow or other they discovered adequate methods and efficient techniques. If our "scientific educators" were indeed scientific, they would not have ignored the knowledge and experience of the foremost masters of self-control and moral education. The failure to explore and apply this knowledge and experience in the fields of contemporary Western psychology and psychiatry, sociology and education, political science, and "social and ethical engineering" explains the crudity and ineffectiveness of the current theories and techniques of character education, of psychotherapy, and of the socialization of criminals. To remedy the situation we must therefore first make a careful study of the experience and techniques of the aforesaid masters. On this basis we may then attempt to make new discoveries and invent new techniques looking toward the establishment of a nobler and happier social order.

Such are the three principal corrections of the fallacious assumptions of contemporary science and pseudo science. Let us now glance at the neglected experience, wisdom, and techniques of the foremost masters of creative altruism.

CHAPTER FOURTEEN

Methods and Techniques of the Great Masters of Creative Altruism

Our knowledge of these ways and techniques is very fragmentary and superficial. However, even this superficial knowledge discloses several things common to the methods of the Oriental and Occidental masters of self-altruization, men responsible for the moral education of millions and for the cultivation of the superconscious in man. Let us note briefly some of the known characteristics of their methods and techniques.

I. Techniques of Contemporary Psychotherapy

The methods and techniques of the Yoga, particularly those of the Raja-Yoga, as a technical part of the Yoga; those of the founders of the great Christian monastic orders at the beginning of the Middle Ages; those of the great mystics and altruists living in the midst of the busy world; and those of the founders of the great religions, the moral educators of millions, these systems contain in themselves nearly all the sound techniques of modern psychoanalysis, psychotherapy, psychodrama, moral education, and education of character. They lacked such techniques as electric-shock therapy, specific surgical operations, and the like. But even there they used good substitutes.

If anything, these techniques were subtler, less mechanical, and richer in their variety and elasticity than the corresponding modern techniques. In addition, as we shall see, the ancient systems employed many techniques scarcely known to the contemporary sciences that aim at the transfiguration of man. Here are a few facts in support of this assertion.

The soundest part of psychoanalysis and the related psychotherapies is the technique of uncovering (through autognosis, or self-analysis, counseling, or suggestion) "repressed" associations, ideas and impulses, unearthing them in all their naked ugliness; followed by that of "transference" and then "sublimation," or rearrangement of the values. These techniques not only were known to the systems discussed but were practiced by the great masters in an incomparably subtler way. The initial ceremonies of many "mystery" religions, like the rite of *taurobolium* (bathing in bull's blood), with its bringing to light of all the hideous impulses of the initiate; the practice of "self-confession"; "examination of conscience"; for which most of the masters often went into solitude, away from all human beings; the private and public confessions provided for by all the great religions; private and public repentance; internal (mental) and public prayer [1] often performed in ingeniously devised technical surroundings; these psychoanalytic and psychotherapeutic techniques in all their varieties were well known to these masterly systems, in which they were, as a matter of fact, merely first steps towards the goal of becoming good or of attaining absorption into the superconscious. We read, for instance, in Raja-Yoga, that "the first lesson [in obtaining control over the unconscious, bioconscious and socioconscious mind or ego] is to sit for some time and let the mind run on. The mind is bubbling up all the time. It is like a monkey jumping around. Let the monkey jump as much as he can; you simply wait and watch. . . . Until you know what the mind is doing you cannot control it. Give it the rein, many hideous thoughts may come into it; you will be astonished that it was possible for you to think such thoughts. But you will find that each day the mind's vagaries are becoming less and less violent,

---

[1] Earnest "mental" prayer is one of the most important techniques of autognosis, still little understood by many psychoanalysts. " 'Mental' prayer is nothing else but being on terms of friendship with God, frequently conversing in secret with Him, who *loves us*," pointedly remarks Saint Teresa. She began to practice it early in the period of her "most grievous sufferings." Saint Teresa of Jesus, *The Life, Relations, Maxims, and Foundations, Written by the Saint* (New York, 1911), p. 24 ff., 49; Pere Poulain, *The Graces of Interior Prayer* (London, 1924); William James, *op. cit.* On the role of private and public confessions see *The Rule of Saint Benedict,* tr. by Cardinal Gasquet (London, 1925), chap. 7.

that each day it is becoming calmer." [2] Here clearly outlined, in essence, is the unearthing of the unconscious, semiconscious, and even conscious impulses through the technique of free association, autognosis, or self-analysis.

"Make known to thy superior and confessor all thy temptations, imperfections and dislikes, that he may give thee counsel and help thee to overcome them." "In all thy actions, and at every hour, examine thy conscience and, having discerned thy faults, strive, by the help of God, to amend them." "Be very exact every night in thy examinations of conscience." [3] These precepts, too, are suggestive of psychoanalytic procedures.

Many pages could be filled with quotations of the extremely detailed technical rules given by the masters in this matter. In their exhaustiveness, variety, and subtlety they far exceed the similar rules of contemporary psychotherapy.

The same is true of the counselor or guide and analyst. The masterly systems recommend such advisers (the Suffist *shaykh*, the Yoga's *guru*, the spiritual advisers, the confessors, etc.) when they are wise and experienced; they do not recommend them when they are unwise, incompetent, and defective morally, mentally, or otherwise. In contradistinction to an indiscriminate use of all kinds of psychoanalysts, counselors, doctors, psychiatrists, among whom there are unwise, incompetent, unprudent, selfish, and unkind practitioners, the masterly systems sharply warn against such advisers as dangerous and harmful. "They harm souls rather than help them along the road." [4] Good spiritual advisers serve as one of the agencies for so-called "transference," though even here the master systems do not limit the transference to such advisers but leave a wide margin for the choice of objects of transference among many idealized or ideal persons and saints. For instance, Saint Teresa chose Saint Joseph as her "patron," "father," and "lord," who "delivered

[2] Swami Vivekananda, *op. cit.*, pp. 69-70.
[3] Saint Teresa, *op. cit.*, pp. 672-674.
[4] *The Complete Works of Saint John of the Cross* (London, 1934), I, 13 ff., 144 ff.; III, 75-91, 176-194. Saint Teresa, *op. cit.*, p. 21 ff., *et passim*. A. Tillyard, *Spiritual Exercises* (New York, 1927), pp. 3-11; Swami Vivekananda, *op. cit.*, p. 66 ff.

me, and rendered me greater services than I knew how to ask for." [5] As to *sublimation*, this procedure is carried out more effectively in the older systems than in the contemporary psychotherapies. The latter often do not succeed at all in it; and when they do succeed in some degree, their sublimation is uncertain, temporary, and fragile, being a sublimation to merely relative values and questionable pursuits. The masterly systems sublimate unconditionally to the Absolute as an object of aspiration and love, certain and unquestionable (God, the Godhead, the Brahman, the superconscious). Such a sublimation proves itself more effective and lasting than the sublimation to such useful but very limited values as hobbies, diversions, politics, art, science, philanthropy, and the like. Besides, sublimation in the masterly systems is inextricably woven into the whole system of their transfiguration of man. [6]

II. Control of Biological and Physical Functions

Though this is only the first — and least important — task in the masterly systems of man's transfiguration, they do not overlook it and are as successful in it as the modern sciences in this field.

Some of the masterly systems, like Yoga, seem to have succeeded even more than modern science, especially in certain fields. Obtaining control over the bodily processes is the first step in the masterly systems. They prescribed a wide range of techniques for that purpose, such as fasting, solitude, austerity, physical work, prohibition of certain foods and drinks, physical hardships, various forms of training of the body, and a most elaborate and ingenious set of exercises, postures, rituals through which ascetic, hermit, worldly altruist, mystic, and yogi successfully subordinated their biological unconscious and bioconscious drives to the control of the conscious sociocultural egos

---

[5] Saint Teresa, *op. cit.*, pp. 30-31. Cf. G. Coster, *Yoga and Western Psychology* (Oxford, 1935); K. T. Behanan, *Yoga: A Scientific Evaluation* (New York, 1937); Swami Pavitrananda, *Common Sense about Yoga* (Advaitu Ashrama, Mayavah, 1944); Swami Vivekananda, *op. cit.*; Swami Akhilananda, *Hindu Psychology* (New York, 1946).

[6] Cf. William James, *The Varieties of Religious Experience* (New York, 1928); E. Underhill, *Mysticism* (London, 1930).

and especially of the superconscious in them. They succeeded not only in the control of these drives but in that of even the least controllable biological functions, regulated by the autonomic nervous system, such as breathing, the heartbeat and the like. Some of these systems, like the Hatha-Yoga and Raja-Yoga (in which the control of bodily posture, breathing, pulse, and other bodily functions is one of the first steps towards the superconscious state of Samadhi, or the union with the divine absolute), seem to have achieved almost unbelievable feats in this respect: willful control of many organs, muscles, and glands; and especially of breathing (prana) and the activity of the heart, whose mastery is one of the preparatory yoga exercises.

After years of training, phases of apnoea (suspension of breath) can last several hours: the longer the suspension of breathing, the greater the mastery of yoga. One of our yogis, as an experiment, had himself buried for ten hours under the observation of the medical corps of Baroda, who noted a tachycardia (rapid pulse) of 160, which quickly returned to normal. In the course of our examinations, the pneumograph registered repeatedly for ten to fifteen minutes these phases of apnoea so superficial that it was accompanied by no expansion of the thorax. By withdrawing what he calls vital energy, the yogi thus puts his body in a state of slowed-up life, comparable to that of hibernating animals. . . . The mastery of the yogi over his voluntary muscular system is such as to permit already such difficult postures, for example, a lateral displacement of the long straight muscles of the abdomen, contracted; the result is abdominal massage. But this elective mastery is also extended to the smooth fibers, regulating at will the peristaltic and antiperistaltic motions, permitting in both directions the play of the anal or vesical sphincters and insuring by simple suction and without the help of any other instrument the penetration of liquids into the bladder or the rectum.[7]

A still more prodigious feat was the willful control of pulse and heartbeat by the yogis, as tested and registered by electrocardiograph, pneumograph, and other instruments.

---

[7] T. Brosse, "A Psychophysiological Study," *Main Currents in Modern Thought* (July, 1946), pp. 77-84, for photographs and electrocardiograms. See Behanan's *Yoga, op. cit.,* which contains photographs and a report on similar findings.

"Thus [concludes the French scientist, who had gone to India especially to study and verify the yogi control of these processes] we find these yogis are masters over diverse activities. Knowing nothing about the structure of their organs, they are however the incontestable masters of appropriate functions. Moreover, they enjoy a magnificent state of health." [8]

With some modification these conclusions are applicable to the successful control of the biological man by other masterly systems described. They do not use the strenuous and intricate system of the Yoga, but in their own way they achieve control of the biological man by the conscious and then the superconscious in man as much as do the yogis. This control is so deep, vast, and effective that it can successfully rival the control achieved through the techniques of modern science. In several ways the former exceeds the latter.

III. The Basic Principle of These Systems

The subjugation and control of the unconscious in man by his conscious will, and of the conscious sociocultural egos by the superconscious in man is the basic principle of these systems in contrast with that of modern psychotherapy, psychoanalysis, psychology, and education.

In modern disciplines the "adjustment" of mental disorders and the development of character consist largely in the liberation of the unconscious from "the repressions" of the ego and the superego, in an adaptation of the conscious (and superconscious) to the demands of the unconscious impulses. Even in the "transference" and "sublimation" techniques it is not so much that the unconditional values of the conscious and the superconscious dictate how the unconscious impulses have to be changed as that the unconscious impulses prescribe the kind of values suitable for the purposes of sublimation. The conscious and superconscious become thus a handmaid of the unconscious. For this reason the modern techniques drag the conscious and superconscious to the level of the unconscious and degrade the whole man to the lowest part of his personality.

[8] T. Brosse, *op. cit.*, pp. 77-84.

His conscious and superconscious become a mere "rationalizing ideology," at the service and command of the unconscious. The modern techniques cater mainly to the unconscious and consist largely in the physical modification of the body processes through various physical agencies — drugs, food, drink, climate, recreation, surgical operation, insulin shock, electric shock, comfortable material environment, and so on. These techniques are based upon an explicit or implicit assumption that changing the body and its processes by means that are mainly physical will automatically change the conscious and superconscious parts in man. In accordance with this assumption they hardly use the forces of the concentrated consciousness and will, especially those of the superconscious (whose reality they deny). Such techniques are in perfect harmony with the prevalent sensate culture.

In contrast to this, the masterly systems demand complete subjugation and control of the unconscious forces by the conscious ones, and of these by the superconscious. They do not cater at all to biological man and his impulses. They categorically insist upon an "adjustment" of the biological impulses to the requirement of the conscious and the superconscious, however difficult it is for the unconscious. They make it a servant of the conscious and superconscious man. As a result their techniques elevate the whole man to the level of the conscious and superconscious, instead of drowning him in the dark waters of the unconscious. In the main their techniques are based upon, and operate through, the concentrated conscious and the superconscious; only in a minor degree do they try to modify the bodily processes by physical agencies. Even the nature of these agencies is largely determined by the nature of the purposes of the conscious and superconscious.

Take no thought for your life, what ye shall eat, or what ye shall drink; nor yet for your body, what ye shall put on. . . . But seek ye first the kingdom of God and His righteousness. . . . Be you therefore perfect, even as your Father which is in heaven is perfect. . . . Our Father, which art in heaven. . . . Thy kingdom come. Thy will be done in earth, as it is in heaven.

If thy right eye offend thee, pluck it out.

If thy right hand offend thee, cut it off.

Whosoever looketh on a woman to lust after her hath committed adultery with her already in his heart.[9]

These maxims of Christianity clearly define the complete subjugation of biological, even of sociocultural man to the supreme superconscious and to its commandments. There is no trace of catering to the unconscious by the conscious and superconscious. The commandments are unconditional and absolute. With variation in the secondary traits they are representative for all the masterly systems discussed.

Saint John of the Cross puts the matter in a way, typical of Buddhist, Hinduist, Taoist, and practically all other "spiritual" systems of man's transfiguration.

The first step for the soul's union with God is "privation and purgation of the soul of all its sensual desires, with respect to all outward things of the world and to those which were delectable to its flesh, and likewise with respect to the desires of its will," including the pleasures given by the sense of sight, hearing, smell, touch; liberation of the soul from the passions of joy, hope, fear, and grief. The whole "sensual part of the soul" must die in order that the divine part of the soul may live. We must "mortify the concupiscence of the flesh, and the concupiscence of the eyes, and the pride of life, from which all the other desires proceed." Liberated from all the pleasures of the senses and all the sensory desires, "in this detachment the spiritual soul finds its quiet and repose; for, since it covets nothing, nothing wearies it when it is lifted up, and nothing oppresses it when it is cast down, for it is in the center of its humility; since, when it covets anything, at that very moment it becomes wearied." [10]

The techniques of all such systems of man's transfiguration

---

[9] Matthew 6:25, 33; 5:48; 6:9, 10. Matthew: 5:29. Matthew 5:30. Matthew 5:28.

[10] *Works of Saint John, op. cit.,* I, 18-63 *et passim.* Compare Yoga's prescriptions in the Raja-Yoga, Bhakti, Jnana, and Karma Yoga; Buddhist *Dhammapada,* and Asvaghosha Bodhisattva, *Life of Buddha,* both in *The World's Great Classics* (New York, Colonial Press, n.d.).

were designed in conformity with these objectives and operated through the concentrated consciousness, will, and superconsciousness rather than through physical means and agencies. T. Brosse, chief of the cardiological clinic of the Faculté de Médicine de Paris, who was sent by the French Government to India for a special study of Yoga techniques, puts the matter as follows:

The specific exercise of yoga, the one which permits it to be reduced to a unique technique, is 'mental concentration' (samyama). It is a concentration pushed beyond anything we can imagine, and divided into three periods. In the first the attention is fixed upon a chosen object (a body organ, a feeling, a philosophical concept, etc.). It is a struggle against automatic mechanisms which have a tendency to distract the attention from it. The attention has to maintain itself upon the chosen object for a period of time determined by the will. It is the concentration of diffused attention and a focusing upon a single point (single-pointedness of mind). The elements making up this first period are therefore triple: subject, object, and act of concentration. In the second period consciousness loses awareness of effort and the inhibition of the unconscious processes is complete. The self has only before it the chosen object upon which the concentration, now happy and easy, can last indefinitely. There is now only a duality of subject-object, the feeling of effort has disappeared.

In the third period (samadhi) this feeling of duality of subject-object in turn disappears. The conscious being is indissolubly united to the object of its contemplation, melts into it and becomes identical with it.[11]

Being identical with the object, the Samadhi-yogi knows it fully. In this process the yogi supposedly develops many extraordinary powers, which he is advised to ignore. The whole process of training for reaching the state of Samadhi is explicitly the process of complete mastery of the unconscious by the conscious will or mind and of the control of the mind by the superconscious self, or absolute.

The essentials of the technique are thus mainly mental (concentration and meditation). Physical agencies and conditions

---

[11] T. Brosse, op. cit., p. 80.

enter the training but only as subsidiary stimuli. "The yogi must always practice. He should try to live alone. Not work much because too much work distracts the mind." Cleanliness, contentment, austerity, certain foods, sexual chastity, and prescribed exercises, these are the main physical conditions and agencies.[12]

Different concretely, but similar in essentials, are the techniques of other great systems of man's transfiguration.

As a "disciplinarian" variation the ingenious and highly scientific techniques of "spiritual exercises" of Saint Ignatius Loyola may be taken. Based upon his personal experimentation, they lay down detailed prescriptions for the complete subjugation of the biological impulses in man and teach him how to discipline and put into the service of the will of God man's sense perceptions, imagination, associations, thoughts, will, even reason; in brief, man's subconscious and conscious energies. The principal way to attain that end is also the utmost concentration of man's imagination and senses upon a chosen religious or moral point. If he has chosen evil as a topic of meditation, the pupil must visualize hell in the utmost detail, its horrors, its wailing condemned souls; its breadth and depth; the pupil's ears must hear in imagination the screams of its victims; his nose must smell sulphur and the putrid odors of hell; his tongue must taste the bitterness of hell; his sense of touch must feel the scorching flame; his eyes must clearly see the horrible convulsions of sinners and other horrid spectacles that hell offers. In this vivid concentration of all the senses, imagination, will, and consciousness upon hell, the pupil lives through his imaginary experience, has his soul shaken to its utmost depths, and his "exercise" becomes an indelible part and parcel of his personality.

Saint Ignatius prescribes in the utmost detail the topics to be concentrated upon, their sequence, what words and exclamations the pupil must utter at each stage of his meditation; how he must systematically examine his conscience — in general and in particular ways; how often he is to repeat each exercise; what

---

[12] Swami Vivekananda, *op. cit.*, p. 69 ff. *et passim.*

actions he must perform at any moment of the exercise; how to breathe, what posture to assume, and so on. In its entirety the system is the most scientific set of techniques for a complete regimentation of all the biological impulses, emotions, associations of images, thoughts, will, and overt actions of a pupil. Saint Ignatius has reason to regard it as infallible. "I can find God at all times, whenever I wish, and any man of good will can do the same [if he follows Saint Ignatius's system]. As a body can be exercised by going, walking, and running, so the will of man can be trained by exercises to find the will of God." [13]

Another variation of these systems is given by the techniques of Saint Francis of Assisi, used by him in his own transfiguration from a sensate youth into the human incarnation of boundless love, the ever-cheerful and singing "jester of God," and into the lover of the Lady Poverty. Here the transfiguration was achieved not so much through will power, or through systematic iron discipline and drill, as by the superconscious power of love, spontaneously exploding and irresistibly permeating the mind, body, and actions of Saint Francis. Through its force he abruptly exchanged the material comforts of a son of a prominent merchant for the utmost poverty and material hardships; pride for limitless humility; ambition for love and service. Through this power he could cheerfully enjoy as a luxurious meal the smelly, wormy contents of garbage cans; could control his body, "brother donkey," fully, and extract from it an enormous amount of endurance and physical effort; through it, at the very beginning of his transfiguration, he could suddenly embrace and kiss the leper he met on the road and devote himself to the service of lepers.

Concretely his techniques were different from those of Saint Ignatius or Yoga, but they were similar to them in their essentials, that is, in their goal and in the forces of the superconscious and conscious used for the transfiguration. Physical means and agencies played only a secondary role in the process. [14]

---

[14] From a purely scientific viewpoint the techniques of Saint Francis have
[13] See *The Spiritual Exercises of Saint Ignatius* (New York, 1914); also his *Letters and Instructions* (St. Louis, 1914).

One may like or dislike the specific goals of transfiguration set forth by these and other masterly systems; but one must concede that their techniques for curbing the unconscious by the conscious and superconscious have been very effective; and, what is still more important, through their pitiless "repression" of the subconscious drives they transformed their practitioners into the great moral, religious, and spiritual leaders of humanity, instead of turning them into psychoneurotics or inmates of insane asylums. These facts, as solid evidence, discredit most of the modern "repressional" theories of psychoneuroses and mental disorders.

In all these systems the mastery over the subconscious is reached mainly by "spiritual exercises and forces." Physical means, very diverse in nature to fit individual cases, are subsidiary, whether they be fasting, mortification of the body, solitude, prolonged silence and certain postures, physical work, acts of service to the needy, or various other practices.[15] In several cases the physical stimuli are spontaneously invented by individual masters, like the sudden act of Saint Francis when he jumped from his horse and embraced the leper met on the road.

It is beyond the scope of this work to give a detailed examination of all the numerous specific technical devices revealed by the experience and teachings of the masters.[16] It is enough to say that they are many and ingenious.

---

been studied little. Such a study can, however, be made through a careful investigation of his life activities, and sayings. See Saint Francis, *Opera Omnia* (Cologne, 1848); Saint Bonaventura, *The Life of Saint Francis of Assisi* (London, 1898); G. G. Coulton, *Two Saints, Saint Bernard and Saint Francis* (Cambridge, England, 1932). See also R. Fulop-Miller, *The Saints That Moved the World* (New York, 1945).

[15] Cf. Sri Aurobindo, *The Life Divine* (Calcutta, India, 1940); D. Suzuki, *Training of the Zen Buddhist Monk*, (Kyoto, Japan, 1934); John Woolman, *The Journal of John Woolman*, (New York, 1903); Rufus Jones, *Spirit in Man* (London, 1941); Saint Francis de Sales, *Treatise on the Love of God* (London and Edinburgh, 1931); M. K. Gandhi, *The Story of My Experiments With Truth* (Ahmedebad, India, 1927-1929); A. Schweitzer, *Out of My Life and Thought* (New York, 1933).

[16] A somewhat dry and mechanical catalogue of some of these techniques is given in such works as A. Tillyard's *Spiritual Exercises*. However, it does not cast much light upon the problem. A systematic survey and analysis of these techniques will be given in my *Types, Techniques, and Varieties of Altruistic Experience* (now in preparation).

IV. INTEGRATION OF THE SOCIOCULTURAL EGOS

These systems of man's transfiguration have been successful also in their techniques for integrating the conscious sociocultural egos into a harmonious unity, subordinated to the superconscious and controlled by it.

One may like or dislike the highest value of God, Brahman, Nirvana, the state of samadhi, the divine Godhead, the superconscious in its various forms to which these systems sublimate the unconscious and the bioconscious, and the sociocultural conscious egos in man. Regardless of personal bias, the fact of their success in sublimation remains beyond question, so far as the outstanding masters and followers of these systems are concerned. They indeed subordinated themselves, their bodies, minds, activities, and lives, to this superconscious absolute value. They became indeed its mere mouthpieces and instrumentalities. All their egos were united into one superconscious self. No traces of split personality, of a disintegrated or unintegrated multitude of various egos, are noticeable in them after they reached their goal. An undisturbed peace of mind, a complete insulation from all fear, doubt, apprehension, disaster, even against death, is their habitual state. Indeed, they are the most conspicuous examples of a complete integration of personality.

This result suggests that their techniques for that purpose have also been sound, efficacious, and therefore scientific. A thoughtful acquaintance with these techniques confirms this expectation. The first reason for the success is their rule: complete subordination of all values, norms, goals, and egos to one *absolute* value, God, Nirvana, Brahman, state of samadhi, union with the absolute. This supreme singleness of value for transcending all relative values is exactly the right formula for integrating a multitude of antagonistic egos, with their relative values and norms, into one harmonious system of superconscious self, with its absolute, unquestionable, universal value and norms. As we have seen in the preceding chapter, there is no other constructive way out of this mutually contradictory multitude of egos. All the other ways are either disastrous or ineffective (the ways of melancholy, suicide, cynicism, animalization, and various mental disorders). In this respect the systems under discussion appear to be more scientific than the modern efforts of sublimation to some conventional, conditional, relative, questionable, and questioned value or goal — hobbies or the superficial pursuits of some artistic, scientific, philanthropic, political or economic value. By their nature all such goals and values are relative, disputed, and objected to by other persons and groups, uncertain and temporary. As such they cannot absorb the whole of the man and cannot give him peace of mind, and freedom from fear, worry, and inner antagonisms.

Look on this world as you would at a bubble [or mirage]. The foolish are immersed in it, but the wise do not touch it; wise men . . . care for nothing in this world. . . .

A man free from all desires sees the majesty of Self, by the Grace of the Creator. . . . He is the greatest of all men.[17]

These Hindu and Buddhist maxims denote the results of this sublimation to the Absolute. When the state of samadhi is reached by the yogi, "then will all sorrow cease, all miseries vanish; the soul will be free for ever." "It cannot be born. It cannot die. It is immortal, indestructible, and ever-living essence of intelligence."[18]

In order to arrive at having pleasure in everything; desire to have pleasure in nothing. In order to arrive at possessing everything, desire to possess nothing. In order to arrive at being everything desire to be nothing. In order to arrive at knowing everything desire to know nothing.

Such is another formulation of the same rule by an eminent Christian mystic.[19]

Saint Teresa tells us of this process of sublimation concretely, describing what she experienced at the moment of her entering the monastery. Suffering from her illness, subject to fits, her

---

[17] The Dhammapada, (New York, n.d.) X:27. Upanishads, II:20, in Sacred Books of the East (Oxford, 1884), XV.
[18] Swami Vivekananda, op. cit., pp. 88, 152.
[19] Works of Saint John, op. cit., I, 62 ff.

personality split by her various egos, values, and attachments, she decided, against the will of her father, whom she deeply loved, to take the habit.

When I left [secretly] my father's house the pain I felt was so great that I do not believe the pain of dying will be greater, for it seemed to me as if every bone in my body were wrenched asunder; for, as I had no love of God to destroy my love of father and of kindred [note this antagonism of her egos], this latter love came upon me with a violence so great that, if our Lord had not been my keeper, my own resolution to go on would have failed me. . . . When I took the habit, our Lord at once made me understand how He helps those who do violence to themselves [i.e. to their unconscious and conscious egos] in order to serve Him. No one observed this violence in me. At that moment I was filled with a joy so great, that it has never failed me to this day; and God converted the aridity of my soul into the greatest tenderness.[20]

This is how the inner conflicts were resolved in her case, and how they are resolved in all these systems by their technique of sublimation to the absolute value. As a result such persons enjoy all creatures in God and God in all creatures. The Cosmos belongs to them and they to the Cosmos. The imperturbability of Job, with his "the Lord hath given and the Lord hath taken away, Blessed be the name of the Lord," becomes their attitude.

Some of the concrete techniques for such a sublimation, as practiced by these systems, also deserve our attention. They are the technique of solitude of the Eastern or Western hermit; or that of leaving the world of conflicting groups and values, and entering a monastery; or dedicating oneself completely to an unselfish service to God and fellow men. These techniques, by their very nature, abruptly sever the membership of a person in various contradictory groups; free him from all these conflicting ties, and thereby eliminate the objective basis for a multitude of contradictory egos in the individual. These are the

---

[20] *Saint Teresa, op. cit.,* p. 14. Like all who unconditionally dedicated themselves to the absolute value, she tells of "the inexpressible bliss," "the heavenly madness," that fills the soul after the "dark nights" of the purgation and illumination of the soul are over and the state of the union with God is reached.

operations that are needed to eliminate the inner conflicts of the individual and to integrate his egos into one unified self.

Instead of the techniques of the hermitage and the monastic vow, other techniques, such as remaining in the world but severing all relationship with the groups, persons, and values contradictory to the main chosen goal, value, and group, and dedicating oneself entirely to the service of this supreme value, are also practiced and serve the same purpose. Many a great altruist remained in the busy world having performed this kind of operation.

In the integration of personality and in the subordination of all egos to one supreme superconscious value, these systems incorporate a great deal of wisdom, of true knowledge and experience, and deserve a most careful study. Their techniques in this field can indeed enrich and improve the theories and techniques of modern science.

V. The Altruization of Man

These systems of man's transfiguration are equally worthy of attention for their aims and techniques for the altruization of man and his "adaptation" and "adjustment" to his fellow men and the universe at large.

In these respects also they differ from modern theories and techniques of the treatment of mental disorders, the "education of character," and the adjustment and adaptation of an individual to his fellow men and environment. The aims and objectives of modern disciplines are fairly pedestrian in these fields. If a person suffering from a mental disorder becomes capable of "muddling through" after his treatment, he is considered "cured." If an individual "can get along somehow" with others, without committing a criminal offense; if he becomes capable of finding a means of subsistence, of doing his job, of satisfying his hunger, his sexual instincts, and his other biological needs without criminal violation of the law, he is regarded as a normal, "adjusted," "educated," and "integrated" person.

If he can do these things by defeating his competitors in sex and business, sport and politics, money-making and social climbing, he is regarded as an outstanding leader, a huge success. *Modern systems demand and cultivate no special development of altruism, beyond the necessary minimum of enlightened self-interest adjusted to that of others (contractual mutual adjustment).* The elements of altruization in school training are effectively neutralized by those of egoistic competition and the cultivation of fighting spirit. In social life at large, if a person violates the interests of others but not to an extent of criminal violation, he is considered to be "adjusted." If he does that and amasses fortune and power, he is admired and respected.

Quite different are the objectives of the great systems in the transfiguration of man. From their standpoint only a person who subjugates his biological part to his conscious part, and both to the superconscious, is considered to be an "adjusted" or educated person. *As a preliminary condition for obtaining control of the unconscious and conscious by the superconscious and for unlocking the forces of the superconscious, they unanimously demand the liberation of a person from all forms of egoism and the development of a love for the Absolute, for all living beings, for the whole universe, in its negative aspect of not causing pain to anybody by thought, word, or deed, and in its positive aspect of unselfish service, devotion, and help to and sacrifice for others.* This altruization is just one of the first, elementary steps for the realization of the main objective. And this is the reason why all these systems are systems of man's altruization and why the true ascetics, true mystics, true religious men, true yogis, are also truly altruistic men. The supreme objective of yogi is *Samadhi,* the union with the superconscious absolute. The first step toward this purpose is *Yama:* not killing, truthfulness, not stealing, continence, and not receiving any gifts; not causing any pain to any living creature by thought, word, or deed; and complete indifference to all the sensory values of this world which are viewed as the roots of egoism. This depreciation of all sensory values goes so far that Raja-Yoga warns the yogi to ignore entirely the extraordinary powers that almost automatically develops in him in the process of his training towards the stage of Samadhi: such powers as creation of mass hallucination by sight; becoming unobservable by others; taming ferocious animals by sympathy; healing sickness; extrasensory perception of remote objects and events; ability to read the mind of others; the knowledge of what happens in the universe; the power of controlling people; and so on. The yogi is advised to neglect completely these powers as pseudo values and to remain steadfast to his supreme goal.[21]

Thus a complete liberation from egoism and actual love for the Absolute, for all human beings, for all living creatures, and for the universe at large is the necessary first condition for reaching the goal. The Christian system formulated the same in a still sublimer form: "Love your neighbor." Even "Love your enemies, bless them that curse you, do good to them that hate you, and pray for them which despitefully . . . persecute you," and do this not in words only but in actions, because "not everyone that saith unto me, Lord, shall enter into the kingdom of heaven; but he that doeth the will of my Father which is in heaven."

The same is true of the systems of all the great mystics, stoics, ascetics, and other true followers of these systems. *They all unanimously say that the practice of kindness and love is one of the best therapies for curing many mental disorders; for the elimination of sorrow, loneliness, and unhappiness; for the mitigation of hatred and other antisocial tendencies; and, above all, for the enoblement of human personality, for release in man of his creative forces, and for the attainment of union with God and peace with oneself, others, and the universe.*

What is still more important, these systems indicate not one strictly mystic or religious method for reaching these goals but several, particularly the method of the realization of the superconscious through cognitive and creative achievement in the fields of truth, goodness, and beauty (Jnana yoga way) and that of altruistic creativity through good deeds and unselfish actions while remaining in the busy world (Karma yoga). (Cf. three ways of altruism and altruistic types of persons, Chapter 4.)

---

21 Cf. quoted works of Swami Vivekananda, Akhilananda, Pavitrananda, of Behanan, Coster, and Brosse; compare *Satori* in Zen Buddhism and "Enlightenment" in Buddhism.

The great mystics and religious creators who attain union with God, or the state of Samadhi, are eminent altruists because without being such they cannot attain that union; and because, as Henri Bergson rightly remarks, the altruistic and moralizing influence of the great hermits and ascetics, such as Saint Anthony, or Pachomius, has been enormous. Their seemingly isolated way of life in the hermitage actually exerted much greater altruizing influence upon humanity than the altruistic deeds of many an unselfish person helping his fellows in the busy world.

The same is true of the great creators. Men of creative genius in all fields of constructive creativity have benefited humanity, mentally, morally, and materially, beyond any calculation. Still more obvious is the influence of explicit altruists of the type of Saint Francis. All three types of creators have generated the superconscious energies of altruism in humanity, have fed its flowing stream, and thus have made possible the creative history of mankind. In this point their main technical rule is: *only love and kindness generate love and kindess; hatred and enmity produce only hatred and enmity; selfishness breeds only selfishness. No creative explosion of the superconscious forces is possible until the minimum of love is achieved by creators, groups, and nations.*

Side by side with the main technical rules, these systems contain a legion of minor, more specific prescriptions for the development and cultivation of this unselfishness and for the overcoming of egoism. These detailed techniques are themselves based upon, and realized mainly through, the conscious and superconscious energies of man, physical means playing only a subsidiary role. Detailed enumeration of these techniques is outside the scope of this work.[22]

This outline of the great systems devoted to the transfigura-

---

[22] These detailed techniques embrace also the methods and techniques operative in true conversions, by which is meant not a mere change of ideology or beliefs, emotional explosions, or revivalistic holy-rolling (which change little and evaporate quickly) but a deep and permanent transmutation of the mind and overt actions of the converts, leading to their altruization and the development of the superconscious. A careful study of such seemingly

tion of man gives an idea of their character; of their essential difference from the prevailing modern techniques and conceptions; and of their superiority over the modern systems in several fields. This explains why these older systems, their principles and techniques largely neglected today, must be carefully studied and incorporated into modern systems, revising these in several respects. In this way we can enrich our knowledge and skill in the field of the altruistic and creative transformation of man. This enriched skill and wisdom we can apply to our own transformation, to that of other persons, and finally to that of social groups and humanity.

In addition, we must discover new ways and techniques, still finer and more efficacious than all the existing ones. If human cognitive and creative efforts are indeed concentrated upon the task, there can be hardly any doubt that a series of epoch-making discoveries and inventions will be forthcoming in this field. Together with the existing wisdom and skill, they will enable mankind to perform its own self-transfiguration in the noblest, easi-' est, and most effective way.

Such in brief is the third line of the total, trilinear, change of culture, of social institutions, and of man himself; a change necessary for the prevention of future conflicts and for the establishment of a new creative order on this planet.

---

sudden conversions discloses many factors, methods, and techniques important for our purpose. Several existing studies disclose a great deal about these "secrets" underlying the sudden transfiguration of converts. But the problem is still far from being exhaustively studied. Cf. William James, *op. cit.*; E. Underhill, *op. cit.*; A. C. Underwood, *Conversion* (New York, 1925); S. de Sanctis, *Religious Conversions* (London, 1927); E. D. Starbuck, *Psychology of Religion* (London, 1899).

PART SIX

Ways of Realization of the Plan

CHAPTER FIFTEEN

HOW THE PROPOSED CHANGE IS TO BE ACHIEVED

I. How It Should Not and Cannot Be Achieved

The proposed trilinear transmutation of man and his social and cultural institutions requires a veritable revolution of the minds and hearts of individuals and groups. In such a revolution no violence is necessary: the whole transformation of culture and institutions, of human conduct and social relationships, can be accomplished in orderly and peaceful fashion through the willing and concerted action of individuals and groups, guided by their consciousness, conscience, and superconsciousness.

The change cannot be effected through rude external compulsion even if applied by a saintly minority to an unwilling sinful majority. Such revolutions and wars are essentially manifestations of the least creative and most destructive forces of the "unconscious" and bioconscious freed from the control of the conscious and superconscious. Hatred, violence, and bloodshed almost invariably engender the counterreactions of hatred, violence, and bloodshed. So it has been, and so it always will be. If peace and constructive measures have occasionally followed certain wars and revolutions, these results have been due to the latent and then reviving forces of creative altruism and solidarity. Only if God saves humanity from the well-intentioned instigators of bloody revolutions and wars has mankind any chance of overcoming its difficulties and of enjoying at least a modicum of international and domestic peace.

On the other hand, if the leaders and dominant strata of the respective societies, groups, and classes prove incapable of unselfish and creative conduct, revolutions and wars are inevitable, proving more unavoidable and more devastating the sharper the deviation from the necessary minimum of creative altruism in the direction of unbridled egoism. In the long run the exploiting groups lose, through their selfishness and shortsightedness, far more than they gain; for wars, revolutions, and other conflicts rob them not only of their wealth and privileges but often of their very lives. Retribution may not follow immediately, but it rarely fails to overtake the guilty in due time.[1]

For these reasons elementary wisdom and self-interest dictate unselfish and whole-hearted co-operation in the orderly realization of any wise, well-tested, and far-reaching plan for the reconstruction of man and his sociocultural institutions. The privileged groups of our time would thereby lose little save the short-lived glitter, the nerve-racking and debilitating pace, of their hollow and spurious mode of living. On the other hand, they would regain their lost freedom, their creative leadership, their conscious and superconscious energies, the real intensity and meaningfulness of life. The nonprivileged and the underprivileged would obviously profit materially, mentally, and morally, from such an orderly reconstruction. Among other benefits, it would free them from the tragic burden of fighting and dying in vain imposed upon them by revolutions and wars.

---

[1] From this standpoint one can only regret the continued prevalence of shortsighted imperialistic power politics. Instead of effecting a just solution of the conflicting interests of the great powers, of the great and small powers, or of the colonial peoples and their masters, the great and small powers strive to seize as much as possible for themselves, relying on war, intimidation, bribery, economic pressure, and the like to coerce their adversaries or competitors. They all seek to provide themselves with the most inhuman means of destruction. Even when they talk of the international control of atomic bombs, they rely mainly upon the coercion each nation or bloc of nations can apply. It would, indeed, be a miracle if lasting peace were to result from such impractical machinations!

In line with the spirit of our sensate culture, there now and then appear puny Machiavellians who fool themselves with the notion that they are "realistic politicians" or "practical doers." They advocate supposedly Machiavellian techniques for achieving peace, social reconstruction, and moral improvement. These techniques consist primarily of deceit, intimidation, gangsterism, and the like, intermingled with a certain amount of utilitarian persuasion, collective discussion, and publicity, and an appeal to the higher values directed toward the persons and groups to be reconstructed, and applied by the collectivity of would-be reformers. It is needless to add that, even if the author of The Prince grievously erred, these Lilliputian imitators of Machiavelli are still worse bunglers!

No person or group must shift to others the responsibility for this task. The rule "Let someone else make the sacrifice while I remain passive and perhaps profit from his efforts" does not apply here. No one can be virtuous through the virtues of others, and no one can attain the kingdom of heaven through the saintliness of others. Such an egoistic attitude would merely hinder the work of reconstruction, engendering conflict rather than peace, destruction instead of construction. In the long run, it must be remembered, egoists and parasites forfeit not only their ill-gained profits but a great deal more: their self-respect and peace of mind, their souls, and perhaps their very lives.

II. How It Should Be Achieved

The transformation should be carried on simultaneously along all three fronts: personal, cultural, and social. (1) The effort-ful transmutation of the individual may slightly precede the others. Without hypocrisy or self-deceit *every individual as such* can begin to work upon himself, developing his creativeness and altruism, increasing the control of his superconscious over the conscious and unconscious regions of his personality. The techniques employed by the masters of the art will prove helpful in performing this difficult task. One of the most efficient procedures at the beginning of this course of self-education is to perform a task which requires a short-time mobilization of all one's higher powers. Once performed it will facilitate subsequent conduct in the desired direction. The impulsive action of Saint Francis in suddenly embracing and kissing a leper furnishes an appropriate, though rather extreme example. Once initiated, altruistic actions must be continued until they become habitual. A break in such a process before it crystallizes into habit may nullify the effects of prolonged effort. Quietly and un-ostentatiously, even secretly (as Jesus rightly stresses), one can carry on this self-education in thousands of specific actions, beginning with minor good deeds and ending with the acts of exceptional unselfishness. If most persons would even slightly improve themselves in this way, the sum total of social life would be ameliorated vastly more than through political campaigns, legislation, wars and revolutions, lockouts and strikes, pressure politics, and pressure reforms.

Every individual can serve the same purpose *as a cultural agent and socius through the responsible performance of his cultural and social functions.* As a *parent* one can produce a vast number of beneficial or harmful effects according to the nature of the care of one's children and the management of the family. As an *artist, composer, painter, poet, writer, journalist, teacher, preacher, or politician, one can* produce vulgarizing trash, debasing plays or novels, demoralizing sermons, unjust legislation, and the like. Or one can create real values generating incalculable positive effects, mental, moral, and social. As a *scientist or inventor* one can discover or invent either constructive or destructive forces. The same beneficent and malevolent possibilities apply to the *role of philosopher or priest, businessman or laborer, farmer or mechanic, clerk or public official.* The same individual, in performing his social roles, may serve either the God of Creation and love or the Mammon of Enmity and Selfishness. None of our actions are lost; each has its constructive or destructive consequences! The total fabric of a given culture is woven of millions of trifling individual deeds. If each of us, imbued with a deep sense of responsibility, "watches his step," avoiding the selfish abuse of his functions, most of our social problems can be easily solved and most catastrophes prevented. On the other hand, without effortful self-education in altruism on the part of every individual, no social transformation is possible.

The second and third lines of attack consist in a well planned modification of our culture and social institutions through the concerted actions of individuals united in groups which, in turn, are merged in larger federations or associations. At the present time their tasks are twofold: first, *to increase our knowledge and wisdom and to invent better, more efficient techniques for fructifying our culture and institutions and rendering human beings more noble and altruistic;* second, *through this increased knowledge and these perfected techniques to draw up more adequate plans for the total process of transformation, to dif-*

fuse and propagate them, and to convince ever-larger sections of humanity of the urgency, feasibility, and adequacy of the proposed reconstruction.

Both of these tasks are important. The first task is especially urgent, since our knowledge, wisdom, and techniques in this field are exceedingly deficient.[2] Sound plans, efficient techniques, and all the related ideas and values are to be communicated to and deeply rooted in larger and larger groups. With their diffusion new associations and organizations will emerge and multiply. Each organization working in its own particular field, they will progressively co-ordinate their activities around the basic values of the entire reconstruction. The co-ordinated activities will progressively translate the values, norms, and ideas into cultural, social, and personal objective realities. They will exert an influence upon governments, the United Nations, and other national and international bodies and their policies. Thus individuals and their conduct, cultural values (science, religion, philosophy, the fine arts, law, and so on), and social institutions and relationships will be modified in orderly fashion in

---

[2] Our statesmen, universities and foundations, business concerns, and philanthropists — to say nothing of the rank and file — do not yet realize that *this is the paramount problem of humanity at the present time.* Without its successful solution the perpetuation of our civilization is highly problematical. Though there are thousands of research institutes devoted to relatively unimportant and even trivial purposes, there is not a single such institute dedicated to this paramount problem. While state governments, universities, and foundations unhesitatingly appropriate billions of dollars for the invention and perfection of atomic bombs, means of bacteriological warfare, and other Frankenstein monsters, I know of no government or other institution that has appropriated even a few thousand dollars for research in this vital field. Hence I and a few other scholars have decided to devote all our spare time to the study of the most strategic subsidiary aspects of this central problem, though well aware of the utter inadequacy of our efforts. Quite unexpectedly, Mr. Eli Lilly generously granted to Harvard University twenty thousand dollars to promote our research work. Several special researches have already been inaugurated. This little volume is a nontechnical, tentative outline of the whole field as I see it. The results of the special investigations will eventually be published seriatim. Even with the aforesaid financial help our possibilities are limited. Much larger funds and more specialists are needed for expanding the project. Anyone who approves of our objectives can assist us by sending a contribution to Harvard University to be applied to the research conducted by P. A. Sorokin and others. It may be added that not a single cent of the aforesaid fund is used for our personal needs. We gladly give to the cause gratis our time and energy.

conformity to the desired patterns. Eventually the whole socio-cultural system will be transformed into a peaceful and creative cosmos.

To be sure, the process of transformation will require considerable time. Now and then it will evolve according to plan; now and then in an unforeseen manner. Now it will move smoothly, now erratically, with many mistakes, deviations, and miscarriages. It is bound to be marked by conflicts, struggles, and crises. However, these will not necessarily be bloody or catastrophic. After its birth throes it will culminate in the dethronement of our decadent sociocultural order and in the rise of a new order ushering in a new constructive period of human history.

III. Can It Be Achieved?

At this point the "tough-minded" reader may be allowed to voice his impatient question: "What assurance is there that this whole scheme is not a mere dream, a mere wishful utopia devoid of any chance of realization? Is it not too vast and difficult to be practicable or even possible? Is there not an easier, more practical way out of the present crisis? Can't we get somewhere by changing certain political or economic conditions, school curricula, divorce laws, or labor-management relationships?"

Our tough-minded practical reader deserves a tough-minded practical answer. It is this: No, there is no easier and more practical way! What seems to be such is highly impractical. In the first part of this volume we examined and tested all the seemingly practical remedies for war and found them wanting. Being a mere patchwork, they do not cure the diseases which they attempt to cure. If anything, they hasten the process of decay. The doctors who prescribe such remedies are grossly incompetent, if not frauds. In brief, there is no short cut for reintegrating the disorganized social system and saving humanity from self-destruction.

If the suggested plan of reconstruction *is* unrealizable, then we should cease beguiling ourselves and others with the false hope that humanity's suicidal mania can be overcome and a nobler social order can be created. Either humanity will be able to transform itself along lines similar to those proposed or it must resign itself to the inevitable "finis" of its creative history.

As to the feasibility of the outlined project, considering its extraordinary inherent difficulties and the selfishness and mental aberration of our decadent society, the prospects are somewhat dubious. However, a genuine fighting chance assuredly exists.

Our first hope lies in the past experience of mankind. Grave crises have happened many times in its history. However desperate the situation was, however hopeless it looked on the surface, humanity, that is, its best elements, has always been able to mobilize its mental, moral, and social forces to meet the crisis and to inaugurate a new constructive phase of its history. Hence there is no certain evidence that humanity cannot once again work out its salvation and that another renaissance is impossible.

Secondly, a shift from the decadent sensate type of culture and society to an idealistic or ideational form has occurred several times in the past. There is accordingly no reason to believe that it cannot recur in the future.

Thirdly, however numerous and grave may have been the mistakes of humanity in choosing wrong leaders and methods for coping with past catastrophes, after many trials and errors, in the final moment of the crisis, it has generally been able to choose the right path, sound plans, and capable leaders, to follow until the danger was over. There is no reason to believe that this cannot happen again.

An attentive observer can already notice signs of the declining influence of false prophets, wrong leaders, and empty values. Partly rationally and partly superconsciously an ever-increasing proportion of humanity is beginning to follow the difficult road that leads to salvation. To be sure, this element is still only a small minority; but it can say of itself what Tertullian said of the handful of early Christians: "Hesterni sumus et vestra omnia implevimus" ("We are only men of yesterday, and yet we fill your world"). Its numbers are rapidly growing.

Fourthly, if the new order were dependent entirely upon "utilitarian rationality" and the ordinary "conscious" energies of sensate man, its emergence and growth would be indeed uncertain. Fortunately, such is not the manner in which a major crisis is overcome and a new social order is established. The replacement of the old by the new is greatly assisted by the historical process itself, by the vast, impersonal, spontaneous forces which animate it, and especially by the superconscious energies released by the crisis.

The spontaneous, impersonal forces inherent in our sensate system have already brought about its phase of crisis and decline. They have undermined its prestige and alienated from it a considerable portion of humanity. They have robbed it of its security and safety, its prosperity and material comfort, its freedom, and all its basic values. Not in the classroom but in the hard school of experience people are being constantly taught by these impersonal forces an unforgettable and indelible lesson, comprehensible to the simplest mind, that the existing order has passed its creative phase and is on the verge of bankruptcy; that it spells bullets rather than bread, destruction rather than construction, misery rather than prosperity, regimentation rather than freedom; confusion rather than order; death rather than life. Its decline is not due to the murderous assault of barbarians, revolutionaries, or plotters, but to its own senility, the exhaustion of its creative forces. The decline is not a case of murder but of disintegration.

Since our sensate culture no longer possesses any fundamental values capable of commanding the allegiance of mankind, an ever-growing number of both high brows and low brows are looking for something new, for some way out of the blind alley, for a new order to supplant the old one.

Such is the result of the vast impersonal forces of the old order. It is crucial for the birth of a new order. These impersonal forces continue to drive humanity farther and farther along the road from the old to the new. Their driving power is irresistible and, if wisely used, may prove of inestimable value in effecting the transition.

Still more important is the role of the superconscious forces released by the crisis itself. Here we observe on the largest scale what has ordinarily happened in virtually all the real "conversions" mentioned above. Almost every true conversion (as a sudden transformation of the personality and conduct of a sinful person into those of a saint, of an egoist into a creative altruist) has been precipitated by the impact of some crisis or calamity. The same is true of a considerable proportion of creative geniuses in the arts and sciences and other fields. In many cases the initial impulse has been illness. Saint Paul, Saint Francis of Assisi, Saint Ignatius Loyola, Saint Teresa, Saint Hildegard of Binger, Mohammed, Luther, Pascal, de Musset, Heine, Dostoevsky, Van Gogh, and a host of other eminent "converts" were launched upon their creative careers *renati in aeternum,* as the result of a grave illness. Others were impelled by some painful shock, the loss of dear ones, the crumbling of their ambitions, persecution, or the suffering incident to such calamities as war, revolution, and plague. Buddha's conversion, as the pampered son of a prince, into one of the foremost educators of humanity was initiated by the shock he received from witnessing the misfortunes of sickness, old age, and death. He came to perceive that these misfortunes were inescapable in this sensory world, that all its values were short-lived and all its pleasures evanescent; and they led him to abandon his princely home in quest of the values that were imperishable and eternal. The loss of his beloved Fiammetta, and other misfortunes, including his illness of 1374, changed Boccaccio, the sensual author of *Decameron,* into a pious and moral stoic. Raymon Lull's sudden transformation, as a rich man who sought to seduce the wife of one of his neighbors, into a saint was due to the sight of the cancerous breasts which this wife exposed in rebuking him for his evil intentions. Saint Augustine's conversion was initiated by the death of a dear friend and confirmed by the loss of his beloved mother. Cardinal Newman's conversion was precipitated by the inner conflict and the loneliness engendered by the rejection of his early tracts. Beethoven's religious and stoical attitude was confirmed by the misfortune of his deafness and by the serious abdominal inflammation which set in during the spring of 1825. "Fervent thanksgiving to the Godhead from one who recovered — in the Lydian mood" was the inscription on the Adagio movement of his Opus 132 written immediately after his recovery.

Similar, though more temporary, conversions are regularly experienced by thousands when their city or community is suddenly stricken by calamity. A typical example of this is afforded by the upsurge of religious feeling, kindness, and unselfishness in Halifax, Nova Scotia, immediately after the serious explosion of an ammunition ship on December 6, 1917.

A systematic study of such cases shows that in the history of great civilizations such as those of ancient Egypt, Babylonia, China, India, Greece, Rome, and the Western countries, the principal steps in religious and moral progress have uniformly been taken either during periods of major and protracted calamity or immediately after their termination. Prolonged periods of prosperity have tended to dull the religious and moral sense rather than to intensify it.[3] Side by side with a release of the superconscious forces in the fields of religion and morality, grave social crises have often stimulated also an upsurge of creativity in all the other cultural fields.[4]

It is true that, hand in hand with this "positive polarization," crises and calamities call forth also a "negative polarization," a portion of the population being freed from the control exercised by the conscious and superconscious forces and falling victim to the chaotic unconscious, biological impulses. Such persons become "worse than the beasts," in the words of Aristotle and Plato.[5]

However, with a few exceptions this negative polarization is a temporary phenomenon, being sooner or later superseded by

---

[3] For a systematic analysis of these facts, see *Calamity*, chaps. 10-12; also the works cited in connection with the discussion of conversion.

[4] *Ibid.*, chaps. 13-14.

[5] For the *law of polarization* and the facts of demoralization in such periods see *ibid., passim.*

the normal situation or by positive polarization. In our time the negative polarization seems to have reached its maximum, whereas the positive polarization is only at its starting point. Recent catastrophes have released a portion of the superconscious forces of this polarization, and these forces have only just begun to "germinate." The prolonged crises that seemingly await humanity in the near future are likely to produce a further release of these forces and markedly intensify their actual, kinetic power. Transforming their potential forces into kinetic forces, these creative energies are likely to assume control of the vast anonymous forces of the historical processes itself, unconscious and conscious, using them for constructive purposes. These energies of the superconscious may prove the most efficacious factors of the desired transmutation. Under their guidance the dangerous bridge may be safely crossed and the epoch-making transformation successfully accomplished. What has occurred thousands of times in individual conversions and in those of groups and nations may happen to the whole of humanity: the process may be effected in the comparatively short space of a few decades instead of requiring centuries.

Since the existing sensate order is moribund, we have no choice, unless we are resigned to the extinction of our civilization, but to follow the road to renaissance and transfiguration. Assisted by the forces of the historical process and especially by the liberated energies of the superconscious, humanity may travel this road until it reaches the haven of the new order of creative peace and happiness. All that is necessary is the supreme mobilization of our available mental and moral forces, control of subconscious drives by the conscious and superconscious factors, and unflinching determination to meet courageously all the difficulties of the pilgrimage. It is for humanity itself to decide its destiny!

INDEX

Absolutism, 105
Adler, J., 103, 189
Advertising, 194
Africa, 43
Africa, South-West, 16
Africa, South-East, 45
Akhilanda, 63, 211n., 225n.
Alexander the Great, 21
Allies, 10, 16, 119
Altruism, 41, 44, 54, 57-89, 148, 153, 183-195, 208-227
Anthony, Saint, 63f., 226
Arab states, 13
Aristotle, 59, 114, 240
Armaments, 10, 41, 51f., 161
Arts, 50f., 96-98, 121-125
Asia, 43
Athens, 8
Atlantic Charter, 16
Atomic bomb, atomic energy, 3, 51f, 79, 111, 113, 161, 193, 235
Augustine, Saint, 114, 239
Aurobindu, Sri, 219n.
Australia, 43
Austria, 9-11
Autocracies, autocratic, 12, 22, 128

Babylon, 156, 175n., 240
Bach, J. S., 123f., 137
Beethoven, L. van, 64, 112, 123f., 168, 184, 240
Behanan, K., 211n., 225n.
Behner, A., 71n.
Belayeff, B. V., 71n.
Belgium, 8, 11, 15, 21
Benedict, Saint, 63
Bergson, H., 64, 187n., 204, 226
Berne, E. V. C., 71n.
Best sellers, 50f., 123
Bethmann-Hollweg, 15
Bhakti yoga, 62, 64, 215n.
Bible, 41, 59n., 77n., 97, 121, 215n.
Bill of Rights, 161
Biological factors, 67f.
Boccacio, 239

Bodhisattva, A., 215n.
Boeck, W., 71n.
Bogardus, E., 72n.
Bolivia, 21
Bonaventura, Saint, 219n.
Bonney, M. E., 71n.
Brahms, J., 123
Brazil, 21
Brosse, T., 212n., 213n., 216, 225n.
Bryce, J., 164
Buddha, Buddhist, 41, 61, 98, 116, 156, 168, 206, 215n., 239
Bulgaria, 21
Burrow, T., 77n.
Byzantium, 11, 31, 33, 171, 175n.

Canada, 49
Capitalism, 25-30, 36, 49, 141f., 171-179
Captains of Industry, 26
Carnegie, A., 27
Cartels, 26, 36
Catholic, Roman, 93f., 177, 200
Cavour, 192
Cervantes, 123
Challman, R. C., 72n.
Charters, W. W., 124n.
Chassell, C. F., 74
Chile, 21
China, 13, 18, 33, 98n.
China, ancient, 31, 99n., 271, 240
Christianity, 41-43, 53, 75-78, 85, 97, 114-116, 118, 121, 131, 157, 225, 237
Cicero, 59
Colonies, 8, 17, 29, 45, 172
Communism, 27, 31-37, 171f., 174, 176
Competition, 28, 150, 167-171, 223f.
Compulsory relationship, 141-147
Confucianism, 41, 116, 156
Congress of Vienna, 16
Contractual relationship, 140-143
Cook, J., 45
Coomaraswamy, A., 205n.

243